Leonardo da Vinci and Anatomy, the Mechanics of Life

EXHIBITION

Exhibition Curators
Pascal Brioist, Professor of Modern History at the University of Tours and member of the Centre for Advanced Renaissance Studies
Dominique Le Nen, University Professor and Surgeon at the Regional University Hospital in Brest

Advisory Committee
Pascal Brioist
Dominique Le Nen
François Saint Bris, President, Château du Clos Lucé

Château du Clos Lucé
François Saint Bris, President
Michaël Petitjean, General Secretary
Diane Junqua, Director of Communications and Sponsorship
Sandra Chupin, Exhibition Coordinator
Eleonora Pavesi, Translator and Italian Coordinator
Nina Germain, Communications Officer
Paul Riffault, Education Officer
Stéphane Darras, Head of the Technical Department, and his team

Institutions loaning exhibits
• Gallerie degli Uffizi, Florence;
• Gallerie dell'Accademia, Venice;
• Bibliothèque interuniversitaire Santé Médecine, université Paris-Cité;
• Bibliothèque municipale, Dijon;
• Bibliothèque municipale, Le Havre;
• Institut national d'histoire de l'art, Paris;
• Bibliothèque Carré d'Art, Nîmes;
• Bibliothèque municipale, Grenoble;
• Bibliothèque humaniste, Sélestat;
• Fondazione Cassa di Risparmio, Bologna (Collezioni d'arte et di storia);
• Biblioteca Nazionale "Vittorio Emanuele III", Naples;
• Château du Clos Lucé.

Scenography
Iris Jasson and Annabelle Jeanne, scenographers, Arc-en-Scène
Livia Marchand, graphic designer, Pangram

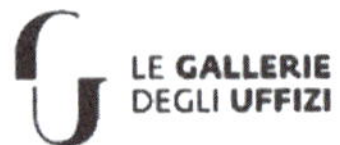

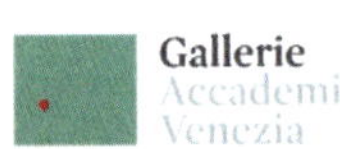

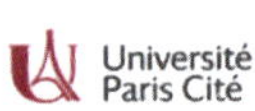

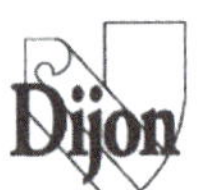

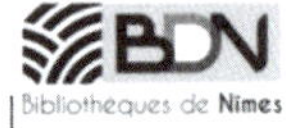

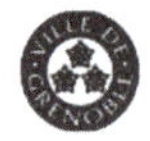
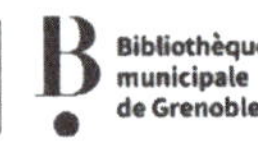

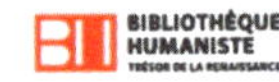

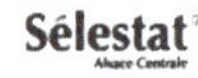

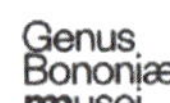

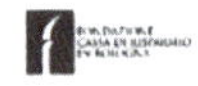
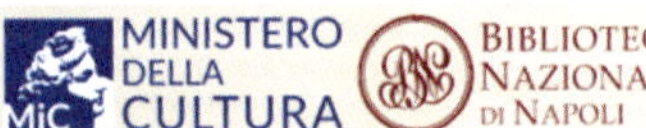

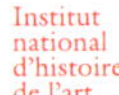

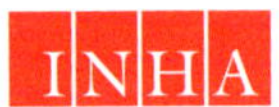

CATALOGUE

Project Management
François Saint Bris, President, Château du Clos Lucé
Diane Junqua, Director of Communications and Sponsorship, Château du Clos Lucé

With the financial support of
the Centre-Val de Loire Region

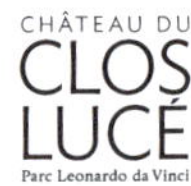

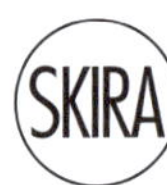

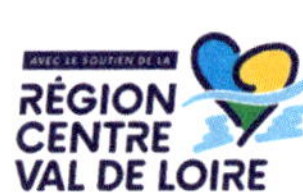

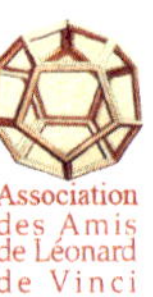

Leonardo da Vinci and Anatomy, the Mechanics of Life

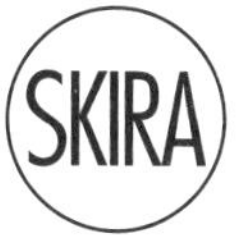

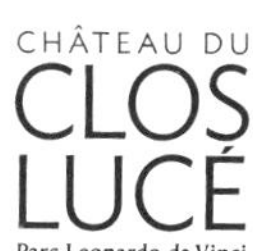

CONTENTS

Unless otherwise stated,
all works are by Leonardo da Vinci

AUTHORS

Dominique Le Nen, University Professor and Surgeon at the Regional University Hospital in Brest

Pascal Brioist, Professor of Modern History at the University of Tours
and member of the Centre for Advanced Renaissance Studies

Bertrand Debono, Neurosurgeon at the Centre Francilien du Dos (Paris-Versailles),
President of the French Society of Private Neurosurgeons

François Gaucher, Surgeon at Quimper General Hospital

Laetitia Guezennec, Marketing and Communication Manager, Dassault Systèmes

Maëlyss Haddjeri, PhD Student in Art History at the École Pratique des Hautes Etudes,
Université Paris Sciences et Lettres

Matthew Landrus, Researcher at Wolfson College, Oxford University,
specialist in the history of art and science in Italy

Jacky Laulan, Hand Surgeon at the Regional University Hospital in Tours

Domenico Laurenza, Associate Professor of Art History at the University of Cagliari

Christian Lefèvre, Professor of Anatomy at the Faculty of Medicine in Brest

Jean-Jacques Monsuez, Cardiologist at René-Muret AP-HP Hospital

Johann Peltier, Neurosurgeon and Professor of Anatomy, Amiens

François Rozet, Senior Surgeon in the Department of Urology
at the Institut Mutualiste Montsouris in Paris

François Saint Bris, President, Château du Clos Lucé – Parc Leonardo da Vinci

Joël Savéan, Technician at the Laboratory of Medical Information Processing in Brest

Anna Sconza, Lecturer in Italian Studies at Sorbonne-Nouvelle Paris-III University

Frank Zöllner, Professor of Art History at Leipzig University

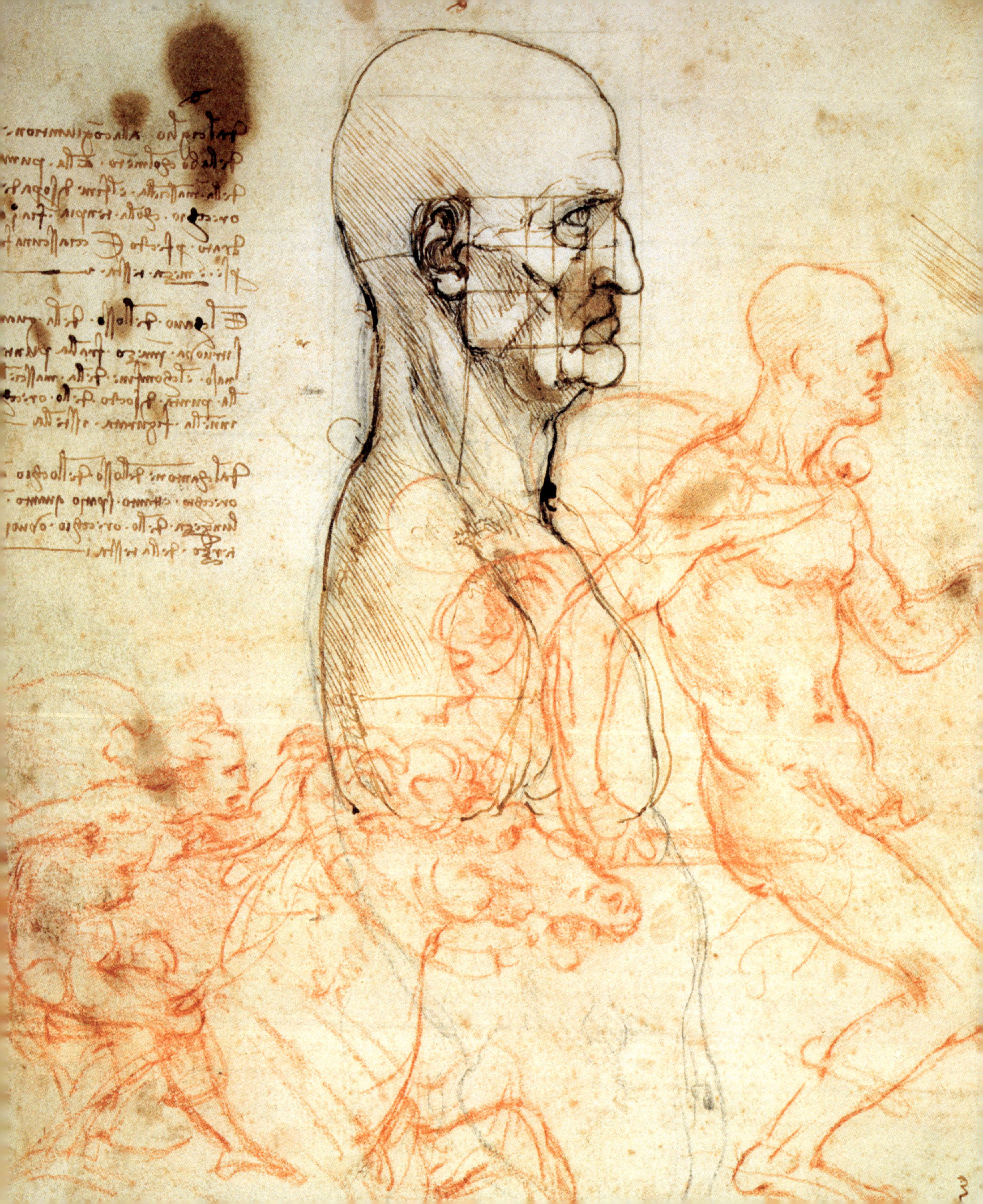

Foreword

François Saint Bris
President
Château du Clos Lucé – Parc Leonardo da Vinci

Previous page:

Torso of a man in profile, the head squared for proportion, and sketches of two horsemen, c.1490 and 1504, pen and ink and red chalk over metalpoint on paper 28 × 22.2 cm
Venice, Gallerie dell'Accademia, Gabinetto dei Disegni e Stampe, inv. 236

The Château du Clos Lucé, in partnership with the Association of the Friends of Clos Lucé, is presenting at the artist's last residence the scientific exhibition: *Leonardo da Vinci and Anatomy, the Mechanics of Life*, from 9 June 2023 to 17 September 2023.

This new exhibition presented by Clos Lucé takes visitors to the heart of Leonardo's experiments and discoveries as an anatomist, revealing also his new scientific methods such as dissection, a little-known facet of his immense talent.

Thirty years (1487–1516) in a relentless quest to penetrate the mysteries of life and decipher the human body in its mechanics, its movement, and the functions of the organs.

Through an educational and immersive tour combining anatomical drawings by the master's disciples, works from the period, facsimiles, a reconstruction of a dissection room and its instruments, anatomical models, interviews with specialists, animated 3D video and contemporary installations, visitors will discover the anatomy of the human body through the eyes of Leonardo.

For the first time, the exhibition will allow the public to discover the inseparable link between the anatomical and psychological studies of *The Last Supper*, a masterpiece of Western painting by Leonardo, through a 3D representation of the painting's anatomy.

Overseen by Château du Clos Lucé, this scientific exhibition was conceived and produced with curators Dominique Le Nen, University Professor and Surgeon at Brest University Hospital, and Pascal Brioist, Professor at the Centre for Advanced Renaissance Studies (CESR) at the University of Tours, a historian specialising in Leonardo da Vinci, the Renaissance, and science and technology. Clos Lucé extends its heartfelt thanks to the commissioners for the generosity they have shown us in curating this exhibition and for the magnificent sense of teamwork they have inspired in all concerned.

Of all the subjects Leonardo da Vinci explored, anatomical studies were his favourite scientific field. He devoted thirty years of his life to it. He dissected thirty male and female cadavers, and recorded in his notebooks his remarkable anatomical work, which was never published.

He has passed on his scientific legacy through 228 anatomical plates, 215 of which belong to the Royal Collection Trust in Windsor, complemented by thousands of explanatory notes and captions, which bear witness to his astonishing exploration of the human body.

Leonardo da Vinci is one of the greatest anatomists of all time, who explored all aspects of anatomy and physiology.

He studied the proportions of the body, the skeleton and the spine, the bones and the thorax, the skull and the brain, the arms, the legs and the hands, the muscles, the nerves and the tendons, the main organs and their vessels, the respiratory and cardiovascular systems, the urogenital system, the embryo and the foetus. He also analysed the expression of emotions and the nature of the senses, particularly that of sight through the use of optics.

Leonardo da Vinci was a pioneer of scientific exploration. In an insatiable quest for understanding, he sought to penetrate the nature of life itself in order to obtain complete and ultimate knowledge. Self-taught, a "man without letters", he created and developed his own scientific method based on hypothesis, observation and experimentation. According to him, "wisdom is the daughter of experience".

He adopted an empirical approach using quantitative and qualitative observations of reality and defined a rigorous methodology by describing the factual results of his own studies and experiments in images and in writing, thus making it possible for new knowledge to be established. In the field of anatomy, Leonardo's method was totally new and multidisciplinary, and it is with this cross-fertilization vision that he laid the foundations for experimental science.

He was the first:

to discover the sinuses by sectioning a skull;

to draw in an accurate and detailed way, with an almost photographic quality, the spine and its curves, by identifying precisely each of the cervical, thoracic and lumbar vertebrae;

to diagnose arteriosclerosis by noting the narrowing and hardening of the coronary arteries of a hundred-year-old man who died in good health;

to identify the four cardiac chambers in the heart, perfectly described in morphological and functional terms, whereas Andreas Vesalius (1514–1564) and René Descartes (1596–1650), much later, described only two chambers;

to explore abdominal and thoracic anatomy;

to study embryology and to represent the anatomy of a foetus in the womb.

According to Professor Dominique Le Nen, Leonardo invented a new method of dissecting: dissection in layers, dissection in sections, and dissection in perspective, offering multiple aspects of the subject before producing a synthesis of all the parts of the dissected body. Thanks to his drawings representing numerous anatomical views in a series of sections, Leonardo also discovered, five centuries ahead of his time, the principle of CT scans and magnetic resonance imaging (MRI).

Although not a physician, he seized on the medical knowledge of the time and advanced it further. Painter and engineer, he became a pioneer of artistic anatomy using his own tools: the scalpel and pencil drawings. The scalpel for clinical experimentation; and black chalk, pen and ink for functional descriptive drawing, recording notes, and reporting his observations, analyses and conclusions. Leonardo both dissected the cadavers and represented the dissections.

He is also one of the greatest draughtsmen of all time. His thinking is pictorial. It testifies to his extraordinary ability to capture and visualise information. Drawing is for him a diagram that makes it possible to see, and therefore to understand. Leonardo structures his thought through drawing. "Drawing was a vehicle for his thought, a way of thinking, a means of reflecting" (Françoise Viatte, curator at the Louvre Museum from 1964 to 2004).

Leonardo da Vinci began to take an interest in superficial human anatomy in order to represent the human body through figurative art, like painters and sculptors of the Quattrocento, such as Masaccio, Pollaiuolo, Verrocchio; and of the early sixteenth century, such as Mantegna, Michelangelo and Raphael.

Artistic anatomy then extolled the study of *écorchés* figures. Artists of the time undertook superficial anatomical observations during autopsy sessions in Milan, Florence, Padua, Pavia and Ferrara, which were the new centres of research on modern anatomy. As the human being became the central theme of painting and sculpture during the Renaissance period, proportions, skeletons, limbs and muscles, bones and tendons were studied to represent the external anatomy of the body and its structure realistically. The *Vitruvian Man* (1490), by Leonardo da Vinci, which places the human being at the centre of the universe, later became the symbol of humanism. Some artists of the Renaissance considered that they were no longer just simple craftsmen, but also scholars trained in the life sciences.

It was at this time, around 1482, that Leonardo painted his *Saint Jerome*, which was exhibited during the summer of 2022 at Clos Lucé, thanks to a special loan from the Vatican Museums. Leonardo's study of ancient sculpture in Verrocchio's studio allowed him to deepen his knowledge of the spatial relationships of the body, even before he completed his physical and physiological studies through anatomical dissections – carried out in 1487, between 1508 and 1510, and after 1510. The painting gives us his first three-dimensional anatomical representation of the human body.

According to his *Treatise on Painting* and his studies on physiognomy, *the movements of the soul* are closely related to those of the body. Leonardo da Vinci, therefore, represents Saint Jerome in penance in the desert. The saint is kneeling on the rocks, with a twisted body and exacerbated suffering, his face glabrous and emaciated, his right arm raised and tensed, and his eyes imploring the heavens. From an anatomical point of view, the painting emphasises the movement of the head and the right arm, the muscles of the neck, the shoulders and the torso. Still in its sketch state, oscillating between drawing and painting, it illustrates with intensity the human soul in the grip of doubt, the tumult of passions, the search for salvation in faith and expectation. The temptation of Saint Jerome evokes the spiritual struggle of faith faced with the limits of the senses and reason.

Later, *The Last Supper* (1495–1498) also marks a major innovation in the history of Western painting. Leonardo da Vinci revolutionised this period by attempting to capture the expression of the feelings, emotions and passions of the Apostles as they learn of the betrayal of Christ. Through a perfect mastery of perspective and movement, he brilliantly details all the protagonists of *The Last Supper*, allowing the viewer to move from the third dimension to a fourth, that of suspended time.

According to him, "The motions and postures of figures should display the true mental state of the originator of these motions, in such a way they can mean nothing else." Christ's last meal becomes the living expression of the *movements of the soul*, a human drama, but also a divine mystery to contemplate.

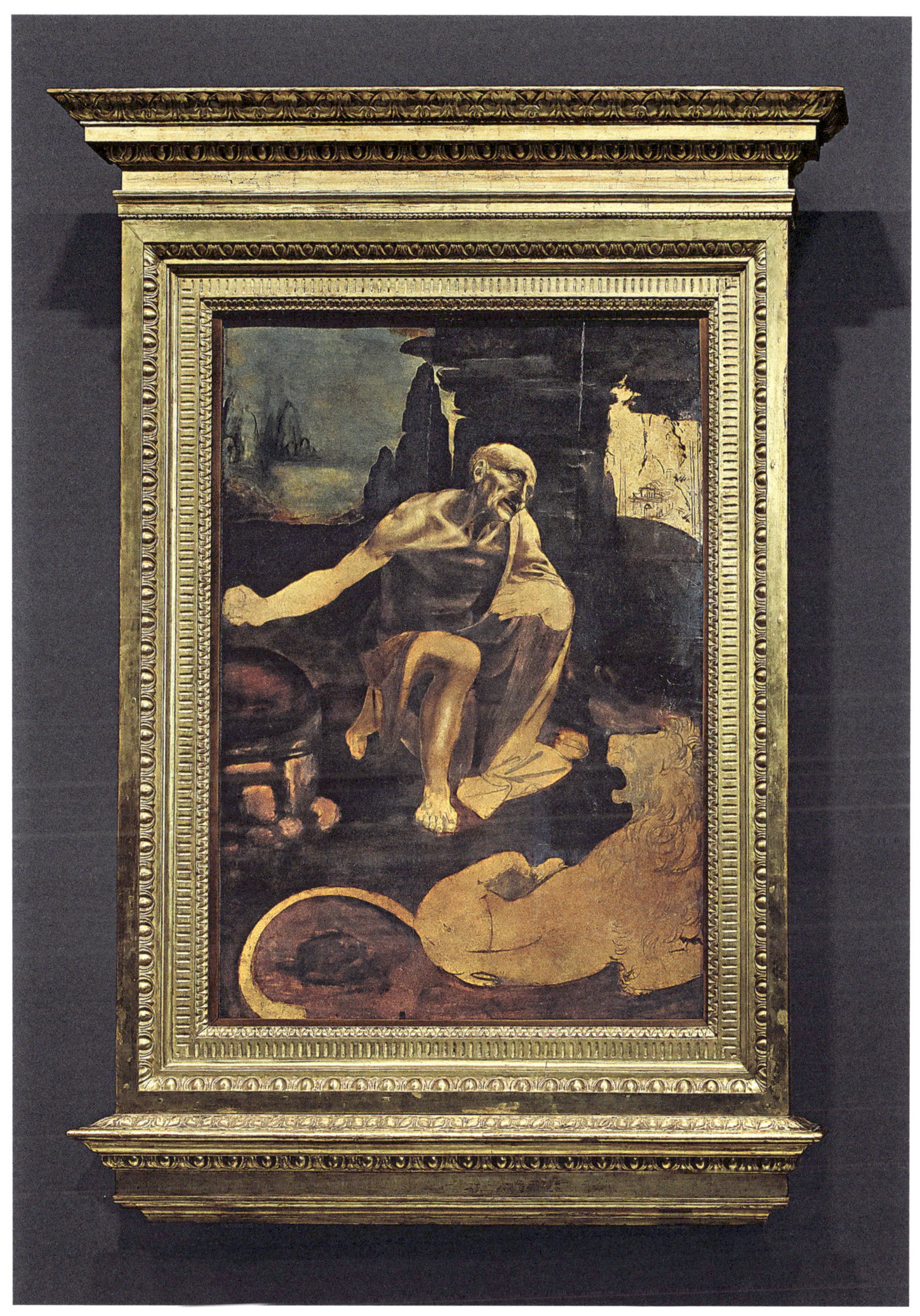

Saint Jerome Praying in the Wilderness, c.1482, oil on wood panel, 103 × 74 cm
Musei Vaticani, inv. 40337.
Presented for the exhibition
Leonardo da Vinci's St Jerome. *An Unfinished Masterpiece*,
8 June – 20 September 2022, Clos Lucé

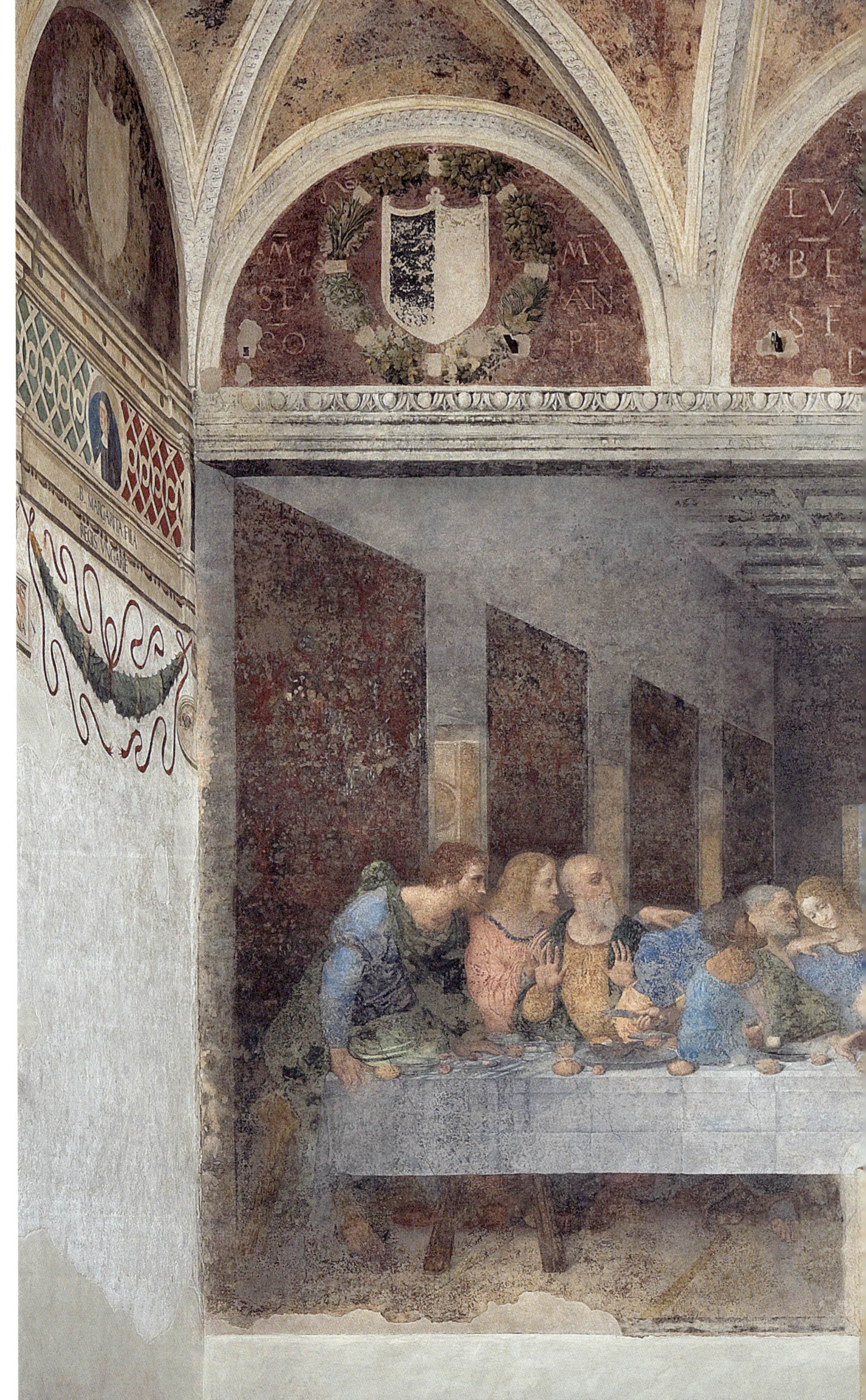

The Last Supper,
c.1495–98
tempera on gesso
460 × 880 cm
Museo del Cenacolo, Milan

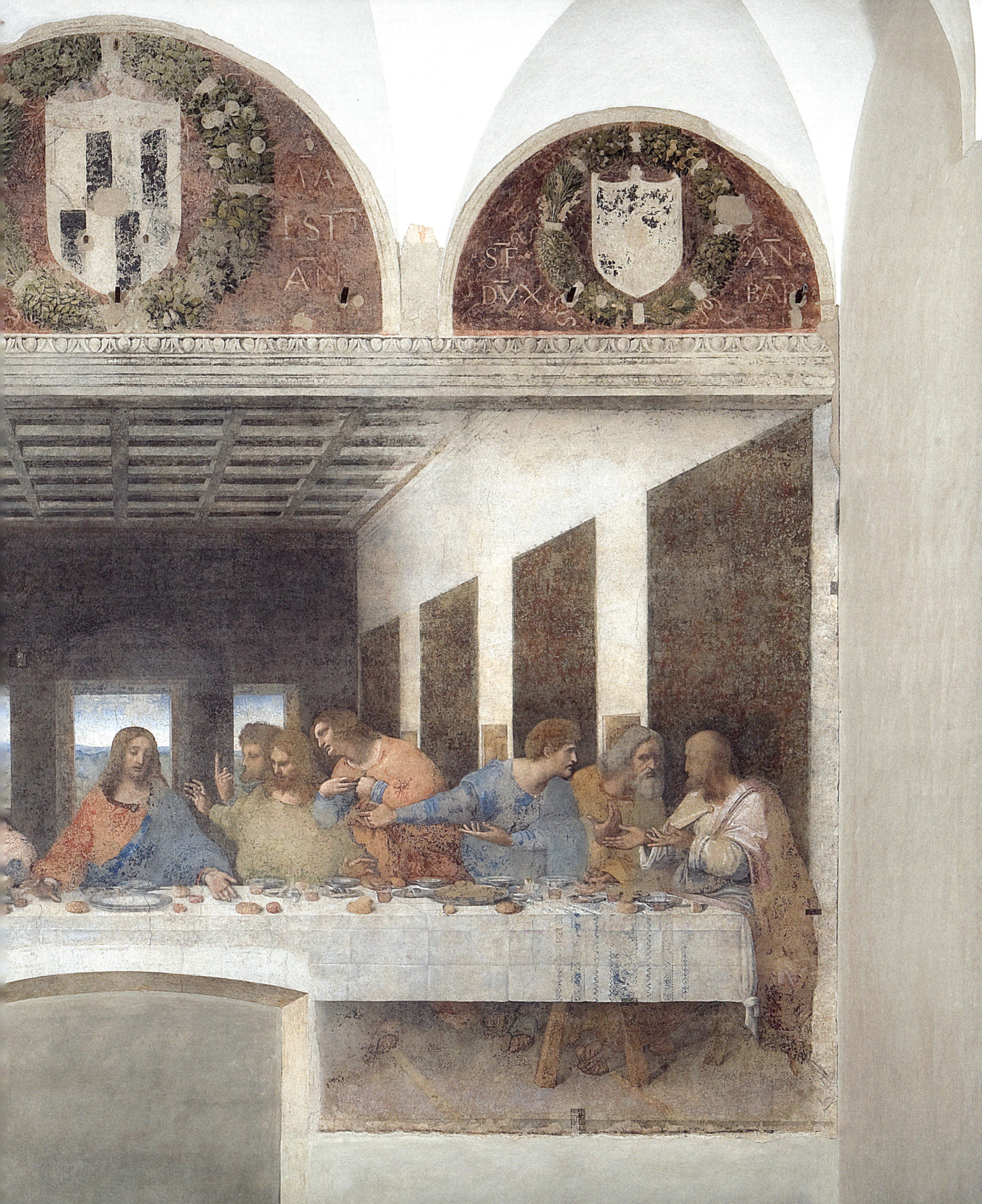
SF
DVX
AN
BAR

Leonardo da Vinci is passionate about this new anatomical study with a scientific end, and is constantly furthering his research to discover the inner beauty of the human body, and the very nature of life.

His influences and sources are multiple and of enduring importance. He read Aristotle, Vitruvius, Ptolemy, Galen, Avicenna, Mondino, Guy de Chauliac, Johannes de Ketham ..., but also met and talked with physicians in the universities and hospitals of Florence, Milan, Padua, Pavia and Rome. Not to mention his mentors, notably Marcantonio della Torre (1481–1511), a young physician specialising in anatomy at the universities of Pavia and Padua, who dissected corpses with Leonardo and died prematurely of the plague at the age of thirty.

In the early years of his research on anatomy, Leonardo, faithful to the ancient tradition of comparative anatomy, was tempted to establish analogies between the functioning of the Earth and that of the human body, the macrocosm and the microcosm. He compared the heart to the ocean and the blood vessels to the flow of river waves. For the artist, "Man is the model of the world."

Subsequently abandoning this early idea, he became fascinated with the structural analogy between man and animals, which he also dissected. He compared man with horses, oxen, cows, pigs, dogs, goats, monkeys, frogs and birds. Leonardo even examined a bear's foot to compare its plantigrade locomotion with the structure of a man's foot. This comparative anatomy allowed him to identify the same anatomical structures for the skeleton and muscles, and the functional role of nerves and blood vessels.

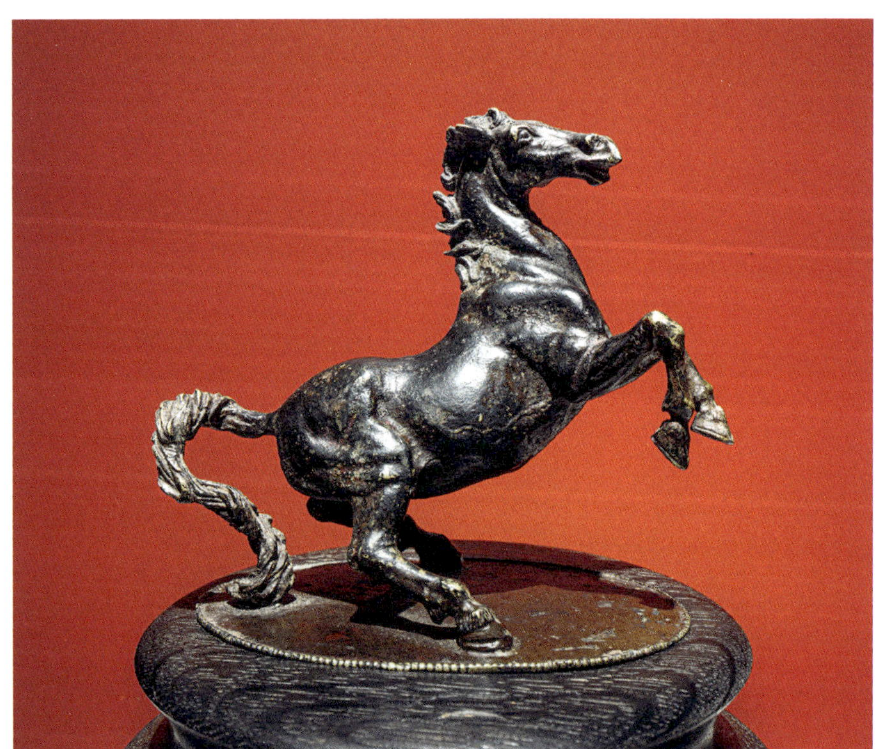

Prancing Horse, based on a wax model by Leonardo da Vinci
Bronze with black patina, Italy, 17th century
Private collection, Château du Clos Lucé

Lastly, Leonardo da Vinci later studied the human body in all its internal aspects, from structural anatomy to physiology; from reproduction to the conception of the embryo in the womb, to the growth and functioning of all the limbs and organs. He even tried to identify the seat of the soul, what he called the 'common sense'.

According to Françoise Viatte, "he was one of the first to be interested in representing what cannot be seen".

His anatomical studies have become a homage to inner beauty. For him: "If this, his external form, appears to thee marvellously constructed, remember that it is nothing as compared with the soul that dwells in that structure."

During his dissections, Leonardo da Vinci compared the human body to a "wonderful machine" whose organs are like gears. He studied the human body as a mechanical science. He modelled the movement of muscles by comparing this to the mechanism of ropes and pulleys. A pioneer of biomechanics, Leonardo, for whom "movement is the cause of all life", was interested in the movements of the body based on the mechanical properties of the skeleton, the muscular system and human gestures.

A visionary anatomist, Leonardo appears to us today as a precursor of bionics, bioinspiration, and biomimicry, the science of the future that draws inspiration from nature and the living to meet the industrial, technological and scientific challenges of our time.

Leonardo's interest in physiognomy, according to which studies of physical characteristics – such as facial features, the shape of the skull and analogies with certain animals – provide keys to understanding the human personality, led him to produce a collection of portraits of grotesque figures.

As no other artist had done before, Leonardo da Vinci gave himself all the means to understand the structure and functioning of the human body in order to be able, better than anyone else, to understand the truth of living beings and the universe; but also to magnify the human being in painting, which he considered to be the supreme and spiritual art, a 'cosa mentale'.

Leonardo da Vinci intended to publish the works of his scientific corpus in the form of a general treatise on anatomy, which he never had the time to complete, and which never saw the light of day. When he died on 2 May 1519, at Clos Lucé, Francesco Melzi, his favourite disciple and legatee, gathered together all his notes, drawings and manuscripts. When Francesco Melzi died in Vaprio d'Adda in 1570, a large part of the drawings was sold by his son Orazio Melzi to Pompeo Leoni, a sculptor, who sorted them by theme and then gave them away. Leonardo's notebooks languished in obscurity, although some of them, including the collection of anatomical drawings, were bought by the English Crown at the end of the 17th century. They were not, however, published until the end of the 19th century, four hundred years after the death of Leonardo. The world then discovered the extent of his immense knowledge. Meanwhile, the Flemish Andreas Vesalius (1514–1564), who had published *On the Fabric of the Human Body* in 1543 and was very successful, earned the title of 'Father of modern anatomy'.

Leonardo da Vinci was the founder of 'scientific anatomy'. His contribution to life sciences is crucial, distinguished by a balance between his artistic and scientific interests. The artist thus perfectly embodies the spirit of the Renaissance, a period during which the boundary between the two disciplines was called into question for the first time. Leonardo da Vinci, for whom "arts and sciences are inseparable", unified and brought them together.

His anatomical studies thus brought two fundamental innovations to the life sciences:

- physiological precision in the results of dissection, with experimental verification;
- drawings of great beauty and unrivalled accuracy, illustrating a scientific understanding of the structure of the human body in its smallest details.

By devoting his entire life to the study of anatomy and the understanding of the human body, Leonardo da Vinci made his mottos "He turns not back who is bound to a star" and, even more so, "Ostinato rigore" ("Relentless rigour"), a reality.

Art and science share the common goal of pushing the boundaries of our knowledge and questioning the world by making 'the invisible' visible. Highlighting the work of Leonardo da Vinci, therefore, makes it possible today to pass on his scientific discoveries to a wider public.

The exhibition catalogue, co-edited by Éditions Skira and Château du Clos Lucé, brings together important and unpublished contributions from numerous international specialists in the work of Leonardo da Vinci. Château du Clos Lucé extends its heartfelt thanks to the curators of the exhibition, Dominique Le Nen and Pascal Brioist, and to all the authors whose research continues to advance our knowledge of Leonardo da Vinci and his work:

Dominique Le Nen, University Professor and Surgeon at the Regional University Hospital in Brest;
Pascal Brioist, Professor of Modern History at the University of Tours and member of the Centre for Advanced Renaissance Studies;
Bertrand Debono, Neurosurgeon at the Centre Francilien du Dos (Paris-Versailles), President of the French Society of Private Neurosurgeons;
François Gaucher, Surgeon at Quimper General Hospital;
Laetitia Guezennec, Marketing and Communication Manager, Dassault Systèmes;
Maëlyss Haddjeri, PhD Student in Art History at the École Pratique des Hautes Etudes, Université Paris Sciences et Lettres;
Matthew Landrus, Researcher at Wolfson College, Oxford University, specialist in the history of art and science in Italy;
Jacky Laulan, Hand Surgeon at the Regional University Hospital in Tours;
Domenico Laurenza, Associate Professor of Art History at the University of Cagliari;
Christian Lefèvre, Professor of Anatomy at the Faculty of Medicine in Brest;
Jean-Jacques Monsuez, Cardiologist at René-Muret AP-HP Hospital;
Johann Peltier, Neurosurgeon and Professor of Anatomy, Amiens;
François Rozet, Senior Surgeon in the Department of Urology at the Institut Mutualiste Montsouris in Paris;

François Saint Bris, President, Château du Clos Lucé – Parc Leonardo da Vinci;
Joël Savéan, Technician at the Laboratory of Medical Information Processing in Brest;
Anna Sconza, Lecturer in Italian Studies at Sorbonne-Nouvelle Paris-III University;
Frank Zöllner, Professor of Art History at Leipzig University.

Clos Lucé thanks the museums and cultural institutions that have loaned works:
Gallerie degli Uffizi, Florence;
Gallerie dell'Accademia, Venice;
Bibliothèque interuniversitaire Santé Médecine, université Paris-Cité;
Bibliothèque municipale, Dijon;
Bibliothèque municipale, Le Havre;
Institut national d'histoire de l'art (INHA), Paris;
Bibliothèque Carré d'Art, Nîmes;
Bibliothèque municipale, Grenoble;
Bibliothèque humaniste, Sélestat;
Fondazione Cassa di Risparmio, Bologna (Collezioni d'arte et di storia);
Biblioteca Nazionale "Vittorio Emanuele III", Naples;

Clos Lucé also thanks Dassault Systèmes 3DEXPERIENCE Lab, its technological partner.

This exhibition has been made possible thanks to the financial support of the Centre-Val de Loire region, to whom the Château du Clos Lucé extends its gratitude for their support, generosity and trust. Finally, the Château du Clos Lucé would like to thank the members of its team, who worked with enthusiasm, professionalism and dedication to bring this wonderful cultural project to fruition, in particular Michaël Petitjean, General Secretary; Diane Junqua, Director of Communications and Sponsorship; Sandra Chupin, Exhibition Coordinator; Nina Germain, Communications Officer; Eleonora Pavesi, Translator and Italian Coordinator; Paul Riffault, Head of Educational Activities; Jordane Mourgues, Executive Assistant; Stéphane Darras, Head of the Technical Department, and his entire team; and the Arc-en-Scène scenographic studio represented by Annabelle Jeanne and Iris Jasson.

This exhibition testifies to the richness and vitality of European relations and illustrates our ability to share and spread a common culture inherited from the humanism of the Renaissance.

✷

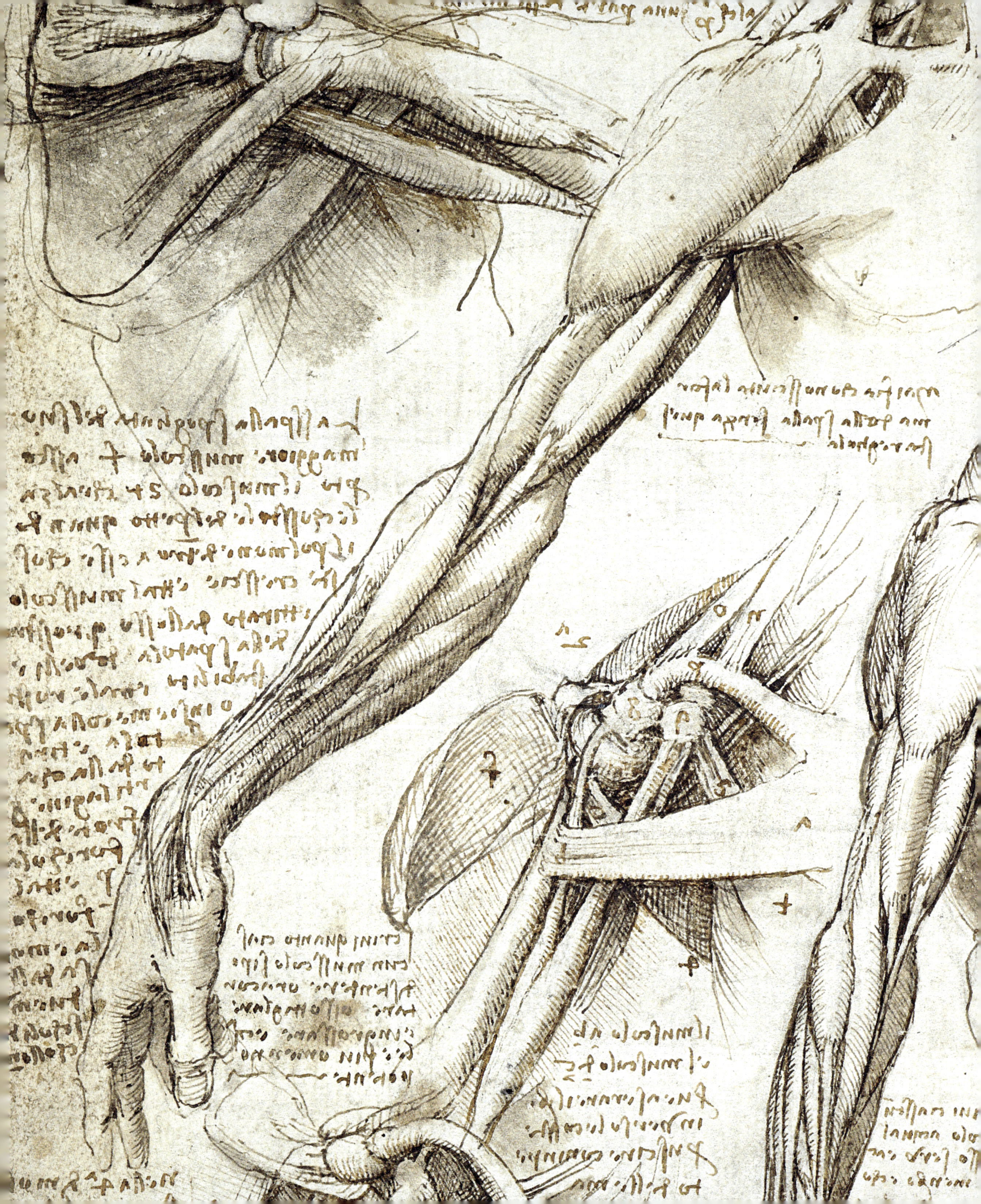

Introduction

Pascal Brioist
Professor of Modern History at the University of Tours
and member of the Centre for Advanced Renaissance Studies

Domenico Laurenza
Associate Professor of Art History
at the University of Cagliari

Dominique Le Nen
University Professor and Surgeon
at Brest Regional University Hospital

Previous page:

The muscles of the shoulder and arm, and the bones of the foot, c.1510–11, black chalk, pen and ink, wash, 28.9 × 20.1 cm (detail)
Windsor, Royal Collection Trust, RL 19013 v

Leonardo da Vinci, renowned for his talents as a painter, inventor, engineer, and prodigious designer of numerous machines (tanks, parachutes, etc.), was no less remarkable as an explorer of nature and the mysteries it conceals. It is no surprise that during the Renaissance, when understanding the human being was the cornerstone of knowledge, Leonardo da Vinci became fascinated with anatomy. For centuries, however, the study of the human body remained hamstrung by beliefs and taboos, which even, through the works of the physician Claudius Galen, imposed the animal as a frame of reference.

Leonardo attended dissections; he then methodically lifted away human and animal flesh using surgical instruments, and layer after layer, in his inverted handwriting and with astonishing accuracy, he transcribed the results of his observations in his notebooks. For him, nothing happened by chance, his approach to work was always carefully thought out, and his method of dissection was highly original. Thanks to a clear talent for observation, coupled with an impressive gift for drawing [fig. 1], he studied everything, from the bodies of men to those of women and children; from the ventricles of the brain to the cavities of the heart; from the bones to the muscles and joints; from the thoracic organs to those of the abdomen. Far from being satisfied with merely describing anatomy, a compelling need to understand led him to study the functions of the dissected tissues, for example by pulling on the tendons to determine their actions.

His anatomical works are, paradoxically, not very well known, even though he devoted himself to the study of the human body from 1487, the date of his first folios, until his departure for France in 1516. From this monumental work, nothing was published, even though this had been his intention. After his death, he left his disciple Francesco Melzi the immense, impossible task of collecting and ordering his countless drawings, sketches and handwritten notes.

The sculptor Pompeo Leoni (1531–1608) acquired them around 1580 before assembling them in albums. One of these, containing his anatomical plates, was bought in 1690 by the Royal Library at Windsor, near London. Today, these plates still belong to the English Crown.

Leonardo da Vinci's anatomical legacy consists of an impressive body of handwritten documents. They form a heterogeneous whole, a compilation of notations, drawings, scientific and artistic observations, testimony to the fields in which he made the greatest advances, through his dedicated and meticulous studies; as for his pictorial output, it amounts to just a dozen paintings.

By presenting his anatomical works in the light of today's knowledge, and by comparing his plates with modern medical imagery [fig. 2-3], the exhibition aims to restore Leonardo da Vinci to his rightful place in the history of anatomy, that of a pioneer – even ahead of the legendary Andreas Vesalius, who published the famous printed work *De humani corporis fabrica* in 1543 – and to retrace the career of this extraordinary visionary by showing the artistic as well as the scientific quality of his work.

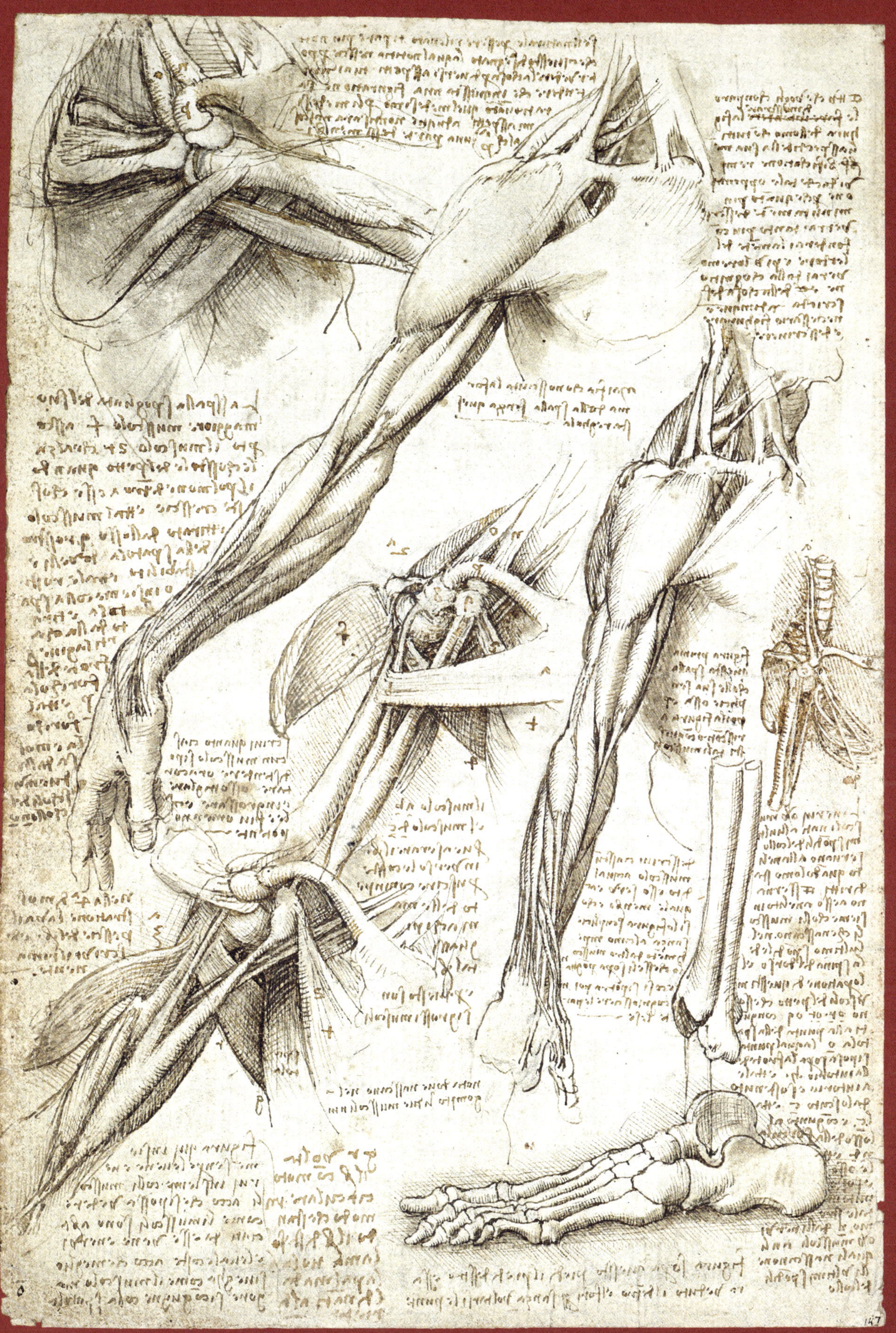

fig.1 — *The muscles of the shoulder and arm, and the bones of the foot*, c.1510–11, black chalk, pen and ink, wash, 28.9 × 20.1 cm
Windsor, Royal Collection Trust, RL 19013 v

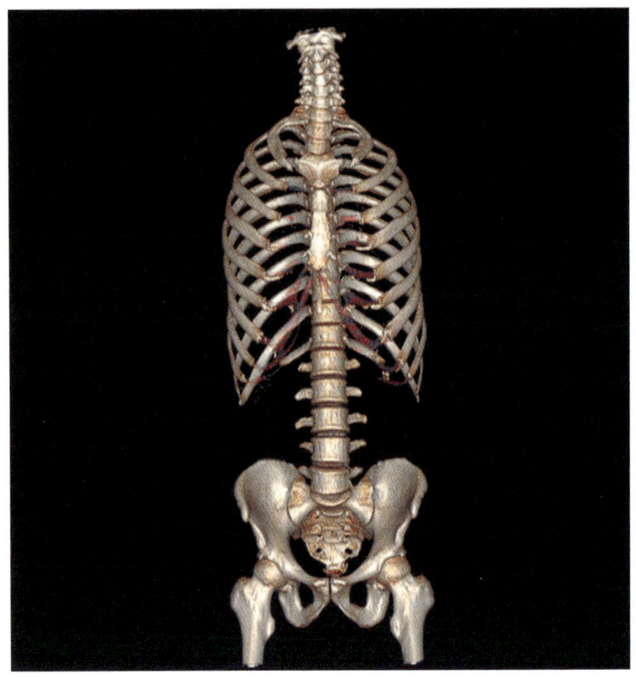
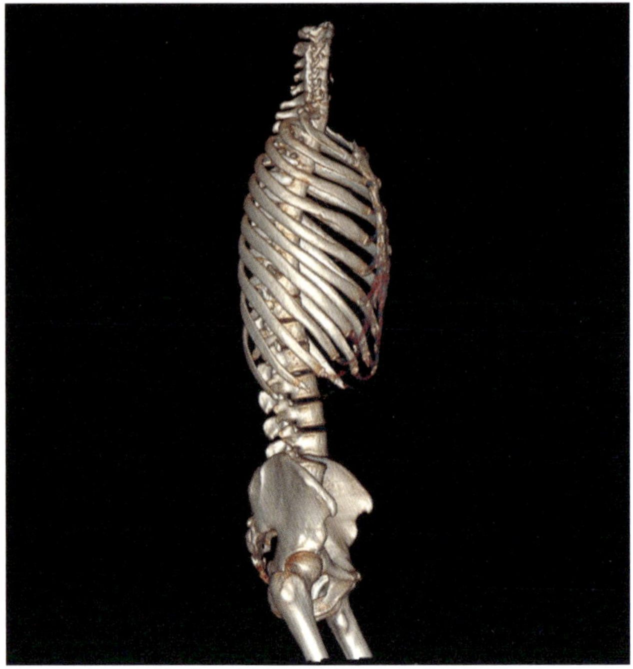

fig. 2 — Modern CT imaging (side and front views)
(Dr Marc Garetier – HIA Brest)

Before undertaking this challenge, however, we must first dispel the perceptions fostered by literature in the vernacular.

The image of Leonardo the 'anatomist' is surrounded by myth: he is said to have secretly dissected human cadavers in order to carry out his studies, in opposition to the Church and medical institutions. Nothing could be further from the truth. In fact, Leonardo was cutting open dead bodies with the tip of his scalpel with the full knowledge of the authorities. It was only very late, as Vasari records, that he encountered certain difficulties, but only because he was at odds with papal opinions on the nature of life in the foetus.

It must also be emphasised that Leonardo's texts and drawings could not, in practice, have influenced the thinking of the physicians and surgeons of his time, nor of the period that followed. In the middle of the 18th century, Leonardo was best known as a painter, and his scientific and philosophical writings were overlooked by the public. It was only in 1773 that the anatomist William Hunter took notice of the folios on the human body, then held in the collection of King Charles II of England. The first printed representations of these plates, engraved by Francesco Bartolozzi, were not actually published until 1796, and it was not until the very end of the 19th century that a complete facsimile edition of the collection at Windsor appeared. It would, therefore, be a mistake to look back and declare Leonardo the inventor of modern anatomy.

The anatomical work of the Tuscan master is that of a 'cultural hybrid'. He was first apprenticed to Verrocchio, then learned to draw bodies with him in a multidisciplinary workshop, and then acquired further knowledge in his encounters with doctors and through his readings. His dissections and methods of observation and experimentation led him further, and in particular to express critical views of his masters.

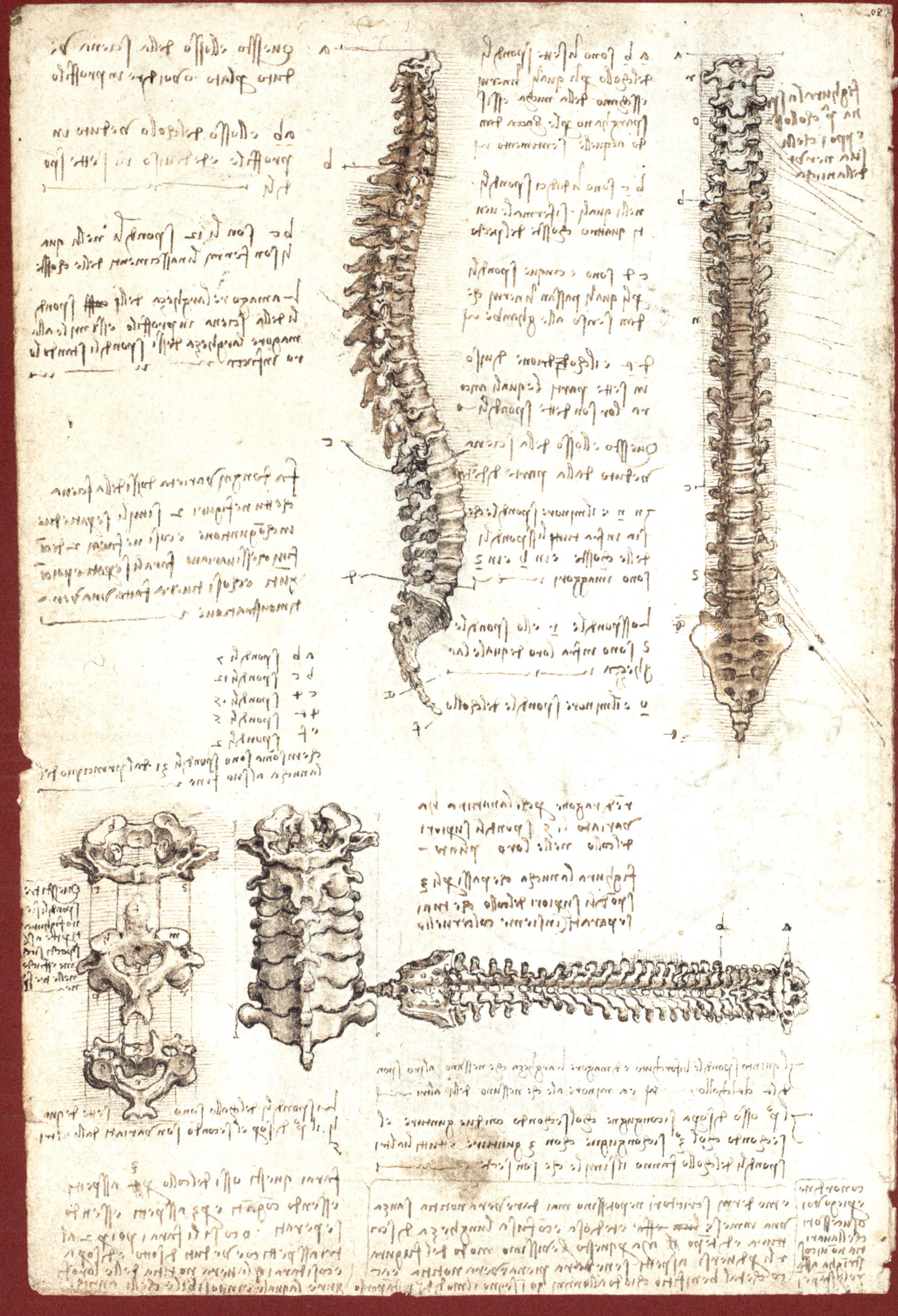

fig. 3 — *The vertebral column*, c.1510–11,
black chalk, pen and ink, wash, 28.6 × 20 cm
Windsor, Royal Collection Trust, RL 19007 v

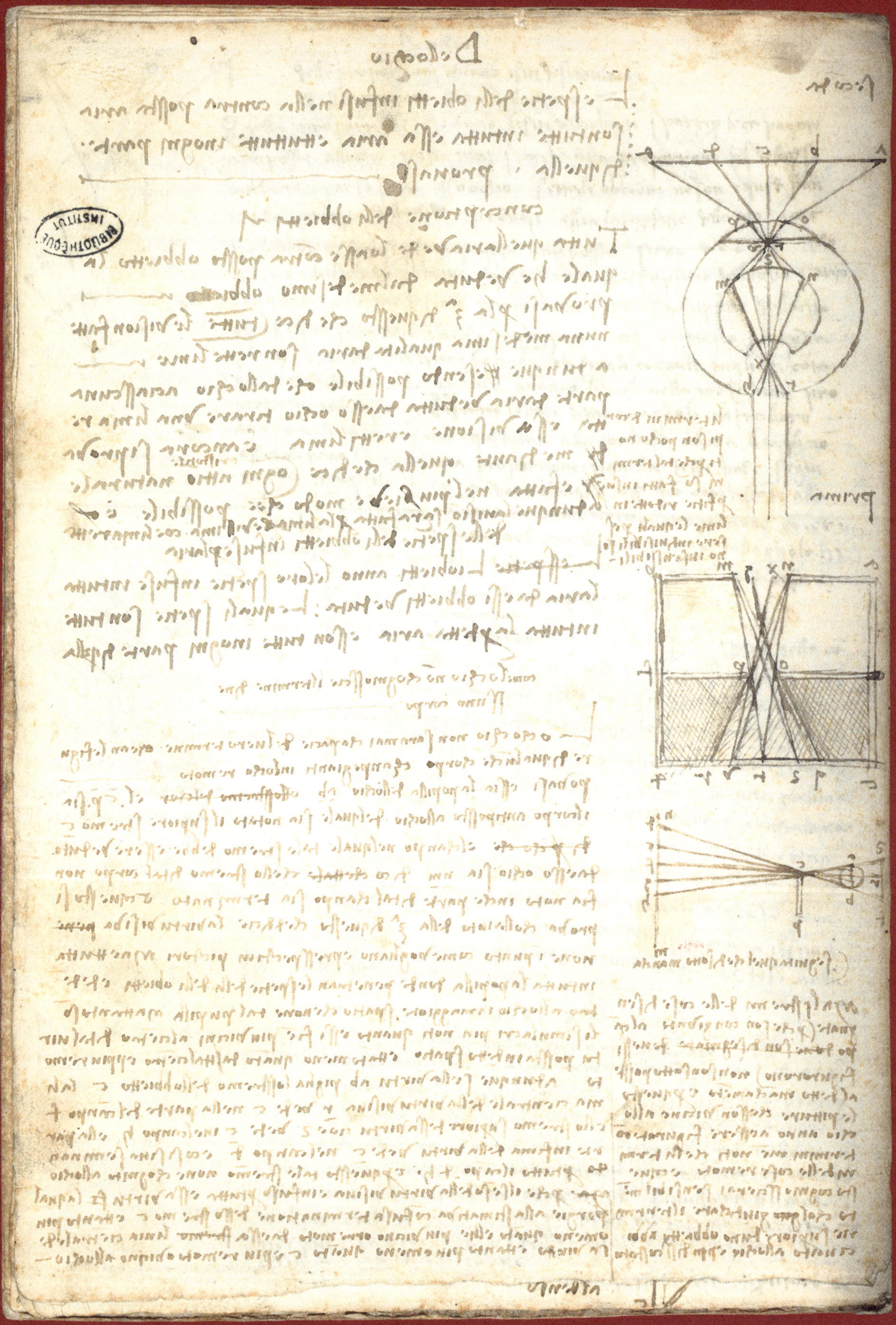

fig. 4 — Sheet of paper representing the camera obscura,
Manuscript D, Institut de France, folio 10 v

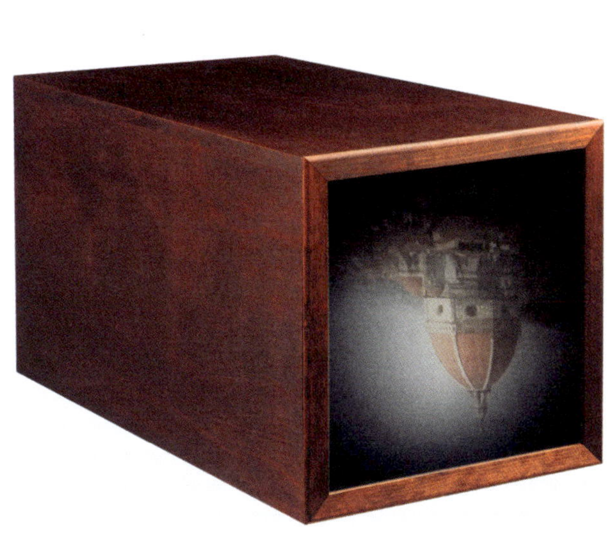

fig. 5 — Camera obscura,
made by Jean-Louis Pironio after the design
of the Manuscript D from Institut de France, folio 10 v

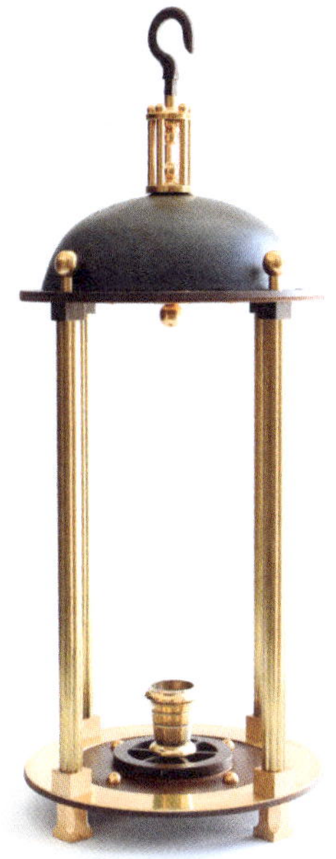

fig. 6 — Candle lamp drawn
by Leonardo da Vinci
and made by Michel Campana

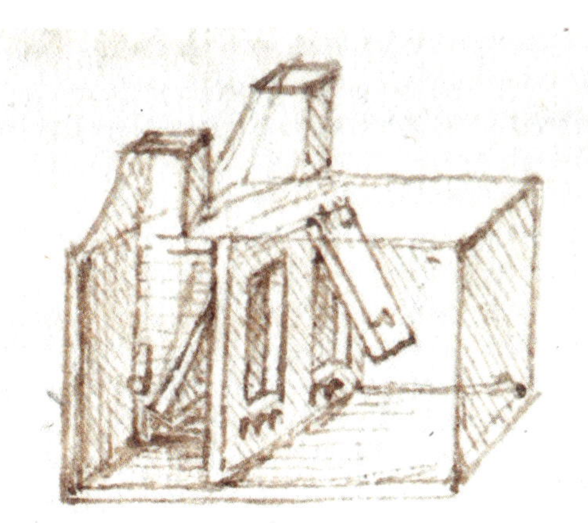

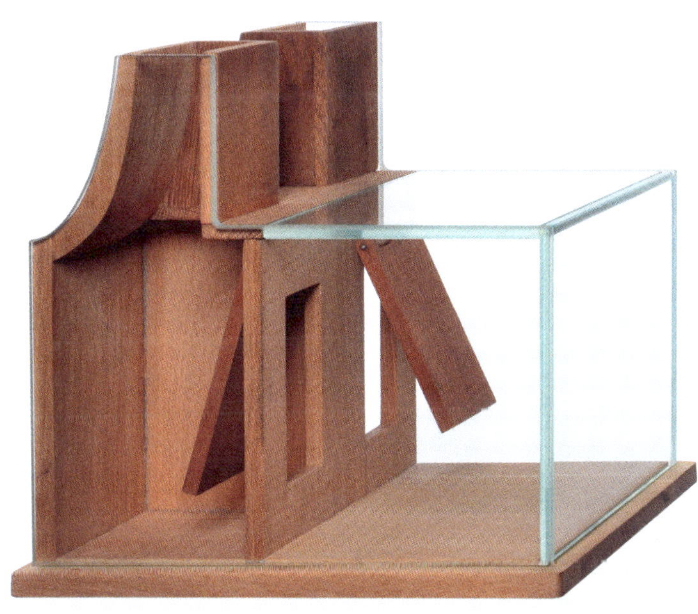

fig. 7 — Model of a mechanism imitating the functioning of the lung
made by Jean-Louis Pironio after the design of the *Codex Arundel*, folio 24 r

Leonardo's method is extremely original, owing perhaps to its hybrid nature. This can be seen in his construction of models to understand the mechanics of the body, the functions of the lungs, the *camera obscura* or the bloodstream (glass model) – a habit of making models that Leonardo acquired in Verrocchio's workshop [fig. 4-7].

Similarly, the idea of showing the body in planes, sections or elevations comes from architecture and sculpture. As for his vision of the mechanics of the human body, it clearly derives from his practice as an engineer. Leonardo's enquiries into the living world prove, moreover, that he could lose his fondness for the academic teachings of which his physician friends had spoken and that he had come across in the course of his reading. He was, therefore, capable of casting doubt on Galen and his theories on the workings of the heart, or on those who sought to simplify anatomy, but who could not present a coherent understanding of the body. This audacity towards the authorities at times led him to contradict the pope himself.

During the Renaissance, anatomists and artists seized upon the human body, some to discover the arrangement of organs, the ramification of nerves, the intricacy of vessels; others to draw, sculpt and model it, to discover the muscles that lie hidden beneath the skin. Leonardo, a man of art and science, went further in the study and representation of the body, using anatomy, first and foremost, for the sake of knowledge; and his drawings, true masterpieces, give us precious messages about the makeup of Man and Woman, compared with the ideas and theories of his famous predecessors.

Leonardo studied all aspects of human anatomy. However, three areas of research are particularly important to understand how his interest in the structure of the human body arose and developed in connection with his work as an artist: the muscles and bones, the heart, and the reproductive organs of the female body.

The first area allows historians to sidestep the debatable idea of genius, and to explain 'Leonardo' in relation to the context in which he lived. From the end of the 14th century (Cennino Cennini's *Libro dell'arte* dates from this period and already deals with the link between art and anatomy), Tuscan artists were making advances on both a theoretical and practical level. Artistic inventiveness with the human body now implied considering muscles and bones as the basis of the external shape of the body and its movements. This is one of the features that characterised Italian art, which based artistic *mimesis* (imitation of nature), in scientific terms, on the understanding of the causes (or reasons) of all natural forms: anatomical reasons in the case of the human figure; mathematical and optical reasons in the case of the representation of space. The mimetic realism of northern European art tended rather towards a recording of what the eye sees directly: "*ut pictura ita visio*" ("As is the picture, so is sight"). In Italy, the link between anatomy and art culminated with the work of Michelangelo and the traditions associated with him. The nude form drawn, painted or sculpted by Michelangelo is a complex study of form and shape based on an awareness of its internal foundations (bones and muscles).

Leonardo's early anatomical studies were also part of this artistic horizon. Produced in 1485–1486, the series of Windsor metalpoint drawings on paper coated with a layer of colour, then variously reworked with pen and ink, mainly includes studies of muscles and bones. The connection with art is clear. The Tuscan also further developed his anatomical study of the neck, as illustrated in his *Saint Jerome in the Wilderness* (c.1481) – one of the last paintings from Leonardo's early period, executed in Florence – one of the best examples of how anatomical knowledge can enhance the dramatic movement of the figure. Another drawing of the same series is the study of the anatomical basis of the movement of the right hand in the *Virgin of the Rocks* (c.1483) [fig. 8-9].

The study of muscles and bones reached its height in 1509–1510, in the Anatomical Manuscript A, which is entirely dedicated to them – anatomical studies of which, however, one would search in vain for any direct artistic consequence. Leonardo's late male nudes conceal any direct morphological relationship with muscles and bones, thus avoiding creating excessive relief; this is in contrast to Michelangelo and the main tradition of artistic anatomy. However, the relationship between anatomy and art also continued for Leonardo, although it became more complex, deeper, more theoretical and philosophical. In the same years, around 1507–1508, at the time of his dissections carried out at the Florentine hospital of Santa Maria Nuova, Leonardo deepened his work on both the cardiovascular system and the reproductive organs of women.

In the natural philosophical dimension of anatomy, the study of the heart had psychosomatic and physiological implications. According to ancient tradition, the heart was the seat of the passions and a particularly well-developed organ in the male body. A courageous and proud character, a typically masculine trait for the culture of the time, derived from the strong constitution of the heart. *The Battle of Anghiari*, painted during the artist's second stay in Florence, dominated by figures of fighters with expressions of anger and daring, is the artistic transfiguration of his psychosomatic research, between anatomy and physiognomy, onto the 'leonine' human figure with the strong constitution of the heart (*cf.* Windsor, RL 19029 r, 12502 r).

The osteo-muscular aspect can be seen in the artistic anatomy of Michelangelo and other artists of the time, dominated by the male form. But it was a different connection with the studies of female anatomy that enabled the introduction of a new, even entirely inverted relationship between art and anatomy. It contributed to the emergence of a new artistic ideal of beauty.

From an anatomical and physiological point of view, Leonardo tried to show that female sperm contributed as much as male sperm to the creation and 'generation' of the body of the unborn child. According to an ancient theory of Aristotelian origin, the female provided matter alone, while the male, through his sperm, provided the active part of the seed.

The value attributed to the female body from the point of view of the physiology of reproduction contributes to define the somatic aspects associated with this vital function: a wider pelvis (seat of the uterus and the reproductive organs) compared with the thorax (seat of the heart). Such a concept caused a discrepancy with the point of view of the anthropometric canons of the Renaissance and classical art. From Vitruvius to Francesco di Giorgio, the ideal body used to model the proportions of architecture was the male body. Leonardo, in some of his anatomical drawings that

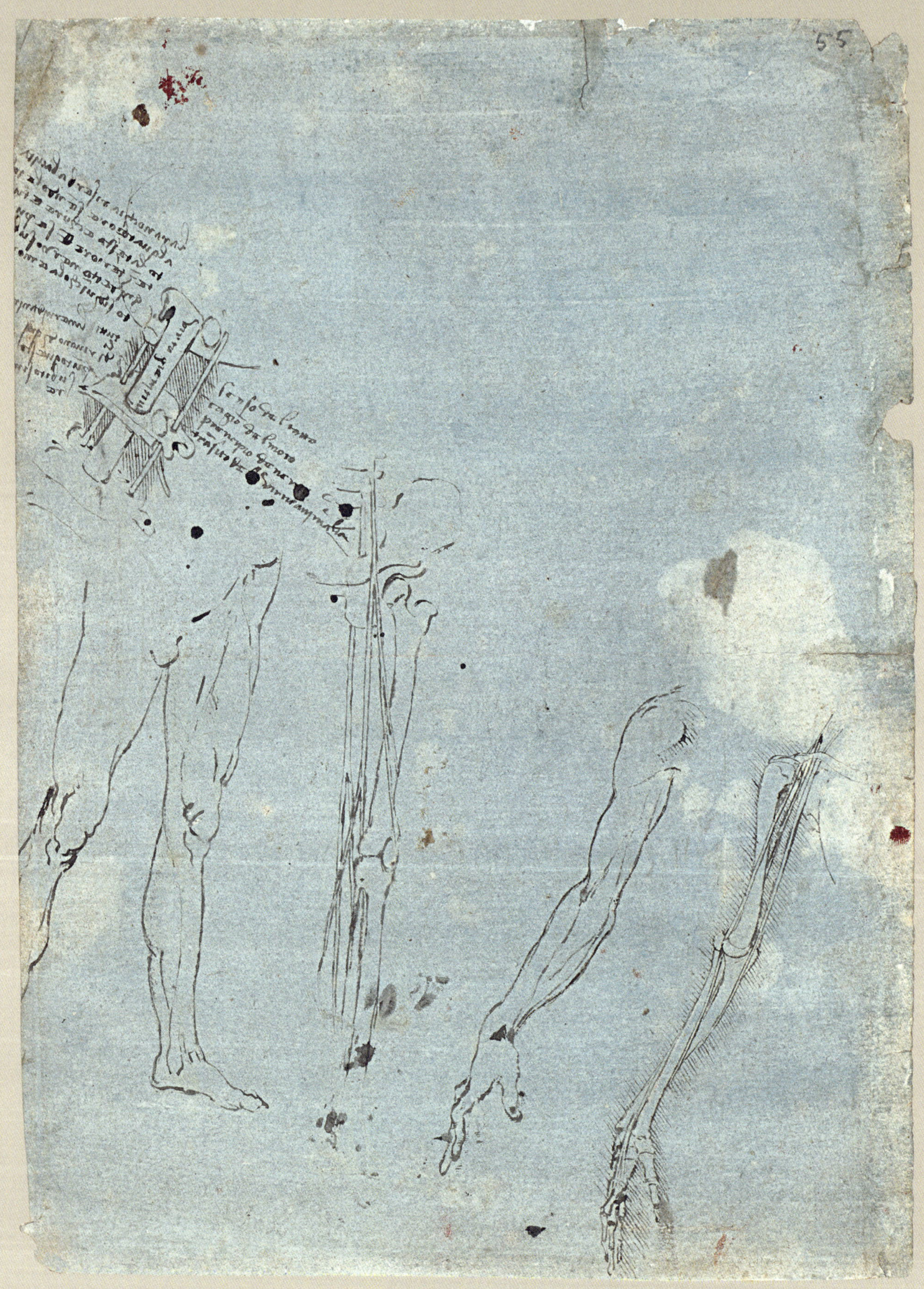

fig. 8 — *Studies of the nervous system*, c.1485–90, metalpoint (faded) and pen and ink on blue-grey prepared paper, 22.2 × 30.4 cm
Windsor, Royal Collection Trust, RL 12613 v

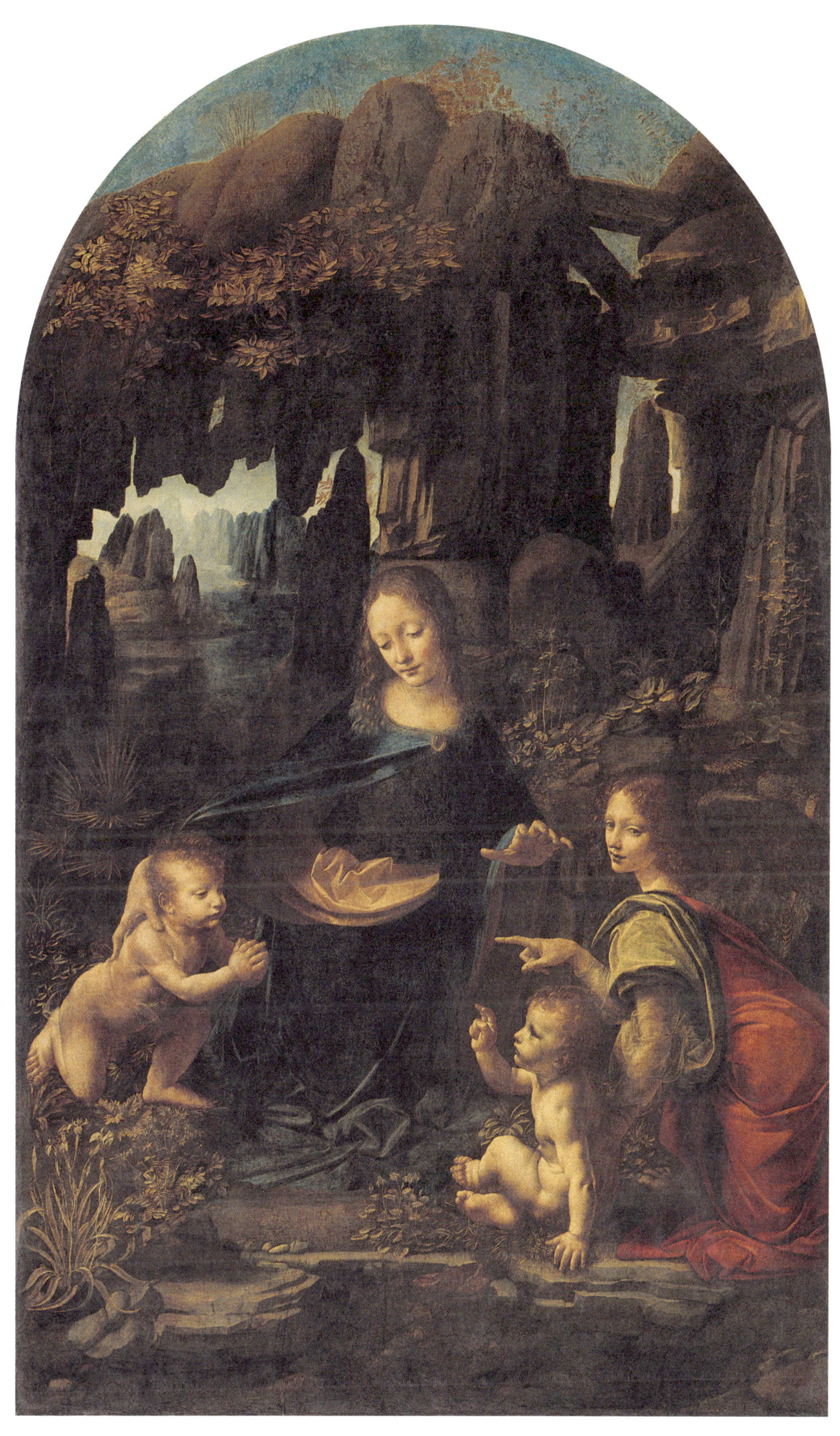

fig. 9 — *The Virgin of the Rocks*,
1483–1494 (4th quarter of the 15th century), oil on canvas, 199.5 × 122 cm
Paris, musée du Louvre, inv. 777

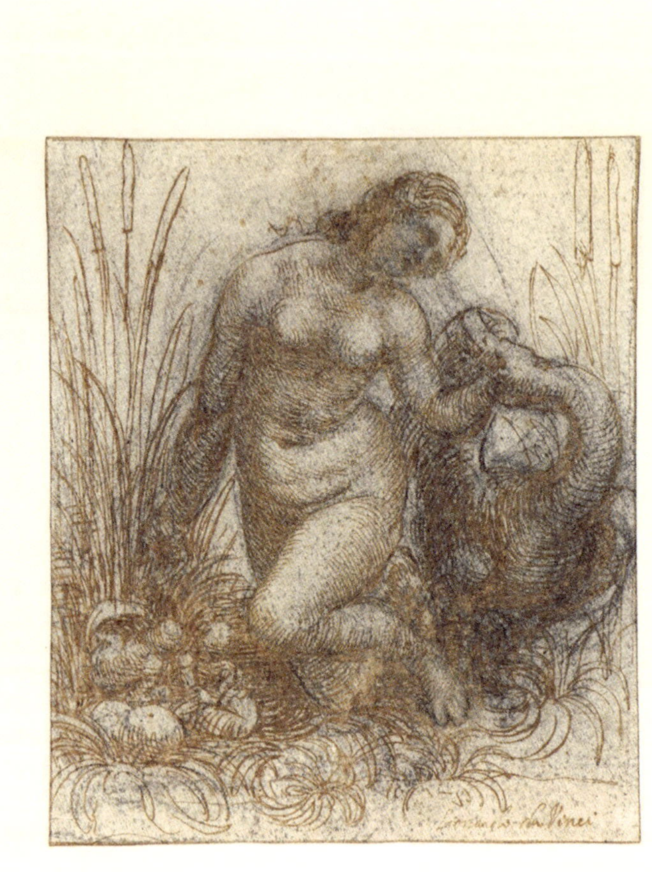

fig. 10
Leda and the Swan,
c.1504–1507
black chalk, pen
and brown ink,
128 × 109 cm
Rotterdam, Museum
Boijmans Van Beuningen, inv. I 466

represented the female reproductive organs, defined the external shape of the body, emphasising the width of the pelvis and, in general, the opulence of a body dominated by curves [fig. 11].

In the preparatory drawings of the figure of Leda, he focused precisely on this type of body [fig. 10].

A new ideal of artistic beauty was born, which, in contrast to the masculine canon of the anthropometric tradition of the 15th century and the muscular style of Michelangelo, was greatly developed between the 16th and 17th centuries, from Titian to Rubens and beyond (we know that Rubens had the opportunity to see Leonardo's anatomical and physiognomic studies). Although one of the fundamental roots of this new ideal of beauty lies in the classical tradition, in Leonardo's case it is also deeply linked to his anatomical research, which represents an original and lesser-known development of what we now call artistic anatomy.

✷

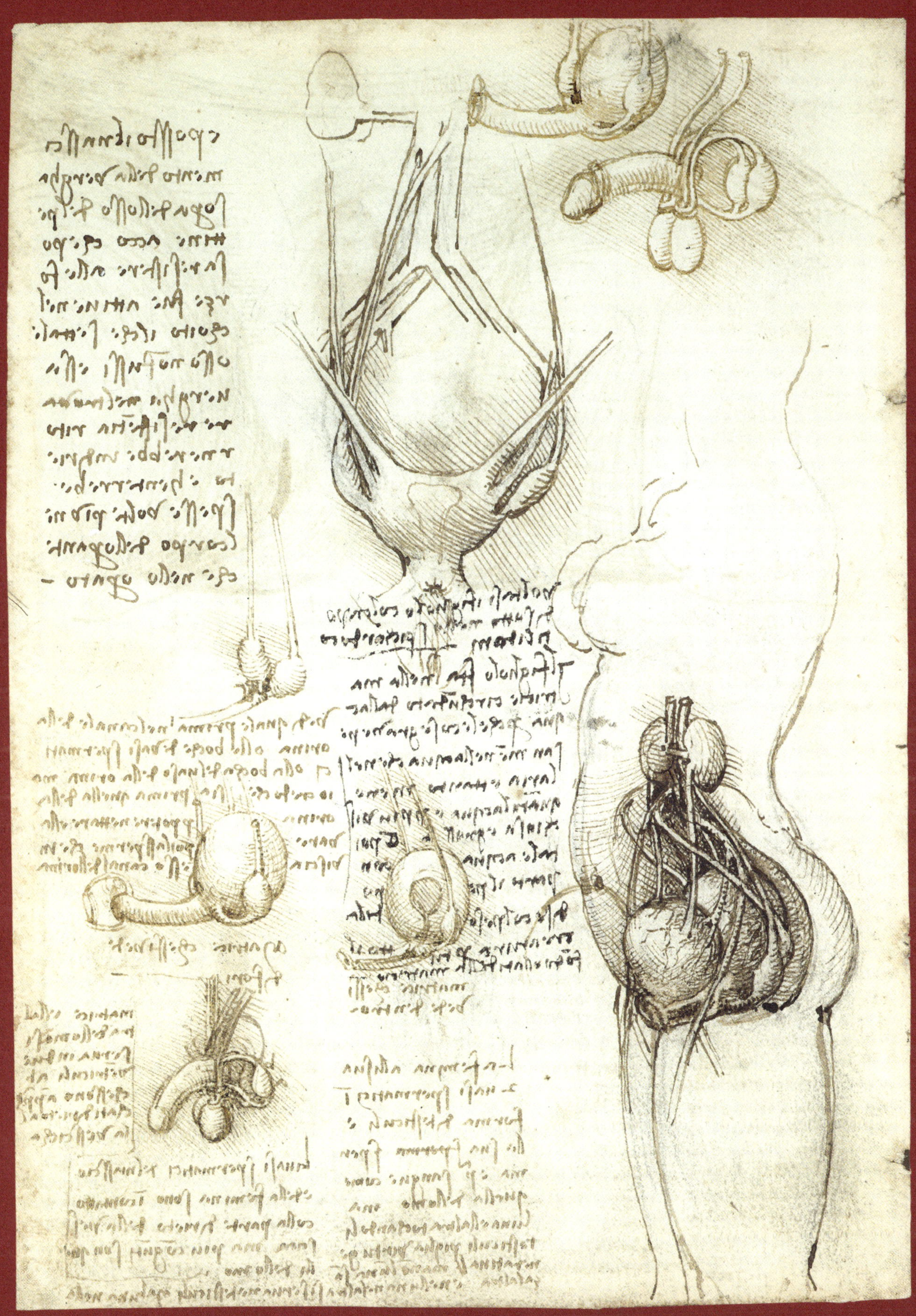

fig. 11 — *The male and female reproductive systems*, c.1508, pen and ink over black chalk, 19.1 × 13.8 cm
Windsor, Royal Collection Trust, RL 19095 v

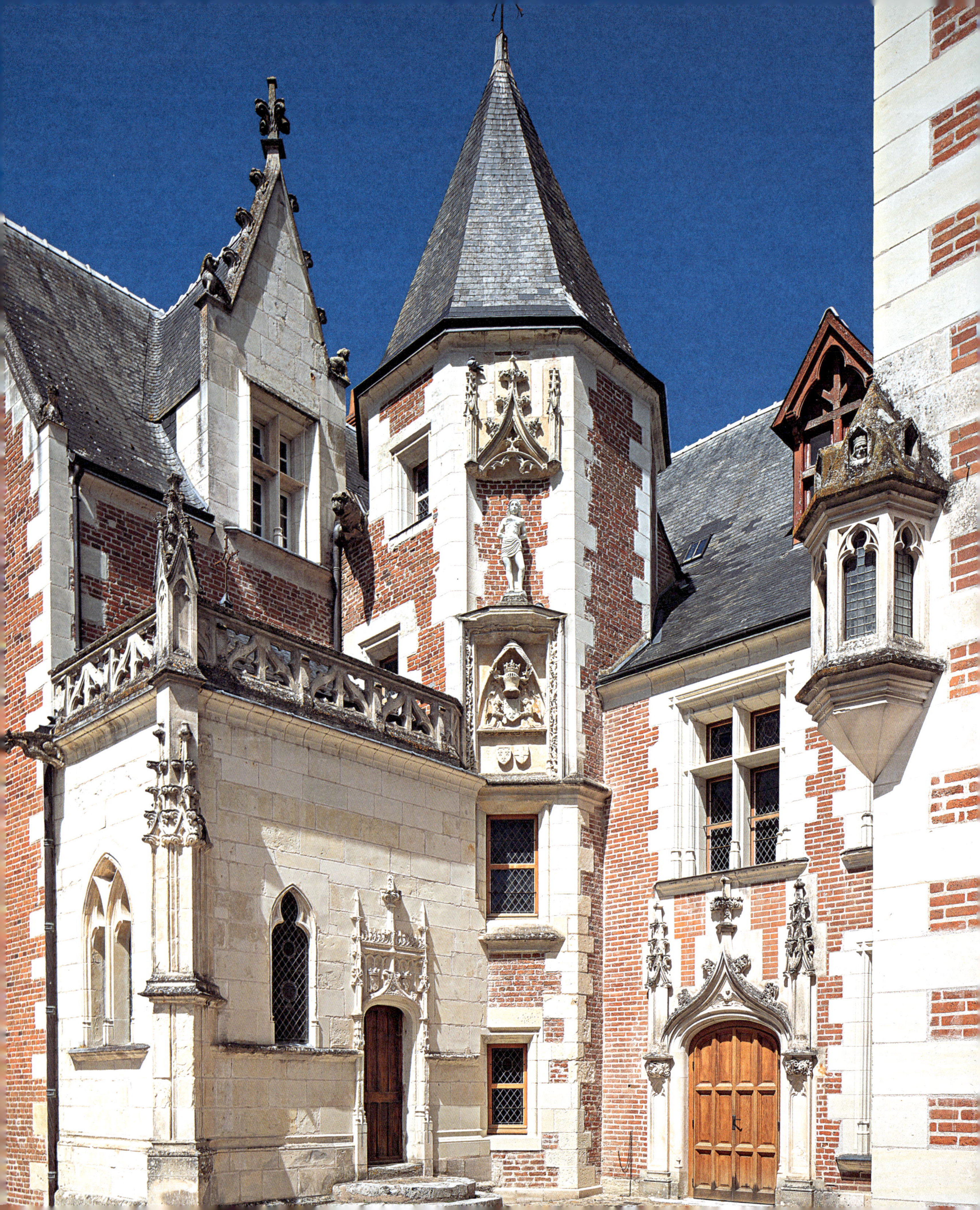

Leonardo da Vinci at the Château du Clos Lucé (1516-1519)

François Saint Bris
President
Château du Clos Lucé – Parc Leonardo da Vinci

Previous page:

The Clos Lucé

Amboise,
Cradle of the French Renaissance

The Renaissance – a vast intellectual, artistic and humanist movement, born in Italy and Flanders – confirmed a return to the founding roots of ancient Greece and Rome and spread across the whole of Europe. It reached France under the successive reigns of three kings, from 1494 to 1547. Fascinated by Italy, the Valois kings were constantly crossing the Alps and, campaign after campaign, sought to entice architects, artists and craftsmen into building and embellishing cities, castles and gardens for them and to promote a new art of living. Great discoveries, bringing massive quantities of gold and spices from the New World, contributed to the prosperity and rapid development of the whole of Europe. Amboise became the cradle of the French Renaissance. Francis I, captivated by the multiple talents of Leonardo da Vinci, invited him to reside in France near him at Clos Lucé.

Three Years
in the Service of the King

In the autumn of 1516, at the age of 64, Leonardo da Vinci left Rome for Amboise, embarking on what would be his last journey. He arrived in France accompanied by Francesco Melzi, his loyal disciple, and Battista de Villanis, his Milanese servant. In addition to the manuscripts and notes he had accumulated throughout his life, he brought with him three of his major works: the *Mona Lisa*, *Saint John the Baptist* and his *Saint Anne*, to live in the Château du Cloux, today called the Château du Clos Lucé [fig.1-2]. The young 22-year-old monarch, basking in the glory of his victory at Marignan, appointed him 'First Painter, Engineer and Architect to the King'. He put his country residence at his disposal and granted him a very generous annual pension of 1,000 gold crowns. The king extended the most generous credit lines to him and showered him with affection. He had an almost filial admiration for him and called him "my father", with not a day spent in Amboise going by without paying Leonardo a visit.

It was thus at Clos Lucé that the French history began of Leonardo da Vinci's three masterpieces, which would join the royal collections before being housed in the Louvre Museum. King Francis I's fascination with these masterpieces, as well as for *The Last Supper*, came from his mother, Louise of Savoy. It was a continuation of the cultural and artistic influence, the admiration and infatuation that the Tuscan master had exerted on the two previous kings of France, Charles VIII and Louis XII, thereby establishing the exceptional link between Leonardo da Vinci, France and Italy during the Renaissance.

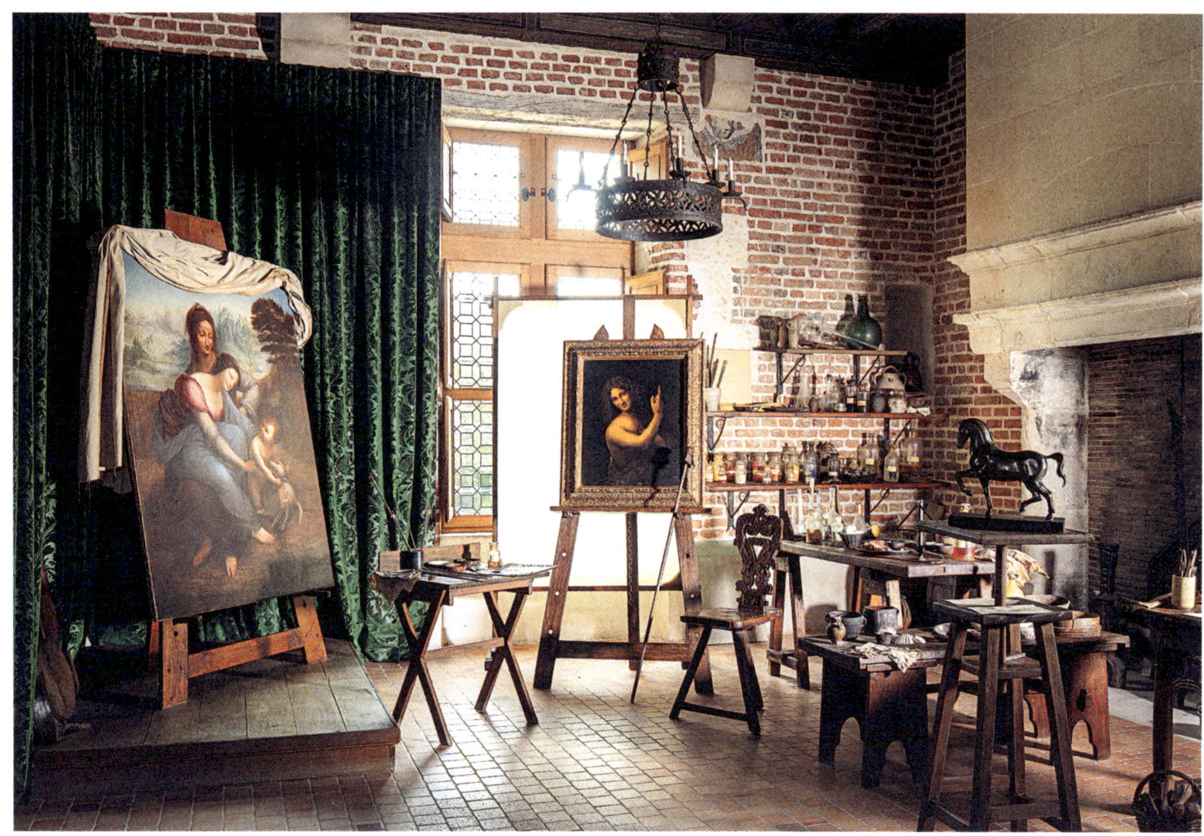

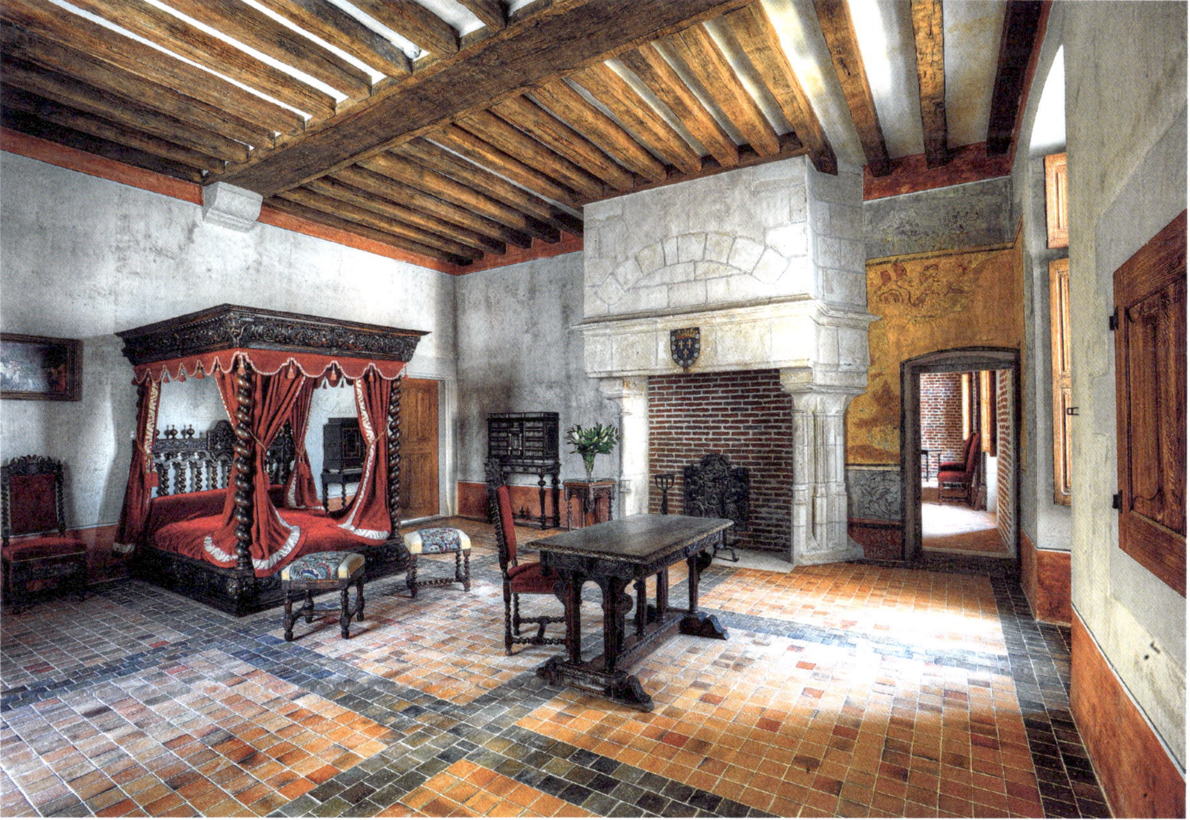

fig. 1 — Leonardo da Vinci's workshops

fig. 2 — Leonardo da Vinci's bedroom

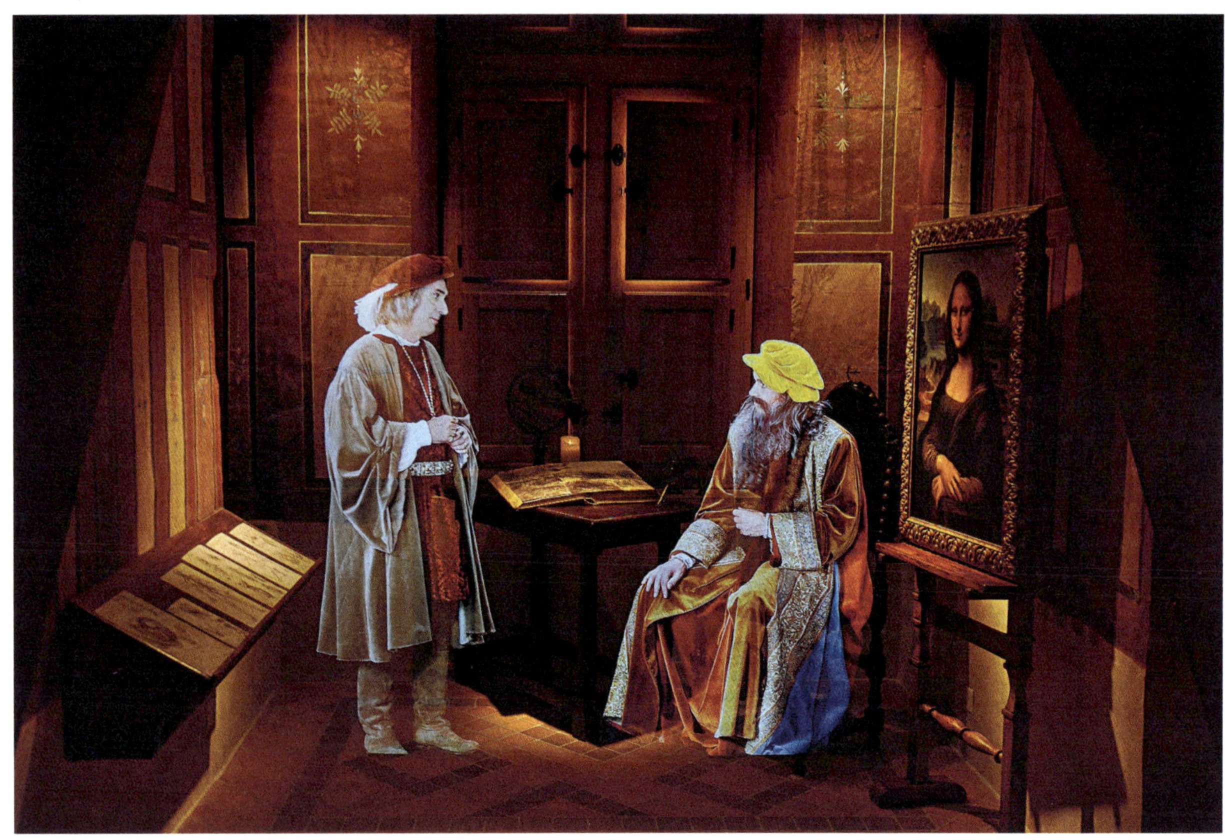

fig. 3 — Cardinal of Aragon visiting Leonardo da Vinci at the Clos Lucé (hologram)

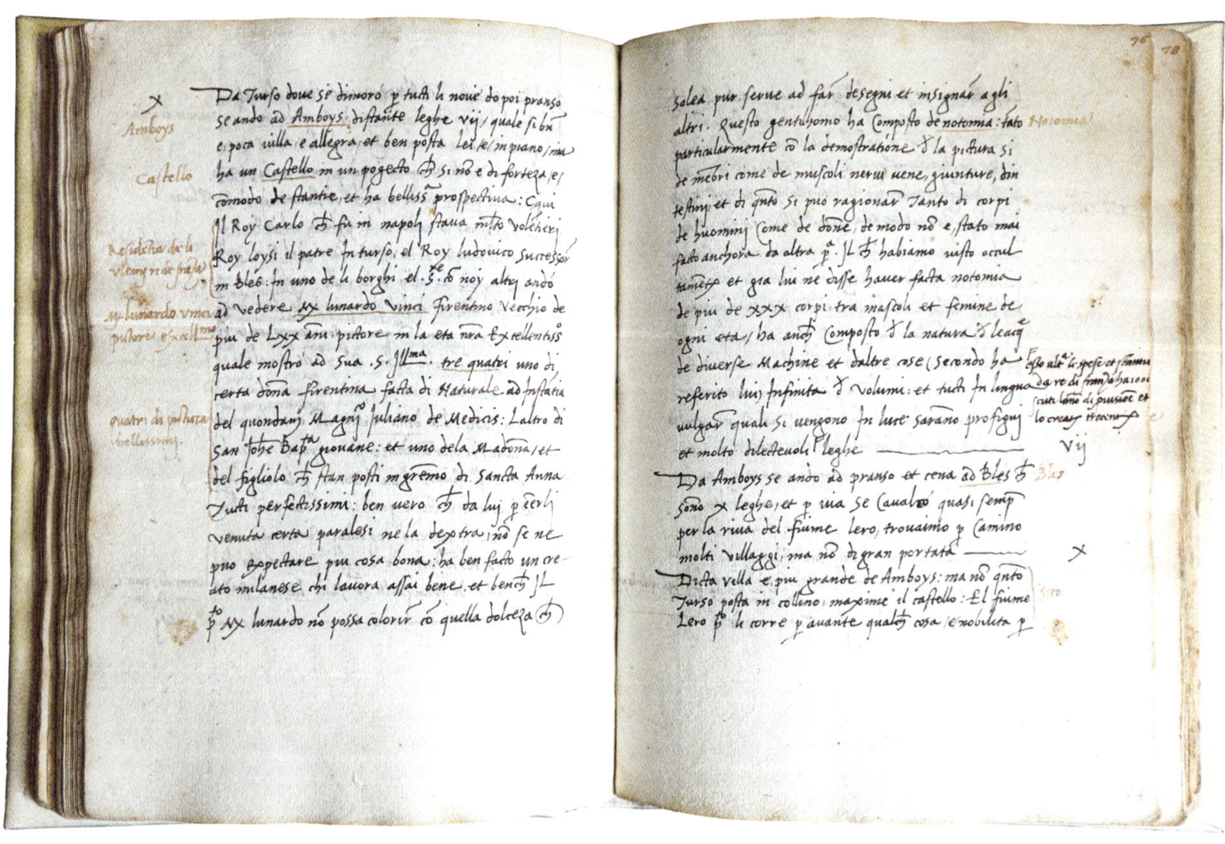

fig. 4 — Antonio de Béatis, Cardinal of Aragon's secretary *Itinerario di Monsignor Reverendissimo et Illustrissimo il cardinale de Aragona* (holographic testimony), 1522
Biblioteca Nazionale "Vittorio Emanuele III", Naples

Leonardo da Vinci's Workshops at Clos Lucé

During his years at Clos Lucé (1516–1519), Leonardo da Vinci remained very active and took on several projects. As Court Painter, Leonardo introduced himself as the "*pittore del re*", the king's painter. In his workshops at Clos Lucé, he put the finishing touches to the works he had brought with him, including *Saint Anne* and *Saint John the Baptist*. As an engineer and architect, he worked tirelessly on several major town planning and hydraulic projects commissioned by the king. Leonardo da Vinci carried out several studies on the hydrography of the region, throughout which he travelled on horseback. He drew maps of the basins of the Loire, Cher and Saône rivers and of the Ile d'Or in Amboise. He devised plans with strategic impact for the kingdom which involved building a system of canals and locks to connect the Loire Valley with the region of Lyon, bringing France closer to Italy. He planned to drain the unsanitary Sologne marshes and, for the court which was always in motion, he designed pavilions which could be dismantled and moved. He designed an architectural project for the king for an immense and grandiose palace, and the plans for an ideal city in Romorantin, the new capital of the kingdom, "a new Rome". Two fundamental concepts of the structure of the Château de Chambord were probably inspired by Leonardo da Vinci: the cross-shaped central-plan design and the 'double helix' staircase. As organiser of festivities for the king and his court, he staged four sumptuous events, including the 'Feast of Paradise', which he gave at the 'Palazzo del Cloux' on 17 June 1518. He designed stage costumes and showed himself to be a past master in the art of special effects. He also designed an equestrian statue for Francis I.

The Visit of the Cardinal of Aragon – Leonardo Anatomist

At Clos Lucé, towards the end of his life, on 10 October 1517, Leonardo da Vinci received a visit from a distinguished guest, the Cardinal of Aragon [fig.3].

The essence of his illustrious visitor's account is recounted by Antonio de Béatis, the Cardinal's secretary, who was present at this exceptional meeting, full of lessons on painting and anatomy [fig.4].

Leonardo confided in the Cardinal, who, upon seeing his anatomical plates, was captivated and amazed by the account of his countless dissections and the extent of his knowledge.

"He showed the Cardinal three paintings: the portrait, painted long ago, of a certain Florentine lady, painted naturally, at the behest of the late Giuliano de' Medici, the Magnificent; an infant Saint John the Baptist; and, last of all, a Virgin with child sitting on Saint Anne's knees. All three works were of a rare perfection.

This gentleman has composed a work on anatomy specifically for the study of painting, of the limbs as well as the muscles, nerves, veins, joints, intestines and everything that may be studied in the body of men as well as on that of women; and this in such a way that no other person before him has ever done. We have seen all this with our own eyes; and he told us that he has already dissected more than some thirty bodies, women and men alike, of all ages.

My lord Leonardo has also written about the nature of water, about various machines, and other things still, which could fill countless tomes and all in common language, which, were they to see the light of day, would be beneficial and pleasing."

In Amboise for All Eternity

Leonardo da Vinci said: "As a well spent day brings contented sleep, so a well spent life brings a peaceful death." On 23 April 1519, on the eve of Easter, Leonardo, "considering the certainty of death and the uncertainty of his hour", drew up his last will and testament with the help of Maître Guillaume Boureau, notary to the Royal Court. On 2 May 1519, with the thought that "no being goes to nought", Leonardo passed away at Clos Lucé at the age of 67. Francesco Melzi, his disciple and legatee, wrote to the artist's brothers: "He departed this life on the second day of May, well prepared, having received the last rites of the Holy Mother Church."

Was Francis I by Leonardo's bedside, as Vasari wrote, or at Saint-Germain-en-Laye, where the court was celebrating the birth of his second son, the future Henry II? The answer will probably always remain uncertain and disputed. Depictions of Leonardo da Vinci's death in the arms of his sovereign, inspired by Vasari's account and made legendary by the Romantic painters, will serve to illustrate, for all eternity, the colourful myth of the royal patronage by the young monarch, protector of the arts and letters, of the greatest artist of the Renaissance. Benvenuto Cellini later recounted the profound respect and immense admiration that Francis I had for Leonardo da Vinci. The king did not believe that "any man had so much culture, in matters to do with painting, sculpture, and architecture, as Leonardo da Vinci, as well as in philosophy, for he was a very great philosopher."

In accordance with his last wishes, his body was buried in the crypt of the collegiate church of Saint Florentin, within the walls of the Royal Castle of Amboise. The procession was made up of canons, chaplains, and young monks and friars, accompanied by sixty beggars carrying torches. The crypt was devastated during the Wars of Religion and the tombs were desecrated and ransacked. In 1807, the collegiate church of Saint Florentin was demolished, as was a large part of the Amboise fortress, by its owner Roger Ducos, a former member of the Convention who became a dignitary at the time of the Second Empire. The first excavations were undertaken in 1863 by the historian Arsène Houssaye, Inspector-General of Fine Arts. They uncovered a stone coffin and fragments of a burial site with bones presumed to be Leonardo da Vinci's, which were transferred, in 1874, to the Saint Hubert chapel at the Royal Castle of Amboise. The Tuscan master now rests there for all eternity.

Clos Lucé's Mission

The core mission of the Château du Clos Lucé, the home of Leonardo da Vinci, is to be a leading centre dedicated to understanding the artist and interpreting his work. In 1855, the Saint Bris family acquired the Clos Lucé estate. One hundred years later, in 1954, Hubert and Agnès Saint Bris embarked on a new adventure and decided to open Leonardo da Vinci's house to the public to give as many people as possible the opportunity to learn about him. They devoted themselves to restoring the house stone by stone, with the help of the 'Monuments Historiques' group of specialist craftsmen, using the same methods as their ancestors in the 15th and 16th centuries to restore the stone, wood and stained glass to the character it had at the time of Leonardo da Vinci during the Renaissance. The mission of the Château du Clos Lucé, a family cultural enterprise, is today to pass on the universal heritage, memory and knowledge of Leonardo da Vinci in the very place where he lived.

In 2016, on the 500th anniversary of Leonardo da Vinci's arrival at Clos Lucé, his workshops were restored and recreated in the spirit of a Renaissance *bottega*.

In June 2019, as part of the 500th anniversary of his death, Clos Lucé hosted an international exhibition *Leonardo da Vinci's Last Supper for Francis I: a Masterpiece of Gold and Silk*, curated by Pietro C. Marani, with the special loan of *The Last Supper* tapestry from the Vatican Museums, together with works on loan from the Louvre Museum, the Uffizi Gallery, the Biblioteca Ambrosiana in Milan and numerous European museums.

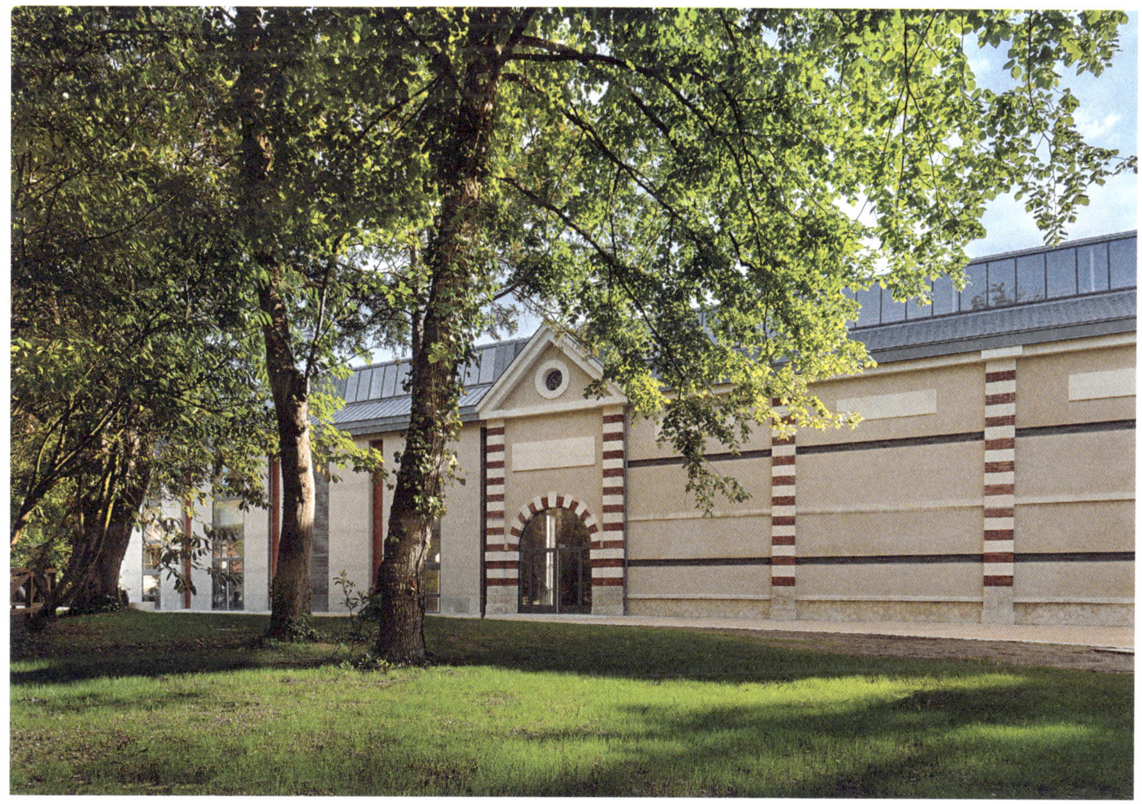

fig. 5 — The Leonardo da Vinci Painter and Architect Galleries

Clos Lucé's Digital Transformation

In June 2021, Clos Lucé, 'a castle for the future', inaugurated a new 500 m^2 cultural facility, the Leonardo da Vinci Painter and Architect Galleries [fig.5].

The first gallery, 'Leonardo, the painter', offers an immersive experience taking you through all Leonardo da Vinci's pictorial oeuvre, providing a new perspective on his creations: innovative staging in a sensitive virtual universe, a new 'ideal museum' presenting a digital monograph of the master's work, dynamic, spectacular and of museum quality. The aim is to illustrate and explain, using his preparatory drawings, the creative process of the masterpieces, while evoking the power and grace of the greatest painter of the Renaissance [fig.6].

The second gallery, 'Leonardo, the architect', evokes his passion for mathematics, spatial geometry and the influence of his contemporaries, whether it be the mathematician Luca Pacioli or the architects Alberti, Brunelleschi and Bramante. It presents and illustrates 'Leonardo and urban planning': his civil, military and religious architecture projects, as well as the architecture of so-called 'ephemeral' celebrations, using tactile models, digital tables and 3D videos.

An experimental multimedia space offers visitors a unique experience through a video game allowing them to fly in an ornithopter – one of Leonardo's flying machines – over a 3D reconstruction of the Royal Palace in Romorantin, the ideal city.

Scientific and technical workshops, designed in collaboration with the Cité des Sciences and the Palais de la Découverte, are also offered to the numerous visiting school groups in this scientific and educational facility. Students can enjoy operating Leonardo da Vinci's inventions. Six machines inspired by Leonardo da Vinci's inventions are available to children aged 9 to 18.

With this new innovative cultural facility, Clos Lucé was listed in *Time* magazine's 2021 top 100 destinations in the world.

In June 2022, Clos Lucé hosted an international exhibition, curated by the Vatican Museums, presenting *Leonardo da Vinci's* Saint Jerome, *an Unfinished Masterpiece*, a special loan from their museums.

Future Projects

Clos Lucé's next cultural and scientific challenge is to become the leading centre on Leonardo da Vinci and the Renaissance. It has acquired a three-hectare plot of industrial wasteland adjacent to the estate. The intention is to create a new cultural facility on the site, the 'International Interpretive Centre on Leonardo da Vinci and the Renaissance'. The aim of this new international cultural and scientific facility is to provide the public with the keys to understanding the work of Leonardo da Vinci and the

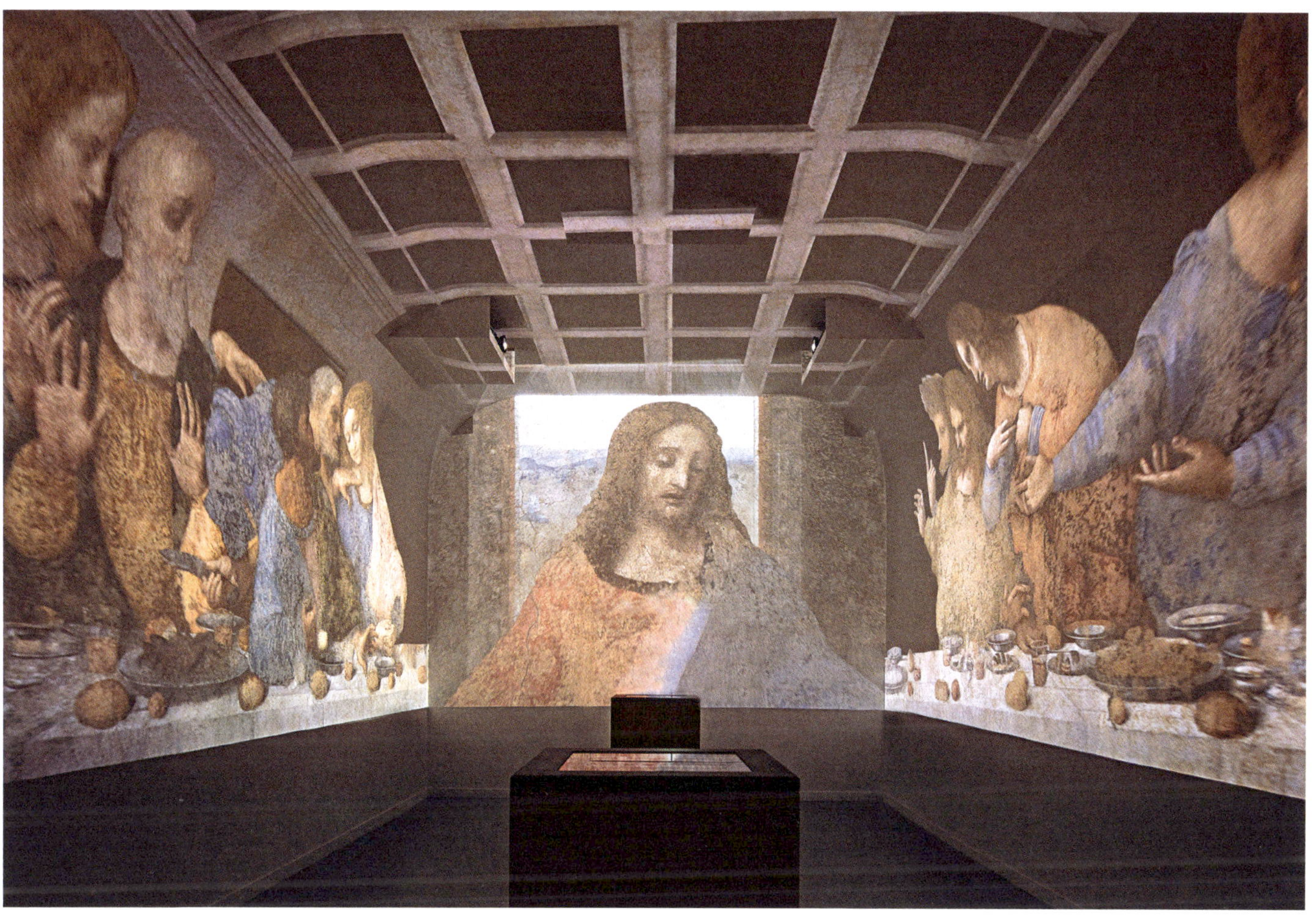

fig. 6 — Immersive show gallery

civilising phenomenon of the Renaissance. Our family cultural institution hopes to make all of Leonardo da Vinci's knowledge available in the only offering of this kind in the world, so that visitors can discover in a single trip and in a single setting the entire world of Leonardo da Vinci. This will be a decisive stage in the life of Clos Lucé and its development. A new lease of life, propelling us into the future...

Leonardo da Vinci was the archetypal Renaissance man who was able to combine the arts and the sciences seamlessly. Five hundred years after his death, he has achieved immortality and eternal greatness. Leonardo da Vinci is at once very current, very present and very modern. He is the all-talented man, in all branches of knowledge. Through his protean and multidisciplinary work, by studying all areas of knowledge, Leonardo da Vinci is truly universal and can enlighten our future.

✷

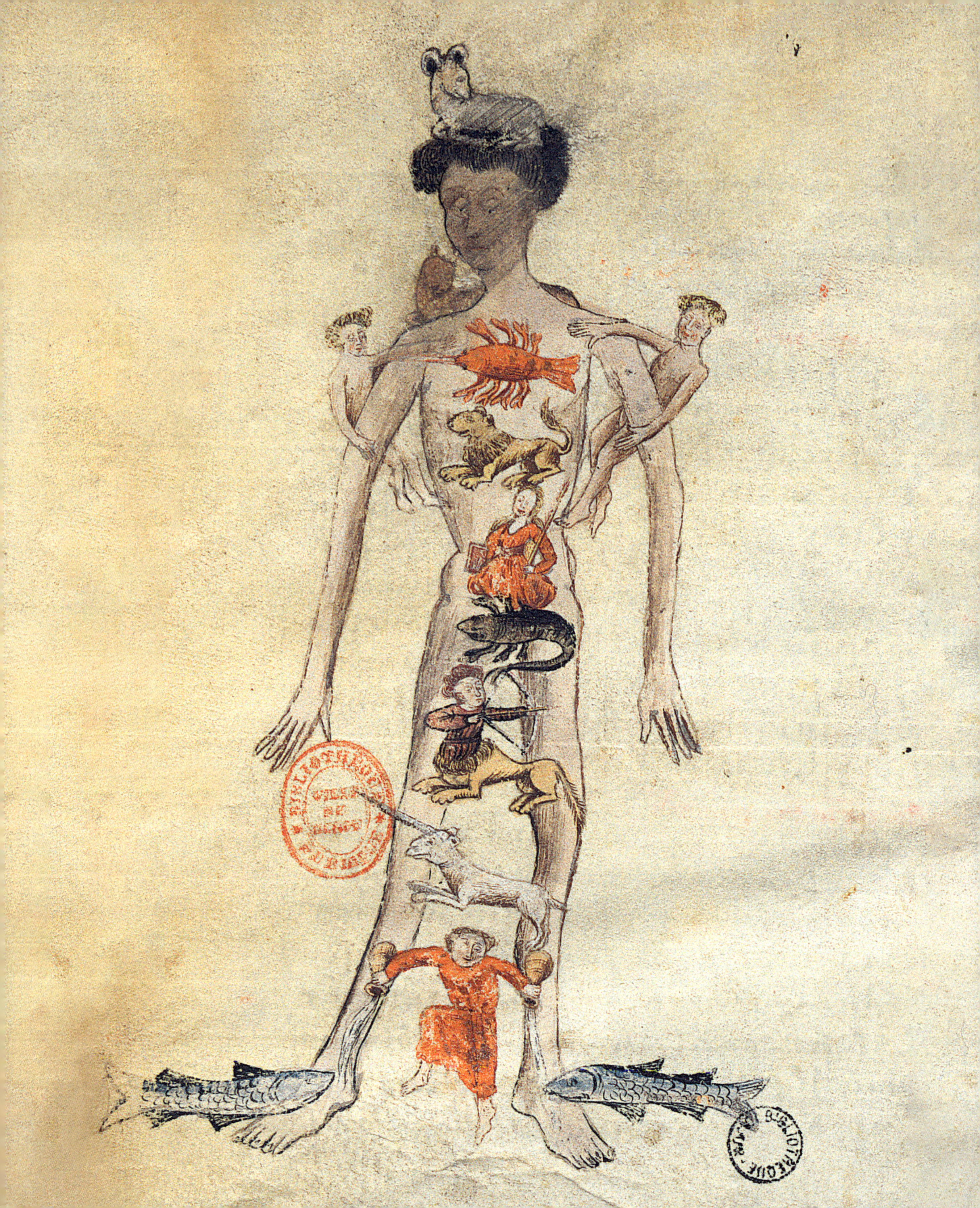

Philosophy on Living Beings and Leonardo's Readings

Pascal Brioist
Professor of Modern History at the University of Tours
and member of the Centre for Advanced Renaissance Studies

Previous page:

Guy de Chauliac, *Traité de chirurgie. Le livre de Guidon*, early 15th century
Bibliothèque municipale de Dijon

Recent studies have made it possible to reconstruct Leonardo da Vinci's library using lists of his books that he kept himself – one dated 1478, the other 1503 – and mentions of works that appear in his writings [fig.1]. It has then been possible to consider what constituted Leonardo's intellectual horizon when he reflected on the nature of living beings, while taking into account that much of his knowledge acquired in the 1490s came from the Milanese oral tradition, which disseminated, among other things, the ideas of Aristotle on the soul or those of medieval Muslim thinkers such as Alhazen or al-Kindi on optics.

This article will examine the major philosophical principles that governed Leonardo's thinking about the human body, and then link Leonardo's folios with his readings on anatomy.

Philosophical Principles

Leonardo's anatomical work was based on a series of preconceived ideas about the soul, the spirits ('animal' and 'vital') and the humours, notions that originated in a culture that dated back to antiquity.

Leonardo borrowed much from Aristotle, especially his concept of the soul. The Tuscan who initially read with difficulty in Latin, and even more so in Greek, as he had not been to university, owing to illegitimate birth, does not seem to have had the works of Aristotle in his library. This did not prevent him from having access to his thinking, both by talking with learned men in Milan and by having texts on Aristotelian thought summarised for him, such as the *Philosophia pauperum sive Isagoge in libros Aristotelis* by Albert the Great (c. 1200–1280), a German philosopher from the medieval period. The same concepts mentioned by Leonardo on cerebral ventricles and psychology can, indeed, be found in Aristotle's *De Anima*. For the Greek thinker, man had 'four different souls': The *organic soul* is, according to him, the source of vital capacity through 'animal spirits'; the *vegetative soul* is responsible for the reproductive functions and the growth of the body; the *sensitive soul* is the one that induces perception through the senses, physical movements, and emotions; finally, the *intellective soul* is the one that enables consciousness and reflection. It is in this context that we must understand the following comment from Leonardo about the senses, which would otherwise remain obscure:

"As the five senses are the ministers of the soul ... The nerves with their muscles obey the tendons as soldiers obey the officers, and the tendons obey the common sense as the officers obey the general, and this common sense in its turn obeys the soul as the general his lord." (Windsor, RL 19019 r)

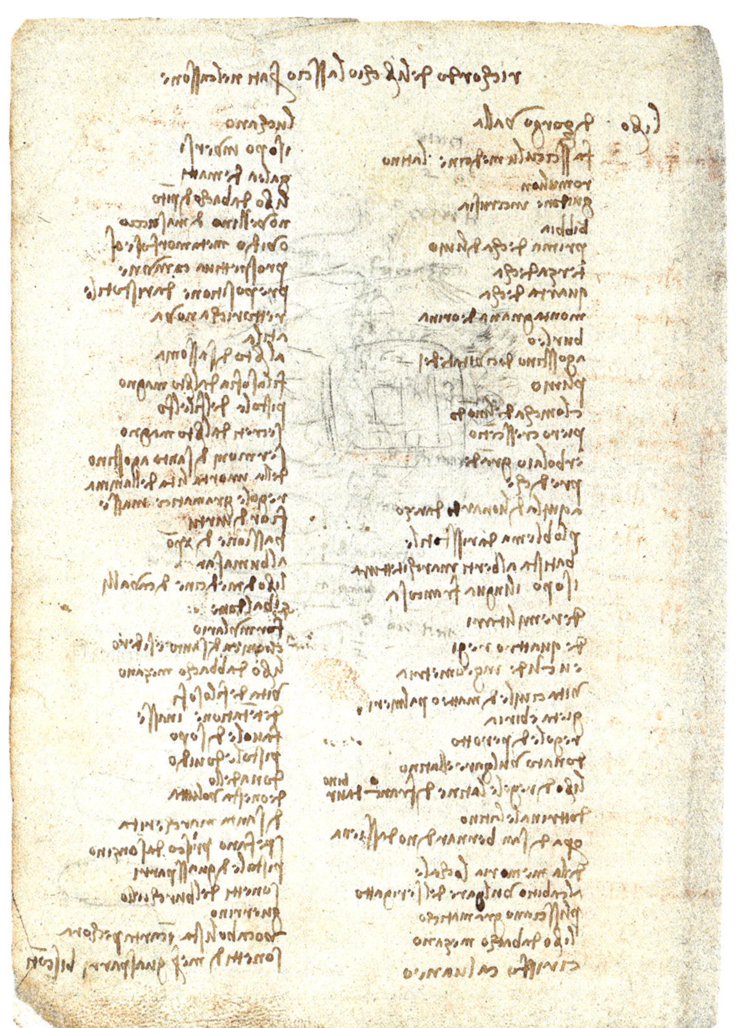

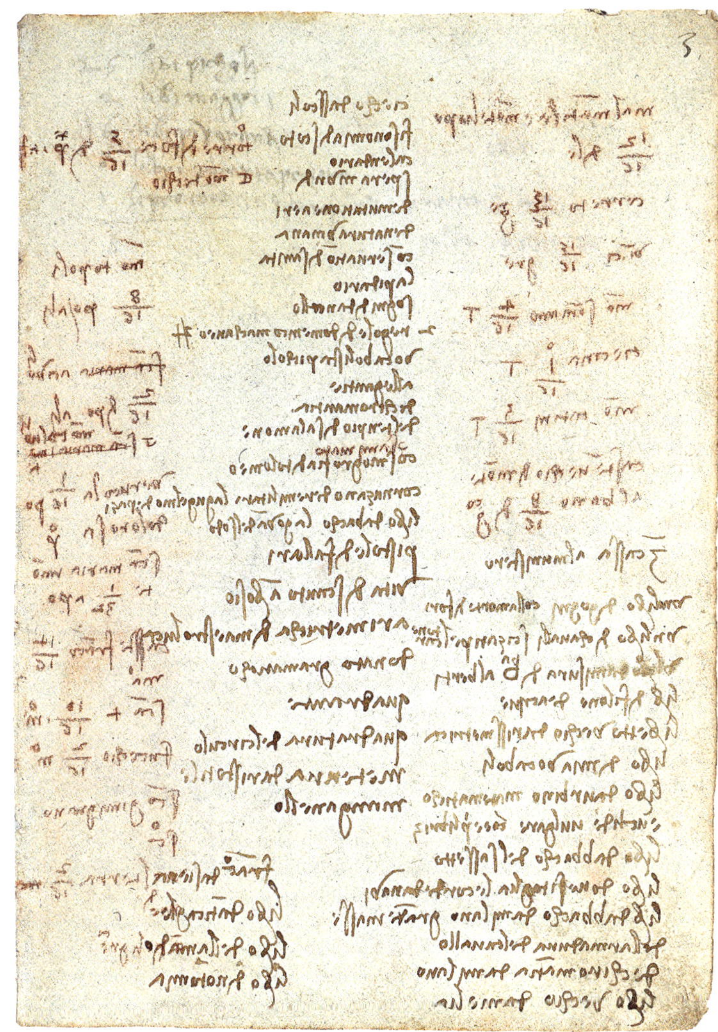

fig.1 — List of books owned by Leonardo in 1504

(Madrid, CM II, folios 2v-3r)

It is again to the ideas of Aristotle, this time in *De animalibus* [fig.3] and *De generatione animalium* (*On the Generation of Animals*) relayed in Tuscan by Dante Alighieri (1265–1321) in his *Convivio* (*The Banquet*) that Leonardo owed his first reflections on the doctrine of reproduction, and his initial interest in embryology.

One of the elements of Leonardo's philosophical approach was based on a profound feeling that there was a harmony to the world and on the conviction that the microcosm of the human body bore close resemblance to the macrocosm of the body of the Earth. Here again, it is his readings that lead Leonardo to say that the four universal states of man (melancholic, choleric, sanguine and phlegmatic) are related to the four elements that make up the Earth (earth, fire, air, water) and their four qualities (dry, moist, hot and cold). While it is not certain that Leonardo had access to Plato's *Timaeus*, he does cite Ptolemy (c.100–168 CE) and his *Cosmography*, which gave him the notion of the microcosm; Ristoro d'Arezzo who established with his *Composizione del Mondo* (1282) a link between human physiology and the form of the Earth; and Nicolas of Cusa (1401–1464), whose treatise *On Learned Ignorance* or *De Docta Ignorantia* (1440) inspired him to reflect on universal harmony, analogies and astronomy.

The Roman physician Claudius Galen (c.131–201), whose writings had survived from antiquity through Arabic and then Latin handwritten translations, also enriched Leonardo's thinking, but less so through direct reading at first, for Galen was printed before the 1520s only in simplified rewritings, and more in conversations with committed Galenists such as Marcantonio della Torre (1481–1511).

When Leonardo met this young physician and anatomist from Pavia in 1508 at the hospital of San Matteo, he began to quote (Windsor, RL 19019 r) *De usu partium corporis humani* (*On the Usefulness of the Parts of the Human Body*) [fig.2]. This is an abbreviated version of *De Iuvamentis membrorum*, which presents a model of his descriptive method: Galen assigns a function to each anatomical form. Leonardo drew on it for his idea of a synthetic concept of anatomy, starting with the components of the body: muscles, nerves, bones; then passing to the complex elements: arm, shoulder, hand, head, foot ...

It is also in Galen that the theory of the humours, to which Leonardo refers, is clearly set out. The Roman physician created a framework by linking not only each humour, i.e. each liquid of the human body, to an element, but also to a particular organ, temperament and quality.

Humour ⟶	Organ ⟶	Element ⟶	Quality ⟶	Temperament
Blood	Heart	Air	Hot and moist	Sanguine
Phlegm	Brain	Water	Cold and moist	Phlegmatic
Yellow bile	Liver	Fire	Hot and dry	Choleric
Black bile	Spleen	Earth	Cold and dry	Melancholic

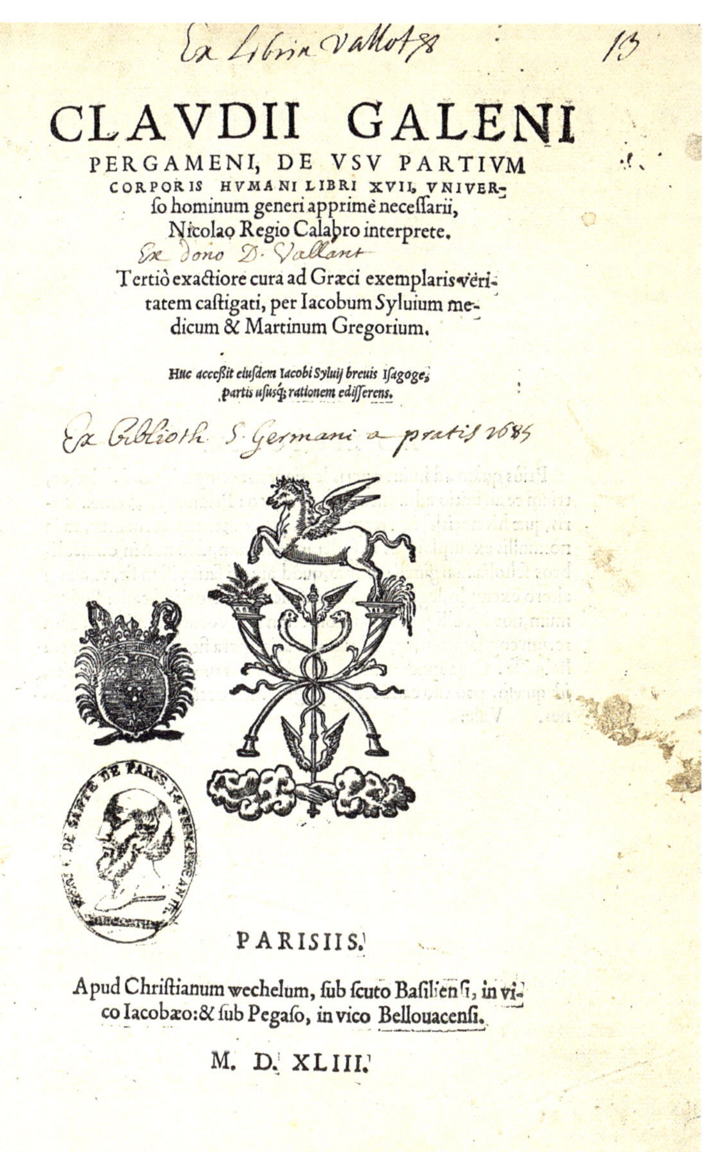

CLAVDII GALENI
PERGAMENI, DE VSV PARTIVM
CORPORIS HVMANI LIBRI XVII, VNIVERso hominum generi apprimè necessarii,
Nicolao Regio Calabro interprete.

Tertiò exactiore cura ad Græci exemplaris veritatem castigati, per Iacobum Syluium medicum & Martinum Gregorium.

Huc accessit eiusdem Iacobi Syluij breuis Isagoge, partis usúsq; rationem edisserens.

PARISIIS.

Apud Christianum wechelum, sub scuto Basiliensi, in vico Iacobæo: & sub Pegaso, in vico Bellouacensi.

M. D. XLIII.

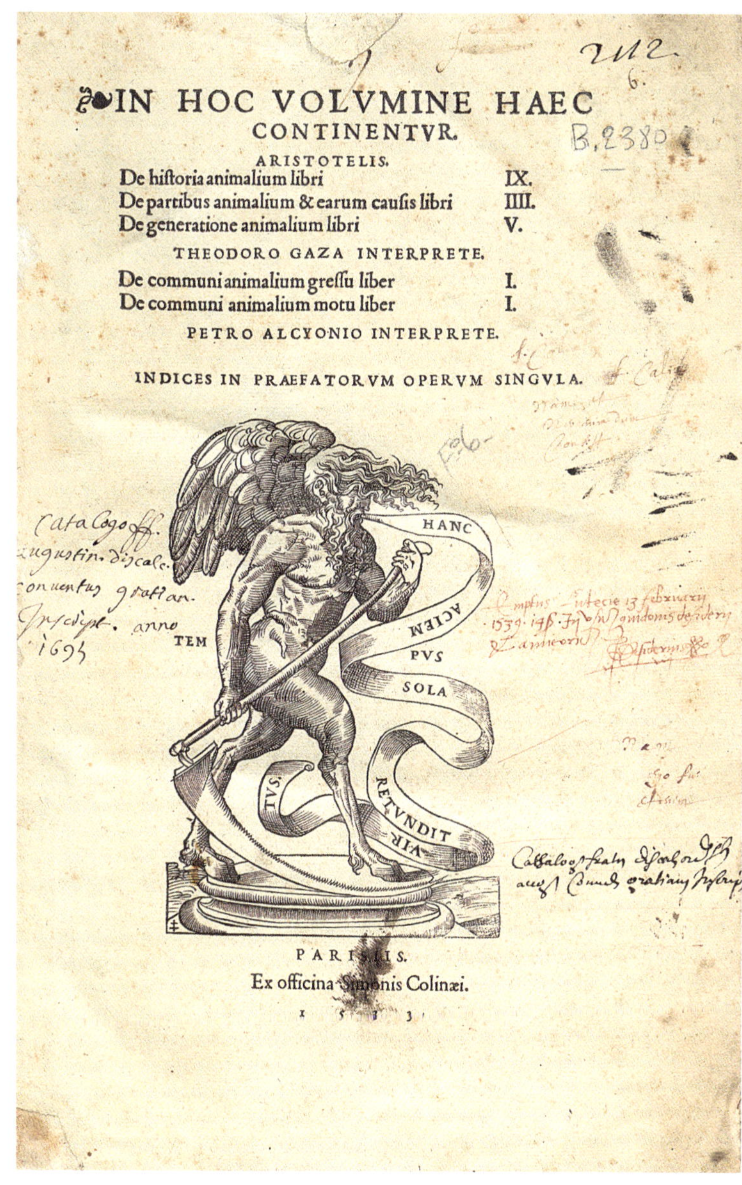

IN HOC VOLVMINE HAEC
CONTINENTVR.

ARISTOTELIS.

De historia animalium libri IX.
De partibus animalium & earum causis libri IIII.
De generatione animalium libri V.

THEODORO GAZA INTERPRETE.

De communi animalium gressu liber I.
De communi animalium motu liber I.

PETRO ALCYONIO INTERPRETE.

INDICES IN PRAEFATORVM OPERVM SINGVLA.

PARISIIS.
Ex officina Simonis Colinæi.
1533

fig. 2 — Claudius Galen, frontispiece of the *De usu partium corporis humani libri XVII, universo hominum generi apprime necessarii, Nicolao Regio Calabro interprete. Tertio exactiore cura ad Graeci exemplaris veritatem castigati, per Jacobum Sylvium medicum & Martinum Gregorium. Huc accessit ejusdem Jacobi Sylvii brevis Isagoge, partis ususque rationem edisserens*, 1543
Bibliothèque interuniversitaire Santé Médecine, université Paris-Cité

fig. 3 — Aristotle, *De Animalibus*, Parisiis : Ex off. S. Colinaeus, 1533
Grenoble, bibliothèque municipale, B.2380

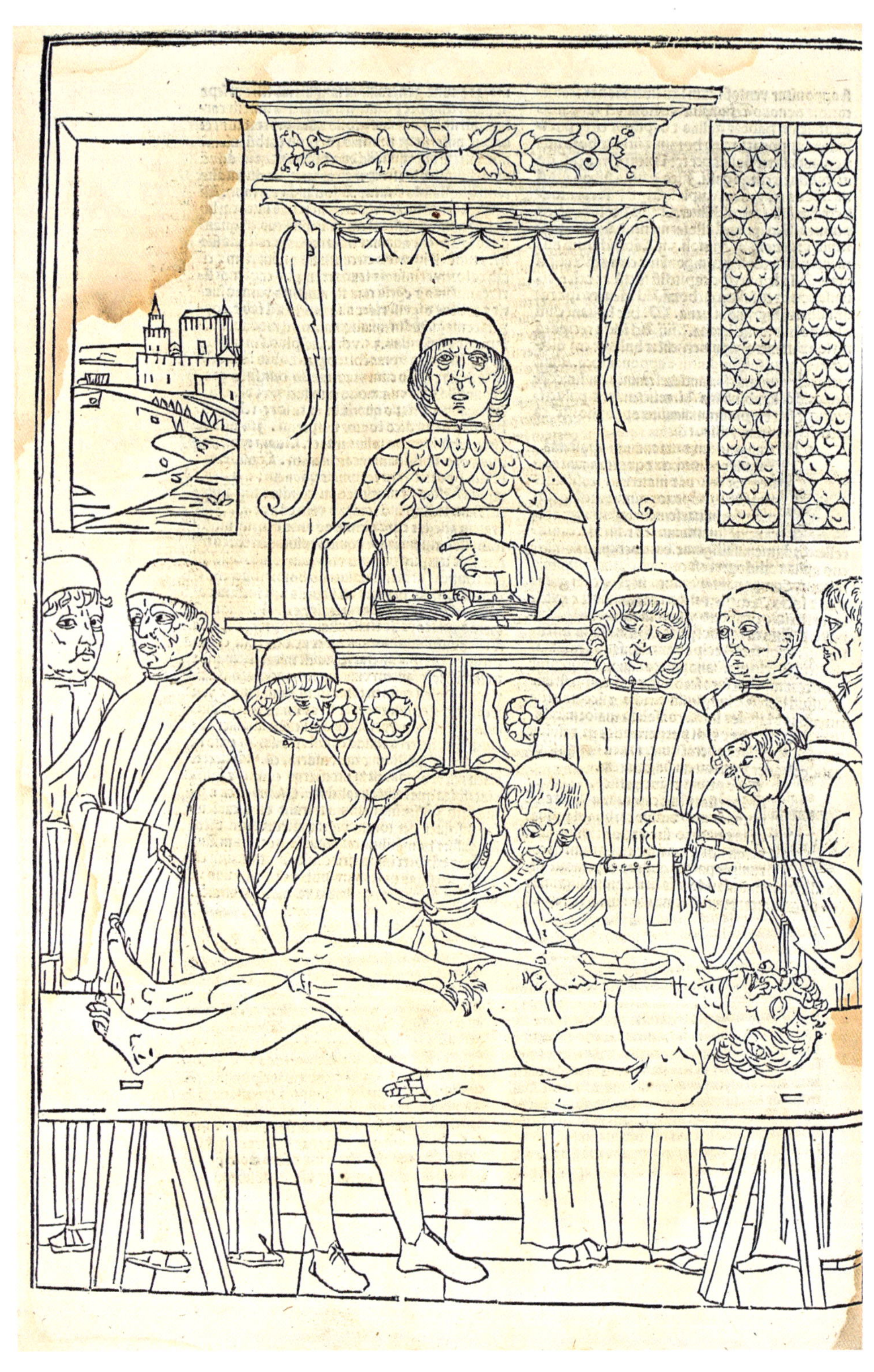

fig. 4 — Johannes de Ketham, *Fasciculus medicinae*,
Venice : Jean and Grégoire de Gregoriis, 1500
Nîmes – bibliothèque Carré d'Art, Inc. 25

For Galenists, the distribution of the humours in the body varied according to age, living conditions and complexions. Thus, a young man was perceived as having a tendency to be phlegmatic, a mature man as choleric, and an old man as melancholic; similarly, a soldier or a nobleman were predisposed to be choleric while a scholar was more likely to be of a melancholic nature. According to them, all illnesses were the result of an imbalance of the humours.

Leonardo's Predecessors and Contemporaries in the Practice of Dissection

Since Galen did not dissect human bodies, Leonardo drew on the medieval tradition of dissection for examples.

In 1503, his primary source was a medical booklet in Italian with the Latin title *Fasciculus medicinae* (Venice 1491). This volume was compiled by Johannes de Ketham (in reality Johannes Kellner von Kirchheim, professor of medicine in Vienna [fig.4]). It included texts by Mondino de' Luzzi (13th century) and Guy de Chauliac (14th century), as well as Bartolomeo Montagnana's treatise on urine (15th century).

Mondino de' Liuzzi (1270–1326), born in Bologna, wrote in the 13th century an *Anathomia* from which Leonardo borrowed the model for anatomical demonstration, distinguishing between the *sector* (who cuts the cadaver), the *ostensor* (who indicates the parts to be cut and shows the anatomical features) and the *lector* (the master who reads the written texts). Liuzzi also mentioned Avicenna's *Canon of Medicine* (Ibn Sina, known as 'Avicenna', 980–1037), a medieval book that dealt with both anatomy – for example, the arrangement of the cavities of the skull, physiognomy (the science of determining a person's character from their physical appearance), physiology – and Aristotelian theories of reproduction. Since 1490, at the time of Leonardo da Vinci, the *Canon* was only available in Latin in a Venetian edition. It was also in Mondino's texts that Leonardo discovered reflections on the muscles of the foot (Windsor, RL 19017 r) and on the urinary system; and it was here that he found the inspiration for his remarkable drawing synthesising the anatomy of a woman (Windsor, RL 12281 r). Perhaps he was thinking of Mondino when he criticised those who sought to simplify anatomy while being unable to present a coherent understanding of the body? Indeed, Leonardo often disagreed with Mondino, especially on his *Expositio super capitulum de generatione embrionis canonis Avicennae.* Unlike Mondino, who thought that there was only a male sperm, Leonardo considered that two sperms were needed, one male and one female, to make reproduction possible. Later, on this theme of reproduction, he also had recourse to Egidio Romano's text entitled *De formatione corporis humani in utero* (*On the Formation of the Human Body in the Womb*, Paris, 1515).

Leonardo's response to the medieval texts was both critical and creative. The *Fasciculus medicinae* also included the writings of a later author than Mondino, Guy de Chauliac (1300–1368), a French physician trained in Bologna who was a canon to the pope. His *Chirurgia magna* was published in Italian in 1498. It clearly articulated, in addition to the ideas of Hippocrates and Galen, the relationship between autopsy, verbal description and illustration. These concepts and the language of study were taken up in Leonardo's anatomical folios (Windsor, RL 19061 r, 19063 v, and 12603 r), as well as in the Codex Forster III and Manuscript A (1509–1510), where he laid out his method based on anatomical considerations.

We also have access to the dissection procedures of Leonardo's contemporaries, thanks to authors mentioned by Leonardo in 1508 (Windsor, RL 19017 r, and 12291 r), such as Gabriele Zerbi and Alessandro Benedetti.

Gabriele Zerbi was a native of Verona, but taught in Bologna. His *Liber anathomie corporis humani et singulorum membrorum illius* (*Book of Anatomy of the Human Body and its Members*, Venice, 1502) is referenced by Leonardo, who had probably heard of it from Marcantonio della Torre (Windsor, RL 19070 v). It describes the ways of cutting up a cadaver or animal parts following the Galenic method, by which it is necessary to recognise substance, complexion, shape, and location; then to collect samples, measure quantities and dimensions, and to analyse the passions.

Zerbi sought, more specifically, to understand the urinary system and embryology, but we can also read in the texts his development on the analogy between Man and the Earth.

Leonardo also associated with Zerbi's name that of Alessandro (Agnolo) Benedetti, a physician from Venice who practised in Padua (Windsor, RL 19070 v). His *Anatomiae sive historia corporis humani* (*Anatomy or History of the Human Body*, Venice, 1505) consists of a commentary on Galen's *De anatomicis administrationibus*. Its five books are arranged as follows:

1. The usefulness of human anatomy;
2. The members of the abdomen;
3. The thorax with the heart and lungs;
4. The brain;
5. The veins, muscles, bones and nerves.

In some chapters, Benedetti went further than Mondino, especially in his understanding of the heart, the cerebral ventricles and the cranial nerves – texts that informed some of Leonardo's writings.

Fluid entities such as the viscera were little discussed in anatomical texts; Leonardo sought information in health regimes such as the *Della conservazione della sanita* (*On the Conservation of Health*) by Hieronimus de Manfredis or the *Trattato circa la conservazione de la sanità* by Ugo Benzi, court physician to Niccolò III d'Este in Ferrara. These treatises mention the spirits that affect the emotions in the body through greater or lesser heat. Reading them, Leonardo was reflecting on the origins of tremors, tears, fevers and various pathologies. In the treatise on the evaluation of urine, *Tractatus de urinarum iudiciis* (1487), by the Paduan physician Bartolomeo Montagnana, one will find an extremely useful 'urine wheel'. It was after 1500, when he became interested in kidneys and urine, that Leonardo came across a version of this book translated into Italian in 1494. On the illustration of the urine wheel, which had already appeared in the *Fasciculus* of 1491, comes the following passage in full from a leaflet in Windsor, RL 19038 r: "Figure to show what causes catarrh, tears, sneezing, yawning, trembling, falling disease (epilepsy), madness, sleep, hunger, lust; anger when it stirs in the body; fear, similarly; fever, disease."

Leonardo's thinking about the body as well as his anatomical study cannot, as we can see, be understood outside of a fairly extensive intellectual context. The anatomical folios demonstrate the self-taught nature of the Tuscan's knowledge, a knowledge informed by numerous readings in the vernacular (Italian), but also, later, in Latin, and by his discussions with physicians in Milan, Pavia, Florence and Rome.

✷

Martin Clayton, Ron Philo, *Leonardo da Vinci: Anatomist*, London, Royal Collection Trust, 2017.
Martin Kemp, *Leonardo da Vinci: The Marvellous Works of Nature and Man*, Oxford, Oxford University Press, 1981.
Leonardo da Vinci's Anatomical World: Language, Context and 'Disegno', ed. by Domenico Laurenza, Alessandro Nova et al., Venice, Marsilio, 2011.
Dominique Le Nen, *Leonardo da Vinci, L'Aventure Anatomique*, Paris, Éditions E/P/A, Hachette, 2019.
Charles Donald O'Malley, John Bertrand de Cusance Morant Saunders, *Leonardo da Vinci on the Human Body*, New York, Gramercy Books, 1952.
La biblioteca di Leonardo, ed. by Carlo Vecce, Giunti, 2021.

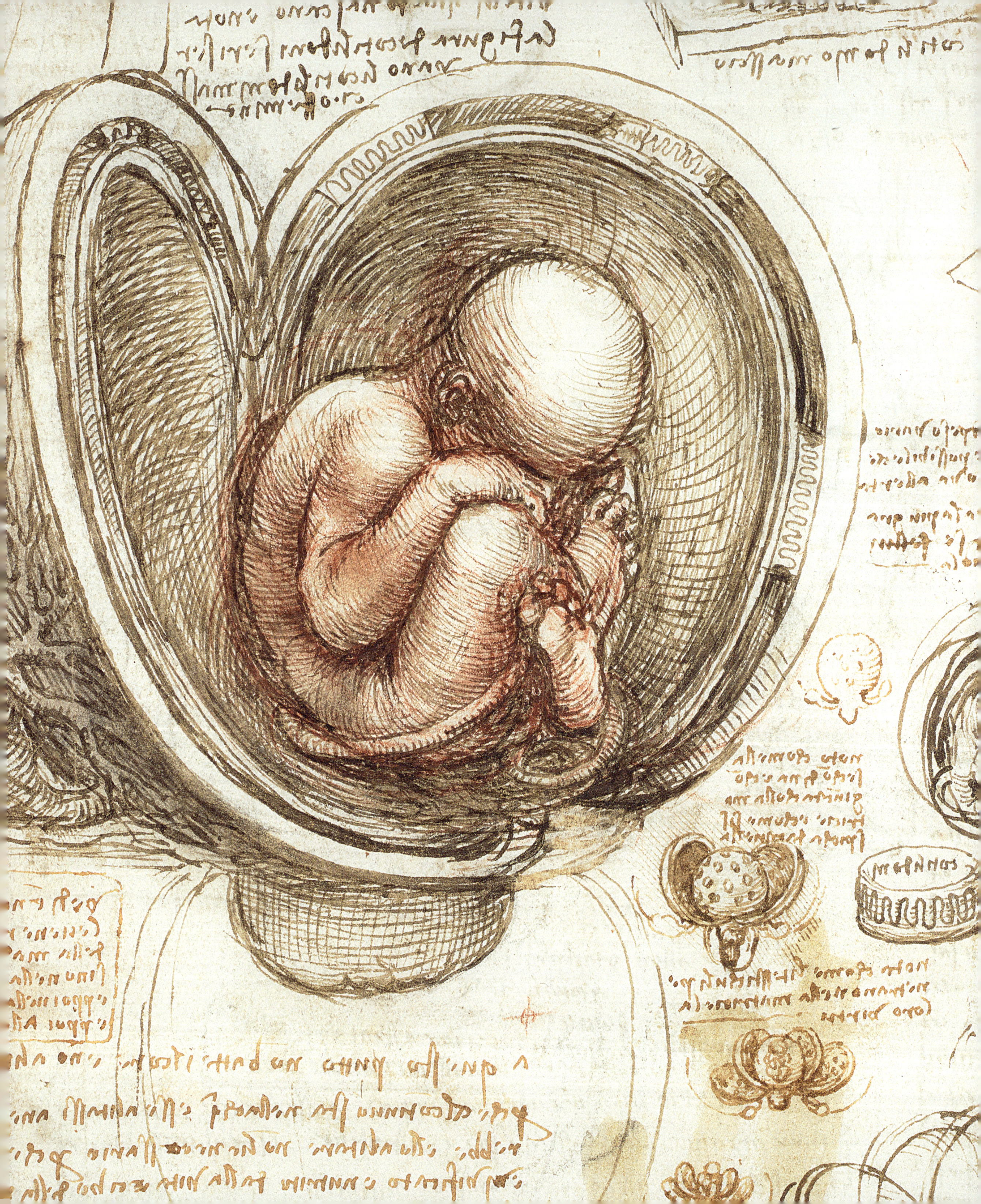

Undoing Nature

Places, Forms and Problems of the Dissections Carried Out by an Artist-Anatomist

Domenico Laurenza
Associate Professor of Art History at the University of Cagliari

Previous page:

The foetus in the womb; sketches and notes on reproduction, c.1511, red chalk and traces of black chalk, pen and ink, wash, 30.4 × 22 cm (detail)
Windsor, Royal Collection Trust, RL 19102 r

In several famous passages dating back to between 1513–14 and 1516, the time he spent in Rome (*Codex Atlanticus*, folios 252r, 500r, 671r, 768r), Leonardo mentions the allegations made against him and the obstacles he encountered because of his practice of anatomical dissections. The whole episode contributed to the creation of the myth of Leonardo as an anatomist who performed dissections in secret places to escape prohibitions imposed by the Church. In actual fact, historians have long since clarified that the Church never hindered the practice of anatomical dissections which, on the contrary, in their public form often became an integral part of a ritual with rules and meanings that were also religious. Leonardo explicitly writes that the problem occurred in a hospital, i.e. in a public, not secret place ("This other prevented me from doing anatomical dissections and so on at the hospital blaming me with the Pope", *Codex Atlanticus*, folio 500r).

What reasons underlay the accusations against the dissections he had performed in Rome? Allegations that in his opinion were addressed directly to Pope Leo X. The answer can be found in the fact that in the same period as Leonardo was an artist-anatomist, anatomy and medicine were integral parts of natural philosophy. Here one needs to historicise the issues without going to historiographical extremes. Of course, the nexus between anatomy and philosophy is something that historically differentiates Leonardo's age from our own. The same applies to the strong permeability between different kinds of knowledge, which was much greater than in the contemporary world and which explains the phenomenon of artist-scientists, from Piero della Francesca to Leonardo. However, greater permeability between different kinds of knowledge did not mean their confusion. Michelangelo, according to Condivi, made it clear that he limited himself to the study of anatomical parts directly useful for art (muscles, bones, body surface) without entering into the 'minutiae' of physicians. Of course by radicalising the connection, Leonardo certainly went beyond the horizon of artistic anatomy: he intended to renew anatomy as a 'science' and studied it in every aspect, from the respiratory to the digestive system. But he does so as an 'artist'. And not only because his research is mainly expressed through images in a period when verbal language definitely prevailed in physicians' anatomy, but also because he has a strongly 'compositive' conception of his anatomical research. While the first of these two aspects has been widely investigated, the other less so. Carrying out an anatomical dissection is an intrinsically analytical and 'destructive' act that implies a separation of parts that nature has put together to construct the human body. To dissect a body is to un-make nature, which is exactly the opposite of Renaissance artistic *mimesis*. In the environment in which Leonardo was formed, the latter consisted instead in re-making nature by trying to understand and imitate the constructive processes it had used to generate the external forms of the bodies represented in art.

On the other hand, in the scientific field, since anatomy was an integral part of natural philosophy, anatomists touched upon problems of theological interest, such as the soul, its origin, its relationship with the body.

Now, this permeability between different kinds of knowledge, in which anatomists entered into philosophical and, often, despite themselves, theological matters, and artists dealt with scientific things such as anatomy, was potentially a source of conflict. And Leonardo, who dealt with anatomy

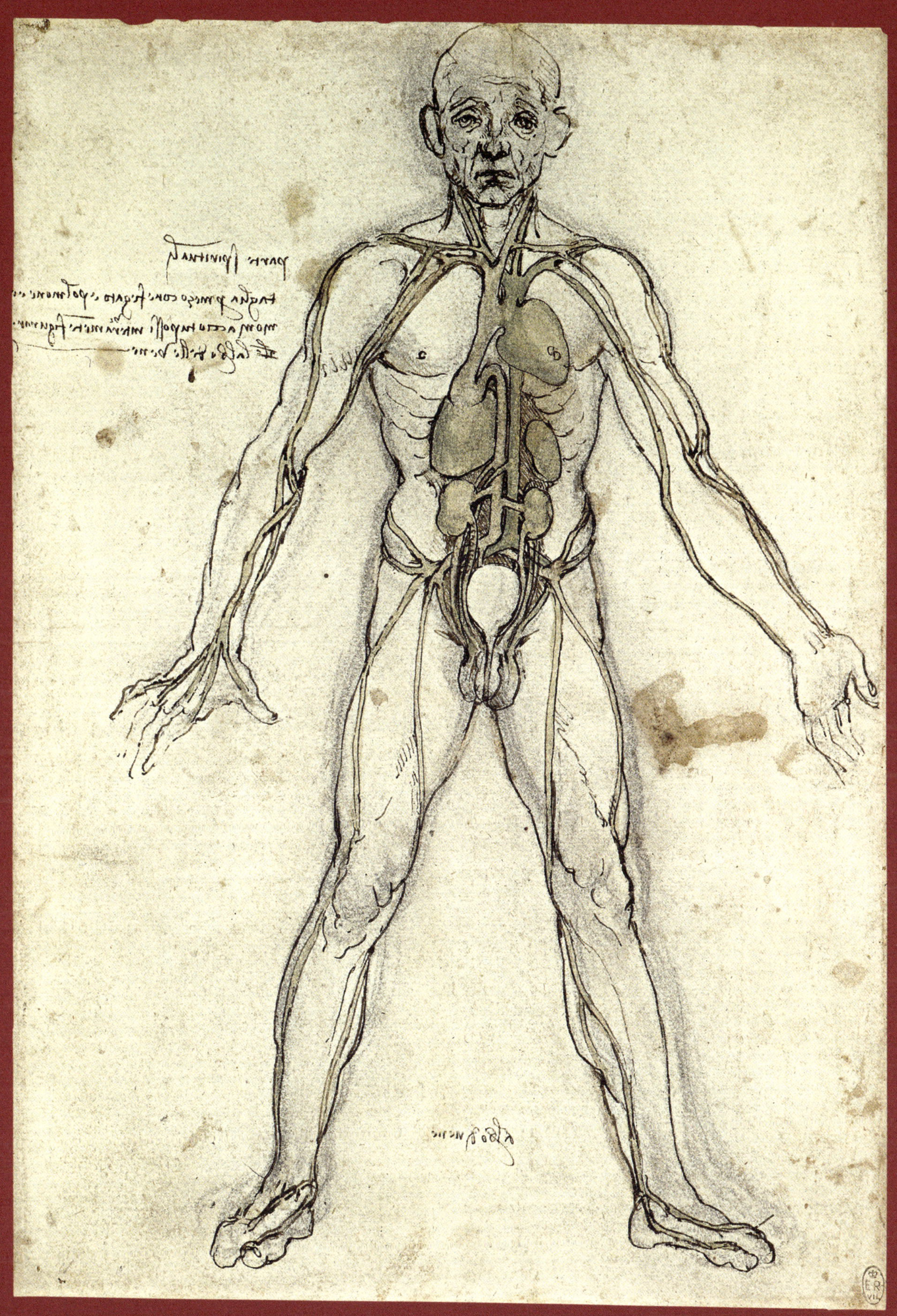

fig. 1 — *The major organs and vessels*, c.1485–90, black chalk or charcoal, pen and ink, brown and green wash, 27.8 × 19.7 cm
Windsor, Royal Collection Trust, RL 12597

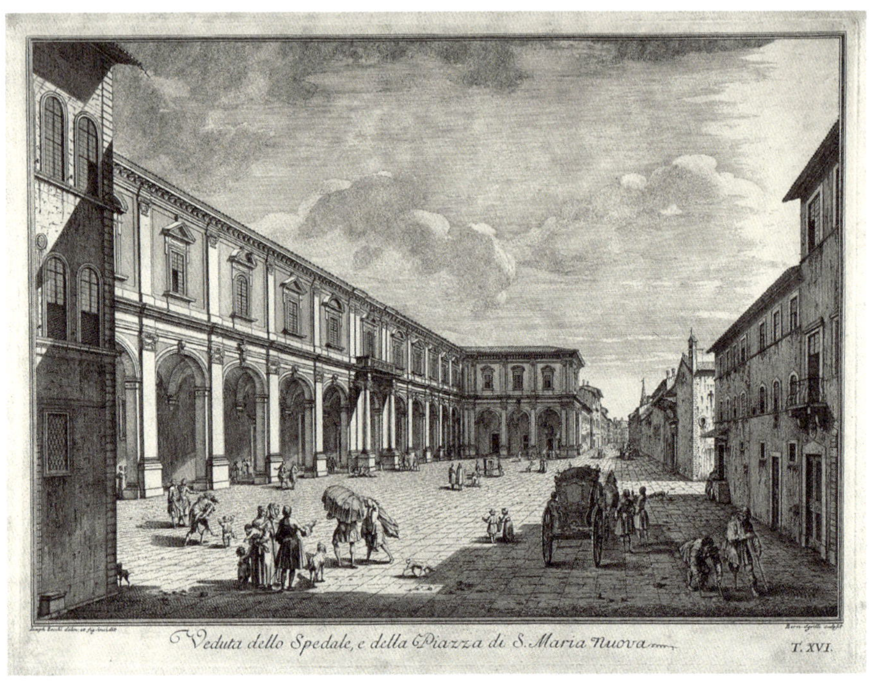

fig. 2—Bernardo Sansone Sgrilli, Hospital Santa Maria Nuova, Florence, 45.5 × 66 cm, engraving after Giuseppe Zocchi

as an 'artist', but also included purely scientific aspects, experienced this in the most complete and dramatic form, coming into conflict with doctors on the one hand and the Church on the other. But this came later, in the most advanced phase of his career as an artist-anatomist.

Before that, at least as far as we know, the relationship between the artist Leonardo and the world of the medical-anatomists was peaceful. We can distinguish three phases: one of inclusion (c.1480–1507), one of collaboration (c.1510), one of conflict (c.1511–16).

If, as I proposed some time ago, the drawing entitled *Tree of Veins* (Windsor, RL 12597 r) dates from 1480–2, and not, as is generally assumed from the 1490s, already in the early Florentine period, the young Leonardo was touching on themes beyond the anatomical-artistic dimension, coming into contact with the world of physicians [fig.1]. After moving to Milan in 1483, he had excellent relations with the medical world active between Milanese hospitals and the medical school of Pavia, for example with Girolamo and Pier Andrea Marliani and with Fazio Cardano (*Codex Atlanticus*, folio 611ar).

This phase of good relations continued after his return to Florence when, around 1506–7, he performed at least two dissections in the hospital of Santa Maria Nuova [fig.2]. In a famous passage, he alludes to the corpses of an old man and a two-year-old child being dissected at the same time (Windsor, RL 19027 v). Dissections conducted by an artist, but in a hospital, where it was usually doctors who performed post-mortem autopsies. This is the phase of inclusion: the world of doctors in the hospital of Santa Maria Nuova allows an outsider, an artist, to perform dissections.

Giorgio Vasari, in *The Life of Leonardo Da Vinci*, writes that the artist made anatomical drawings on behalf of the young anatomist Marcantonio della Torre, who worked at the University of Pavia in 1509–10. Conversely, in one of Leonardo's anatomical sheets from the same period, a physician, perhaps Marcantonio himself, inserted the scientific names for the placenta (Windsor, RL 19102 v). This was the phase of collaboration.

But things soon changed. In 1513, following the election of a Florentine pope, Leo X, Leonardo moved to Rome and here, as we have seen, he was accused of having performed dissections. This was the phase of conflict. A double conflict: on the one hand, with the world of doctors, on the other with the Church.

Thanks to a text in the *Codex Arundel* (folio 147v: "Have the Sancto and the other give you the definition and remedy of the case and you will see that men are elected as doctors of diseases not known to them") we know that Leonardo came into conflict with two doctors working in Rome. Ironically and rather polemically, Leonardo invites a person to consult two doctors to realise just how incompetent they were. One of the two doctors, named Santo, is almost certainly Mariano Santo da Barletta, active in the Roman hospital of Santa Maria della Consolazione, which stood at the foot of the Capitoline hill and had a ward reserved for women. It is very likely that this is the hospital where Leonardo performed dissections when he was in Rome.

Santa Maria della Consolazione is where a conflict arose between the artist-anatomist Leonardo and the world of hospital doctors. What were the reasons behind this clash? Let us not forget that the physicians had been trying for centuries to assert the theoretical nature of their knowledge compared with those so-called 'practitioners', such as barbers and charlatans, who often practised medicine and surgery abusively. Perhaps the Roman doctors saw the presence of an artist-anatomist in the hospital wards as yet another improper invasion of their field. But, in addition to these social and professional reasons, it is also necessary to consider that the conception of anatomy held by Leonardo and more generally by the artist-anatomists of the Renaissance differed in many aspects from the conception that would increasingly prevail among 16th century physicians. From this point of view, the conflict phase began perhaps as early as the last years in Milan, if we can confirm the dating proposed by scholars of certain anatomical sheets in which Leonardo inserts long passages against certain doctors, polemically defined as 'abbreviators' of anatomy and dissections (Windsor, RL 19063 v, 19084 r). By the term 'abbreviators' Leonardo basically means that in order to highlight an anatomical part during a dissection, the part has to be cut off to eliminate the other parts that surround and cover it and this, according to Leonardo, is a shortcut, an 'abbreviation', deleterious from a cognitive point of view, because it destroys the perception of the relationship between the individual parts and with the body as a whole. Leonardo and the artist-anatomists of the time were primarily interested in how the internal anatomical parts contribute to defining the external form of the body to be represented in a painting or sculpture. Leon Battista Alberti, in *De pictura*, and other art theorists discuss the usefulness of artists' anatomical study by connecting it to the 'compositio', the process by which the artist 'puts together' the various limbs to compose the body as a whole. Leonardo follows this principle when he 're-composes' vessels and thigh bones in their relationship with the surface of the body ([fig.3-4],

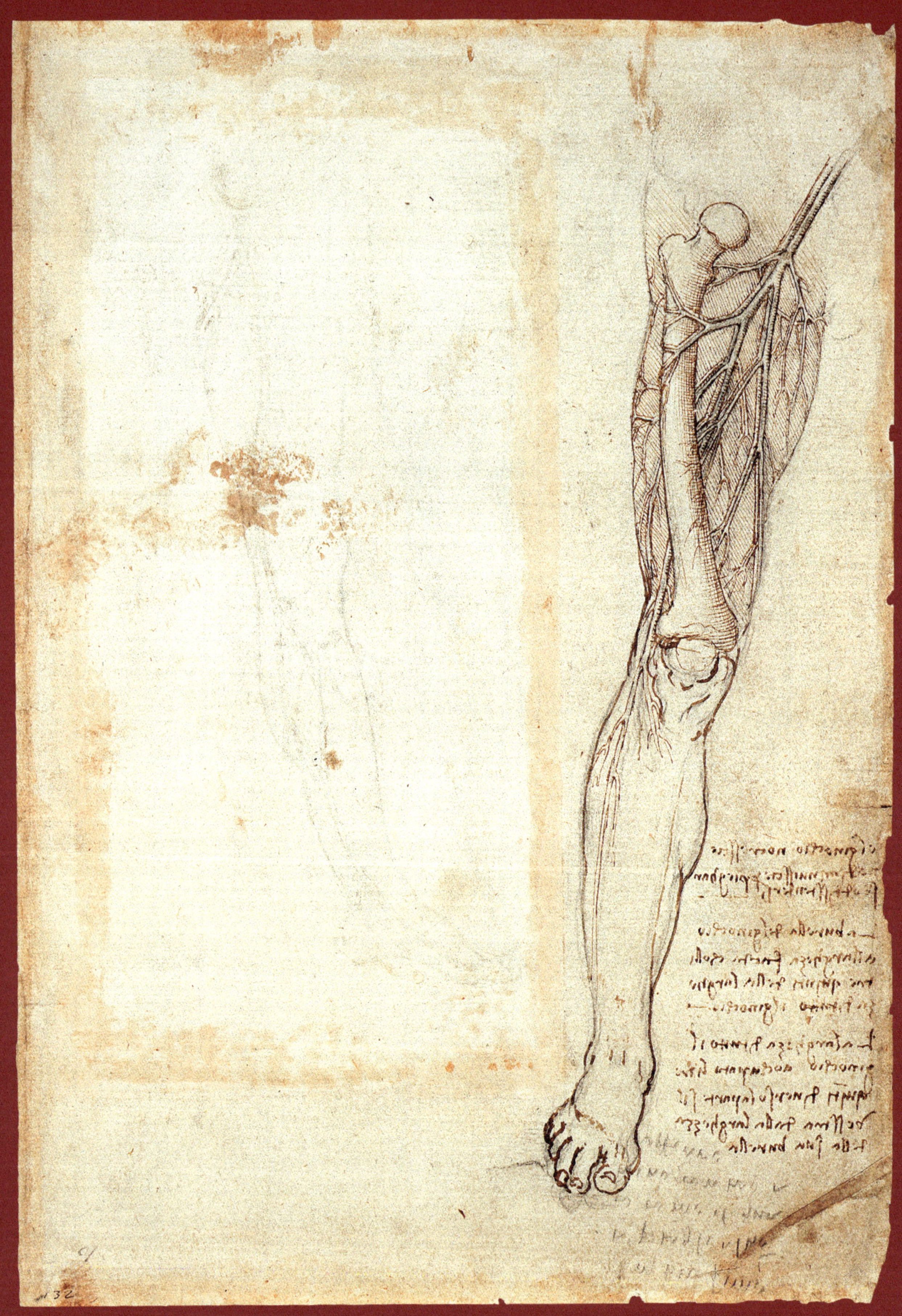

fig. 3 — *The bone and vessels of the thigh*, c.1508–10, pen and ink and black chalk, 27.5 × 19.5 cm
Windsor, Royal Collection Trust, RL 12624 v

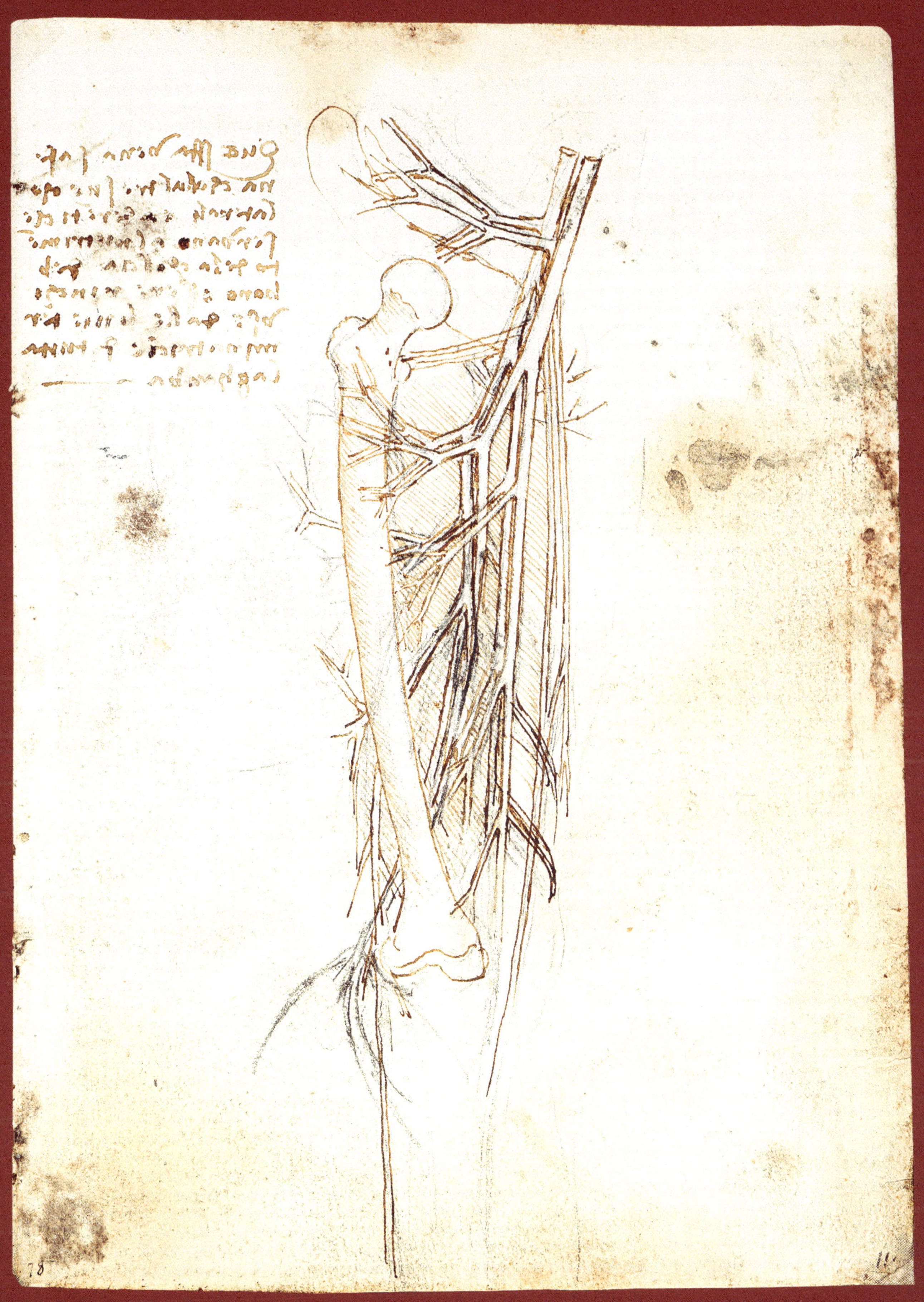

fig. 4 — *The vessels of the upper leg*, c.1508,
pen and ink over traces of black chalk, 18.9 × 14.1 cm
Windsor, Royal Collection Trust, RL 19025 r

Windsor, RL 12624 v and 19025 r). In contrast, the *De humani corporis fabrica* (Basel, 1543) by the Flemish physician Andrea Vesalius, a masterpiece of Renaissance anatomy, is dominated by representations of systems and parts in isolation.

But Leonardo, as we have seen, went beyond artistic anatomy and also studied embryology and the origin of life in a famous series of sheets he began in Milan in 1509–10 and continued in Rome in 1514–16 ([fig. 5], Windsor, RL 19102 r). And it is these studies that show us the reasons for the other conflict with religion. As already mentioned, while Leonardo was in Rome, he performed dissections not in a hidden place, but in a normal hospital and, from a general point of view, the 16th century Church never obstructed the practice of dissections performed under normal conditions. Instead, it was the natural philosophical level of anatomy of that age that created all the problems. The bull *Apostolici Regiminis*, promulgated by Pope Leo X in 1513, instructed the natural philosophers, i.e. the scientists of the time, to always uphold the immortal nature, and thus the divine origin, of the soul, when their research led them to investigate the relationship between soul and body. And this was precisely what happened to Leonardo: his embryological studies include questions concerning the relationship between the soul of the foetus and the maternal soul. For example: "To this baby neither beats its heart nor breathes ... and the same soul governs these two bodies and the desires, fears and pains are common to this creature as to all the other animate members [of the mother] ..." (Windsor, RL 19102 r). Themes on the verge of heresy. Although the content of his embryological research is hard to read in the private note version of his papers, it nevertheless emerged in the environment of the papal court where Leonardo lived. And as can be deduced from Leonardo's texts, the pope himself was certainly informed,

This is only the beginning of a historical phenomenon. In the years that followed, the conflict between science and faith would become more and more severe. Similarly, the divergence of anatomical conceptions between artists and scientists will deepen with the discovery in the 17th century of the microscopic dimension of anatomy and more generally of natural forms. Scientists, first through dissection and then also through the use of the microscope, will increasingly un-make the external, direct and surface form of the body, while artists, compositionally, will continue to mimetically re-make nature.

✷

Monica Azzolini, 'Leonardo da Vinci's anatomical studies in Milan: a Re-examination of Sites and Sources', in Givens, Jean A., *Visualizing Medieval Medicine and Natural History, 1200–1550*, Aldershot, Ashgate, 2006, pp. 147–176.
Maurizio Brunori (a cura di), *Leonardo. Il corpo dell'uomo*, Roma, Accademia dei Lincei e Bardi Edizioni, 2019.
Martin Clayton, Ron Philo, *Leonardo da Vinci Anatomist*, London, Royal Collection Publications, 2012.
Ascanio Condivi, *Vita di Michelagnolo Buonarroti*, Roma, 1553.
Kenneth David Keele, Carlo Pedretti, *Leonardo da Vinci, Corpus of Anatomical Drawings in the Collection of Her Majesty the Queen at Windsor Castle*, New York, 1979.
Domenico Laurenza, *De figura umana. Fisiognomica, anatomia e arte in Leonardo*, Florence, 2001.
Domenico Laurenza, *Leonardo nella Roma di Leone X (c. 1513–16): gli studi anatomici, la vita, l'arte*. XLIII Lettura Vinciana, Florence, Giunti, 2004.
Domenico Laurenza, *Leonardo. L'anatomia*, Florence, Giunti, 2009.
Dominique Le Nen, Jacky Laulan, *La main de Léonard de Vinci*, Paris, Springer-Verlag, 2010.
Alessandro Nova, Domenico Laurenza, *Leonardo da Vinci's Anatomical World. Language, Context and "Disegno"*, Venice, 2011.

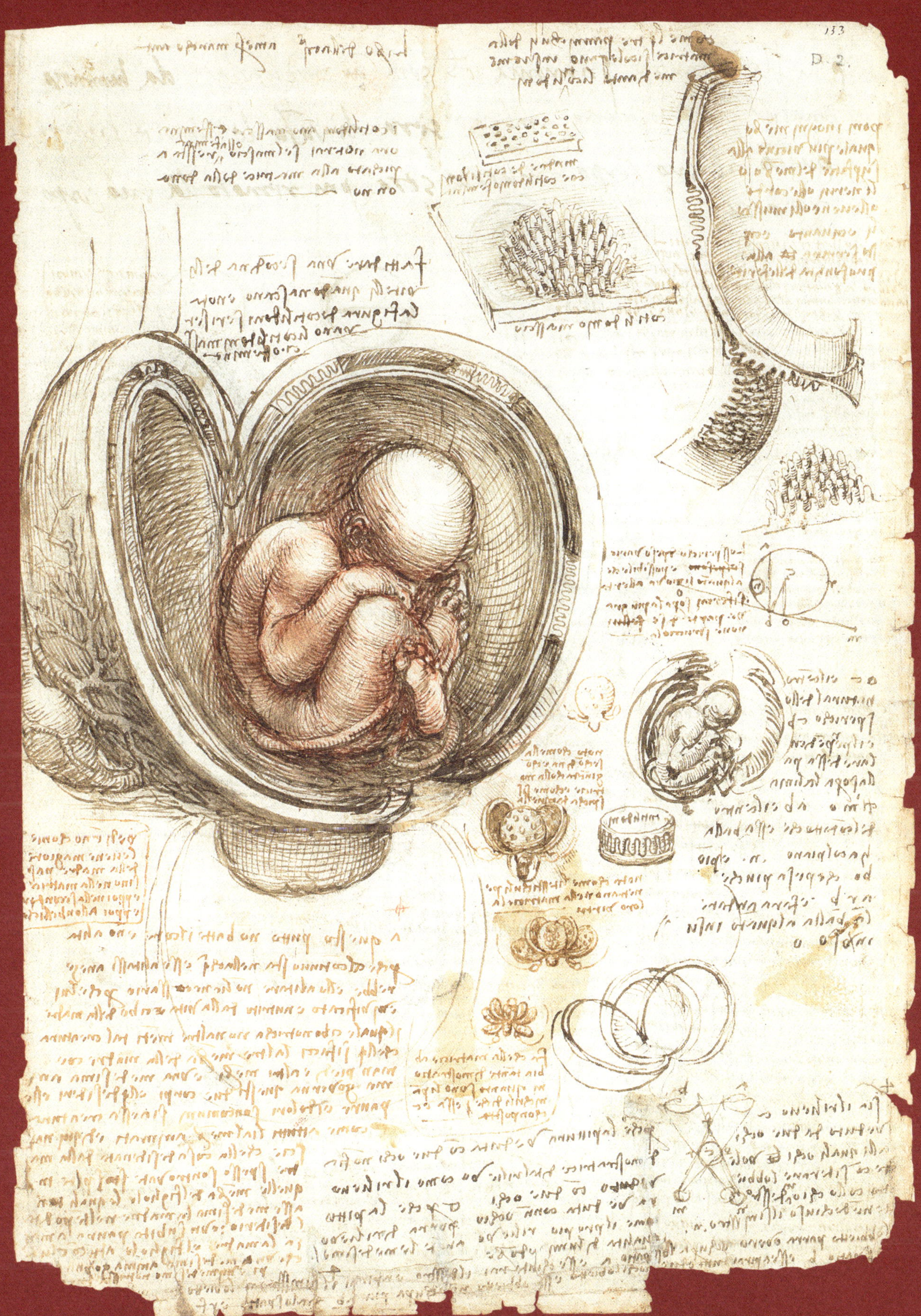

fig. 5 — *The foetus in the womb; sketches and notes on reproduction*, c.1511, red chalk and traces of black chalk, pen and ink, wash, 30.4 × 22 cm
Windsor, Royal Collection Trust, RL 19102 r

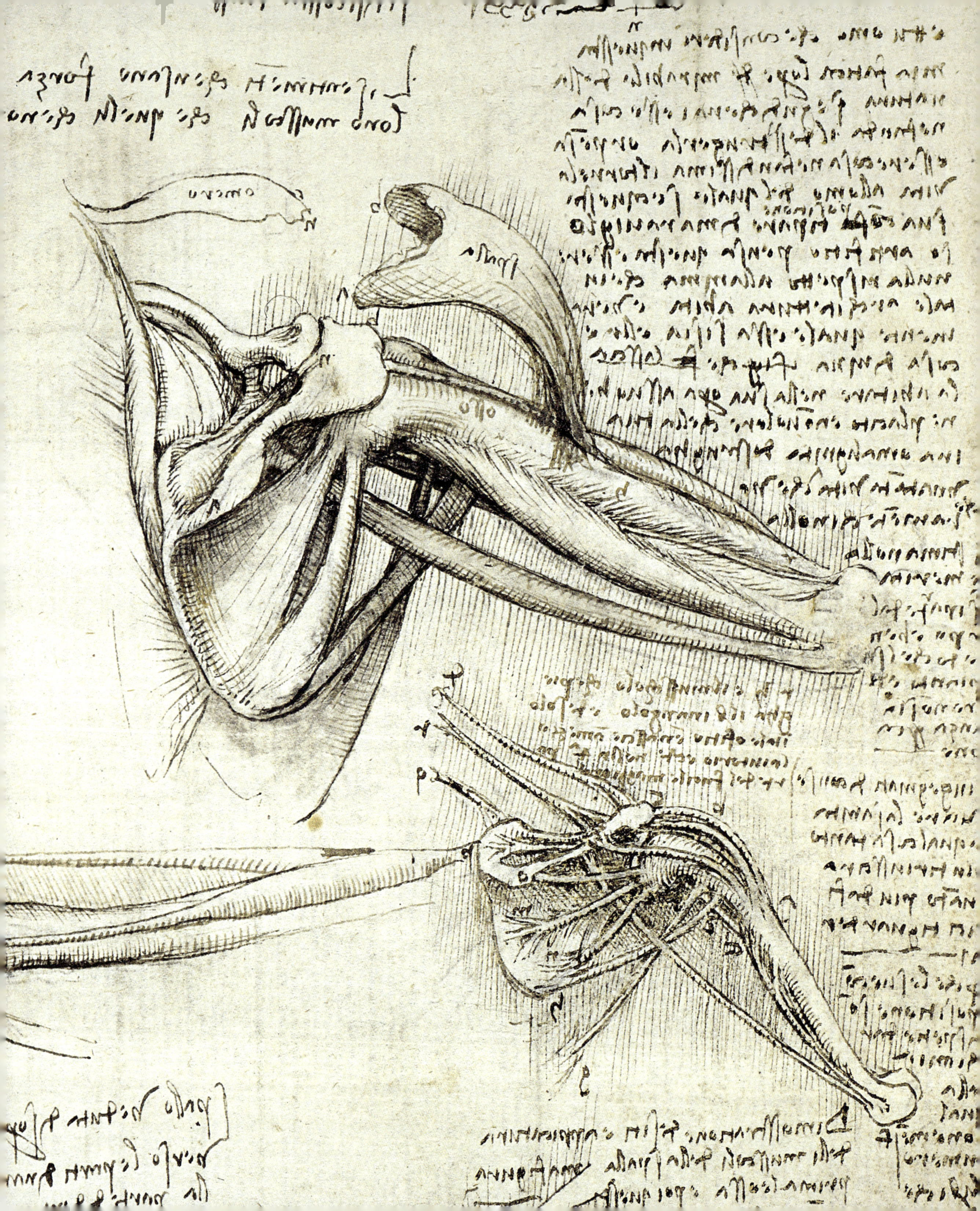

Leonardo da Vinci's Methods of Dissection

Dominique Le Nen
University Professor and Surgeon at Brest Regional University Hospital

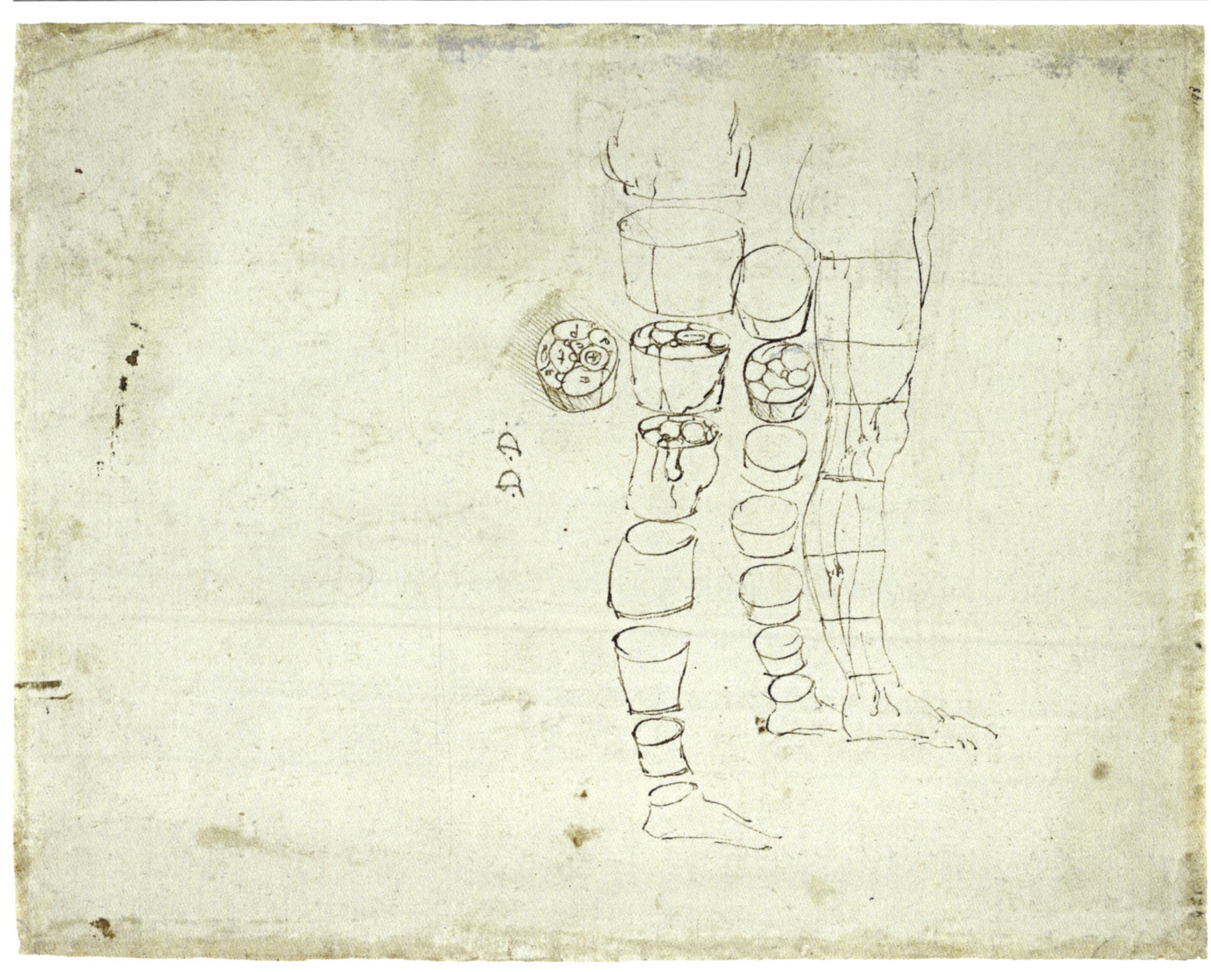

fig. 1 a—*The leg sectioned*, c.1485–90, pen and ink, 22.2 × 29 cm, Windsor, Royal Collection Trust, RL 12627 v

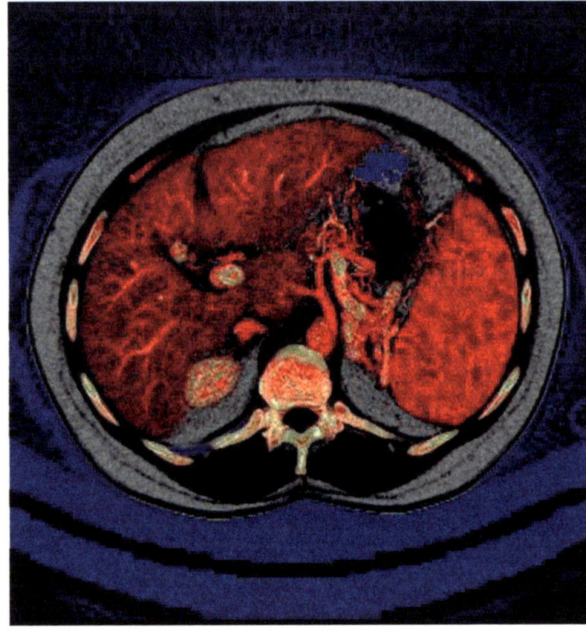

fig. 1 b—Application of the cross-sectional view with a CT view of the abdomen
© Ronan Bouttier, CHRU BREST

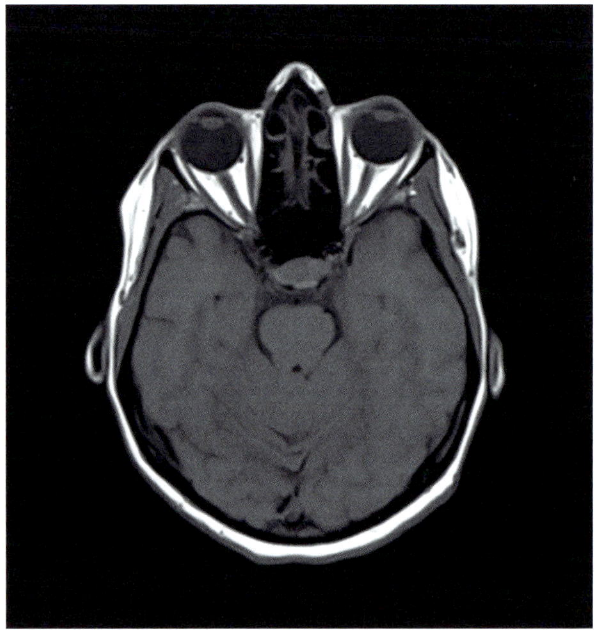

fig. 1 c—Application of the cross-sectional view with a brain MRI
© Marc Garetier HIA BREST

Leonardo da Vinci advanced the study of the human body. He methodically depicted what he observed and wrote commentary in his famous inverted handwriting in the course of his dissections. He considered the human body to be a 'machine' endowed with a soul, each part of which could be modelled, thus allowing the study of its anatomical position, its mechanism and its interactions. His plates are among the finest in the Royal Windsor Collection. His work is an outstanding achievement, going from anatomy to biomechanics and from biomechanics to aesthetics. He left to posterity a remarkable body of anatomical work, of astonishing sensibility, challenging Galen's thinking that considered animals to be the frame of reference for the human body.

Let us take a look at some examples of his methods of dissection and representations of his anatomical observations, in relation to 21st century imagery.

Page 64:

The bones and muscles of the shoulder (detail), c.1510–11, black chalk, pen and ink, wash, 28.9 × 19.8 cm
Windsor, Royal Collection Trust, RL 19001 r

Cross-sectional View of Man

As early as the end of the 1480s, Leonardo dissected or attended dissections of legs. He discovered the compartments housing the muscles and endeavoured to represent them from a slightly angled view [fig.1a]. The illustration speaks for itself. In a single view, Leonardo intended to give a direct and complete picture of this part of the anatomy.

A few centuries ahead of his time, he prefigured CT scans and MRI [fig. 1b-c], allowing him to 'read' the human body without having to 'open' it. From these elementary cross-sections, three-dimensional static or even dynamic reconstructions provide a global picture of the structures, making it possible to study the detailed anatomy of a whole area.

Multiple Views for the Complete Picture

In at least two plates devoted to the anatomy of the upper limb, Leonardo da Vinci employs a technique offering 'multiple views'. The reader, thus, has an immediate picture of a body part thanks to views from all around the part and from above. One of the plates shows several successive images of an upper limb (Windsor, RL 19008 v/c.1510); it provides a complete view of what the eye sees when it moves 90° around the upper limb from an anterior to a side-on view, and vice versa [fig. 2a]. A very simple diagram at the bottom of the plate represents a star that illustrates the eight points of view that Leonardo recommends in order to understand and represent the anatomy of the arm: "I turn an arm into eight aspects of which three are from outside, three from inside, and one from behind, and one from the front...". Here Leonardo takes up a theory of Benvenuto Cellini, goldsmith and sculptor, for whom relief gave sculpture its superiority over painting [fig. 2b]. The dynamic images that scanners make possible today perfectly evoke Leonardo's perspectivist method [fig. 2c].

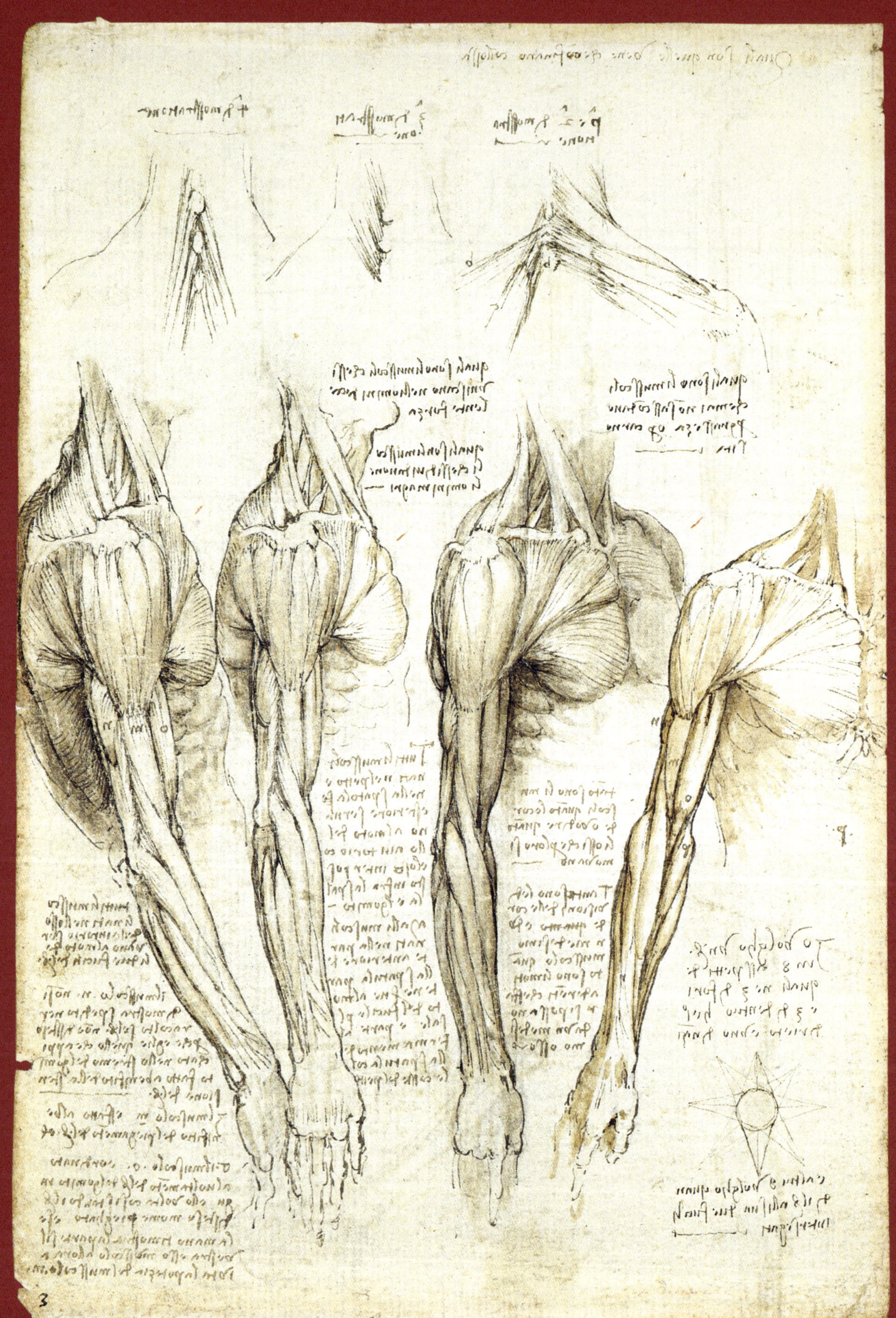

fig. 2 a — *The muscles of the shoulder, arm and neck*, c.1510–11,
black chalk, pen and ink, wash, 28.8 × 20.2 cm
Windsor, Royal Collection Trust, RL 19008 v

fig. 2—Views around the limbs

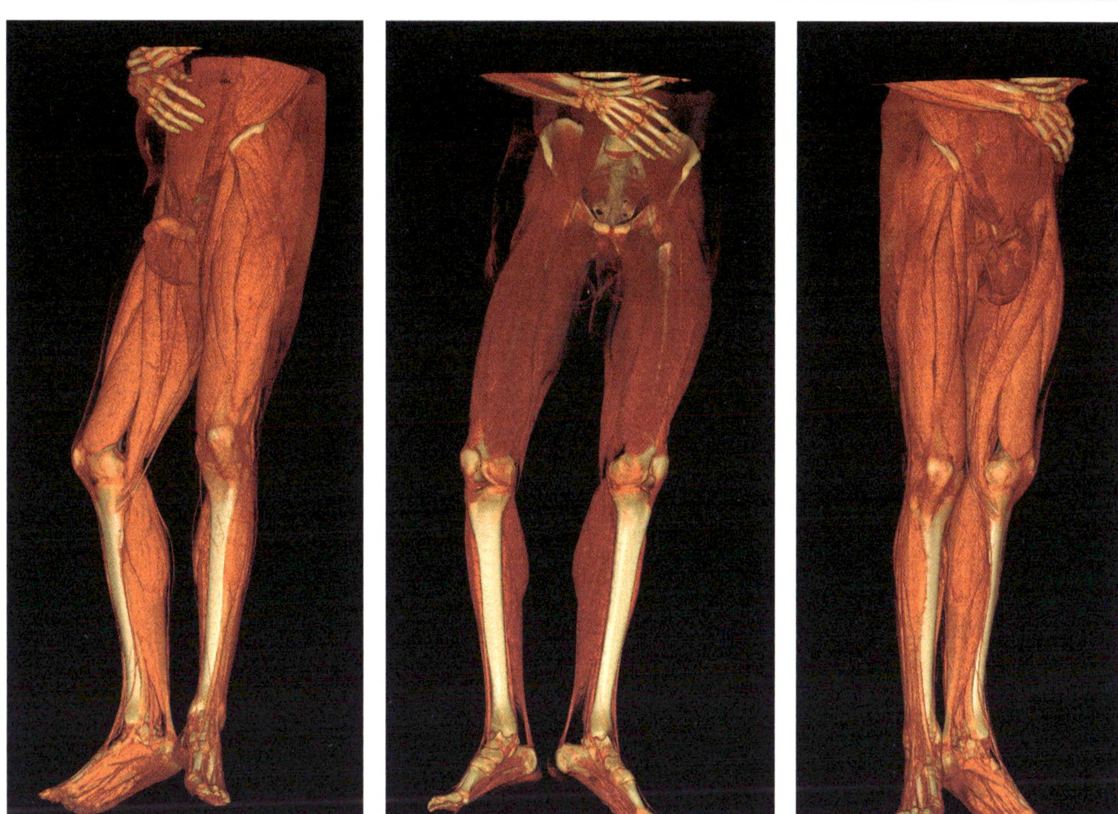

fig. 2 c — Dynamic CT images of lower limbs
with three sequences shown here

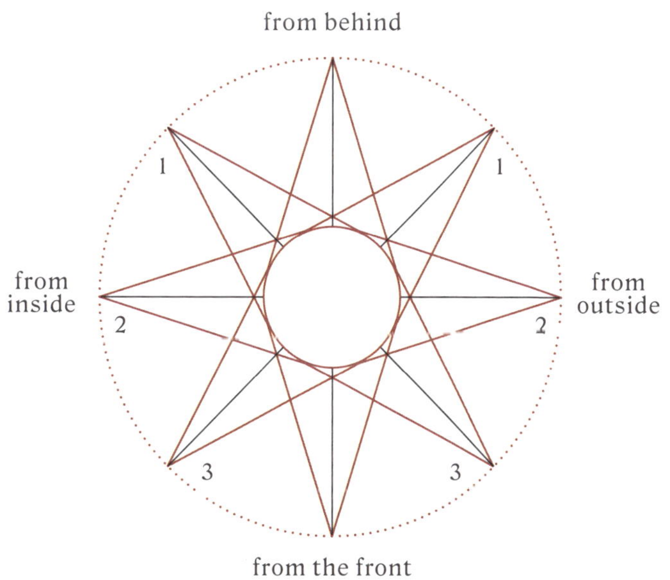

fig. 2 b — Enlarged diagram of the drawing at the bottom of the plate

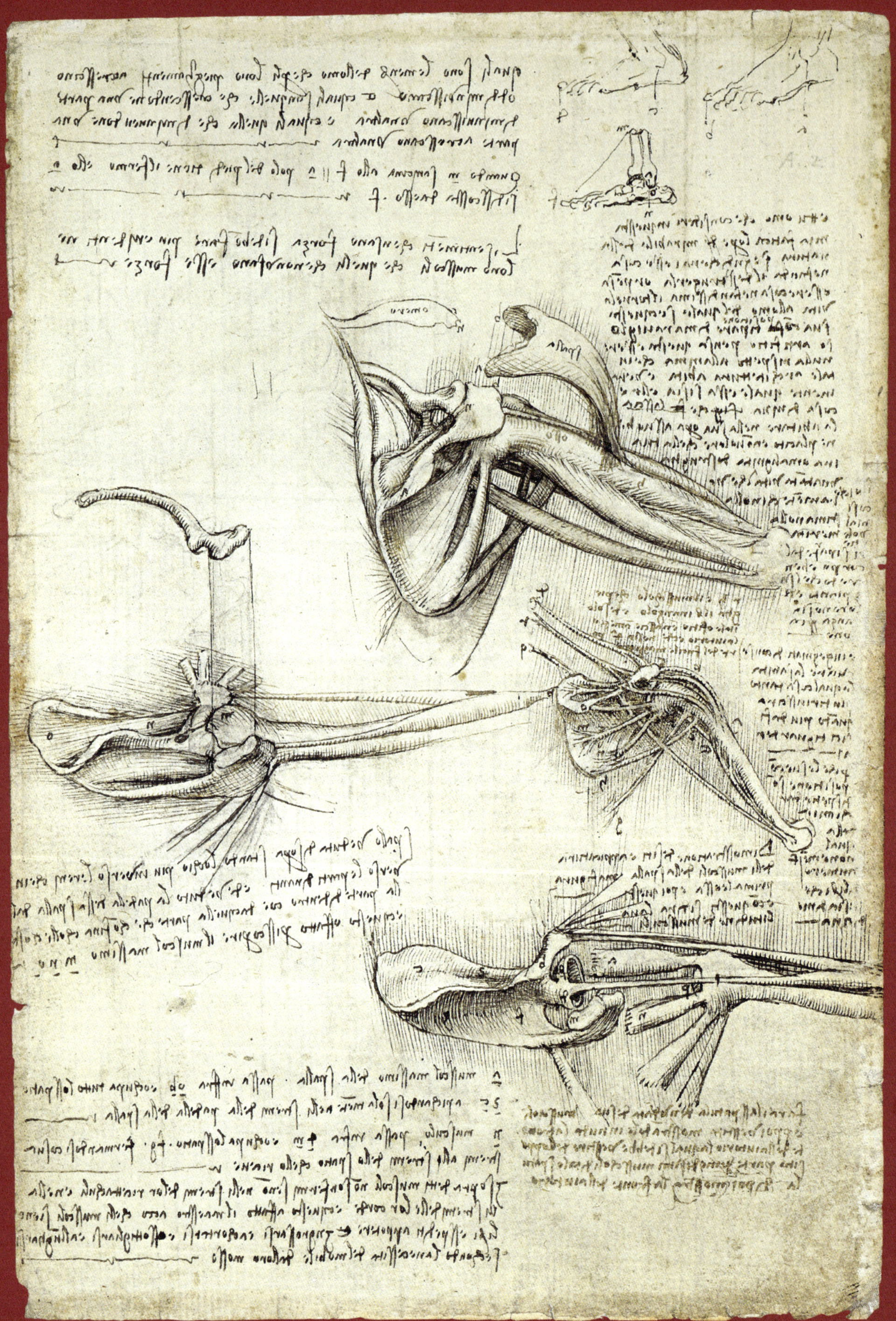

fig. 3 a — *The bones and muscles of the shoulder*, c.1510–11,
black chalk, pen and ink, wash, 28.9 × 19.8 cm
Windsor, Royal Collection Trust, RL 19001 r

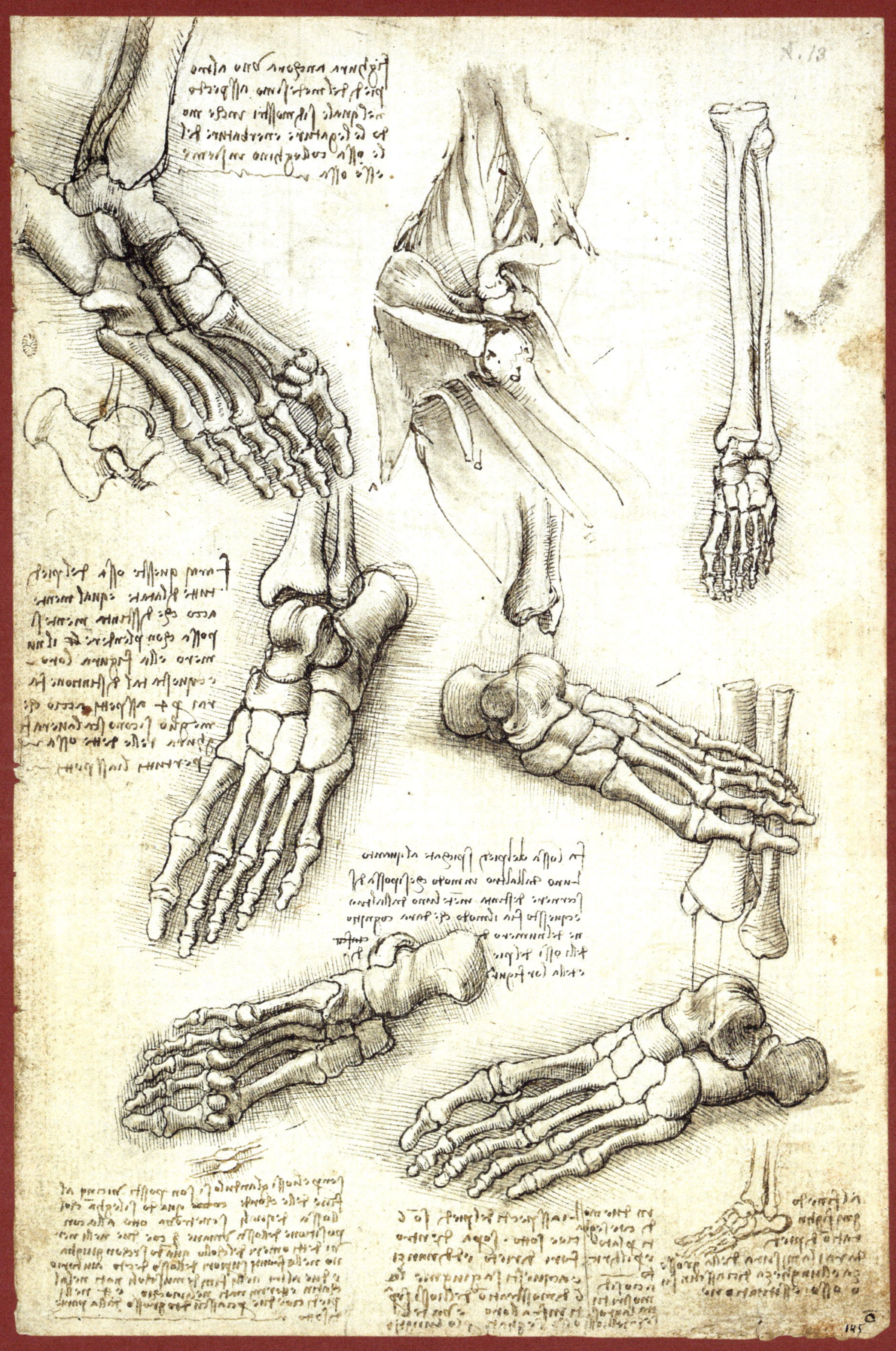

fig. 3 b — *The bones of the foot, and the shoulder*, c.1510–11, pen and ink with wash, over traces of black chalk, 28.7 × 19.8 cm
Windsor, Royal Collection Trust, RL 19011 r

Multiple Views for a Full Understanding

In the process of dissection, Leonardo lifts away the various planes in order to study the layers of tissue in detail.

His study of the hand, for example, which requires no less than ten anatomical 'preparations' for the palm, is remarkable in its accuracy (see 'The Hand, from Anatomy to Function', p. 89). The description is done layer by layer, from deep to superficial, according to the precepts of the painter Leon Battista Alberti. This method is the one we still adopt today in learning anatomy or in designing medical courses.

Removing Parts from the Body

For Leonardo, man also seems to be composed of 'removable parts'. In a plate devoted to the shoulder, he extracts the clavicle, with lines connecting it to its original position, reflecting his intention to remove this bone in order to show the underlying anatomical structures more clearly – as is now done in medical schools or on mannequins or plastic joints for educational purposes [fig. 3a]. On the same plate, he represents an arm on which an imaginary traction reveals the joint between the scapula and the humerus. He proceeds in the same way in a plate devoted to the bones of the ankle [fig. 3b].

This type of representation, applied to other parts of the body such as the cervical vertebrae, helped him to gain a detailed understanding of the anatomy. Nowadays, in the manner of Leonardo [fig. 3c-d], scanners allow certain structures to be extracted virtually, in order to study them more closely or to uncover others.

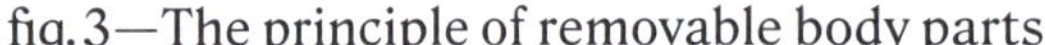

fig. 3—The principle of removable body parts

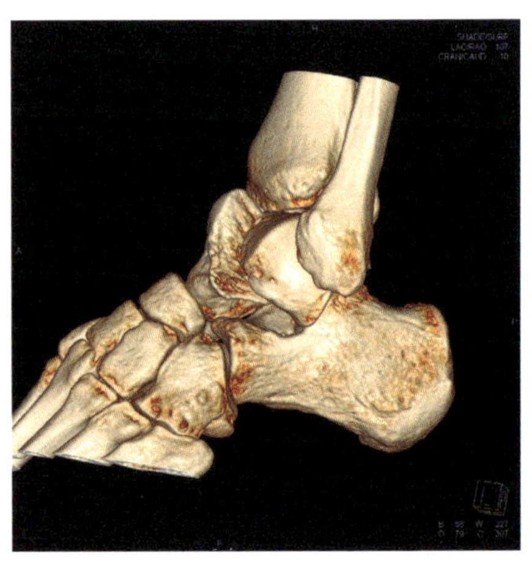

fig. 3 c—CT scan of an ankle showing a fracture of the talus
© CHRU BREST

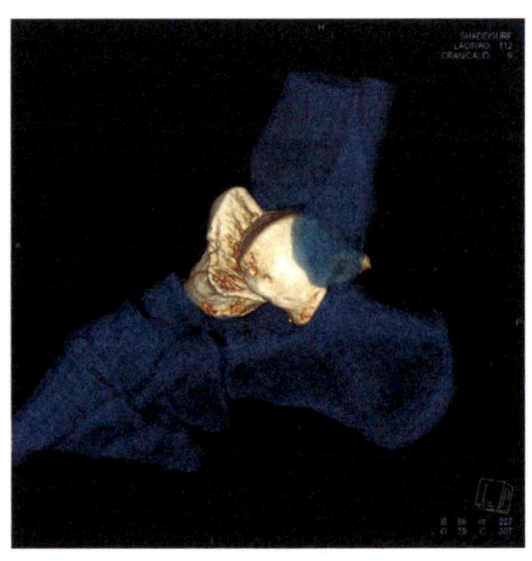

fig. 3 d—Digital removal of other ankle bones to better study the fracture
© CHRU BREST

fig. 4—Function of the fingers

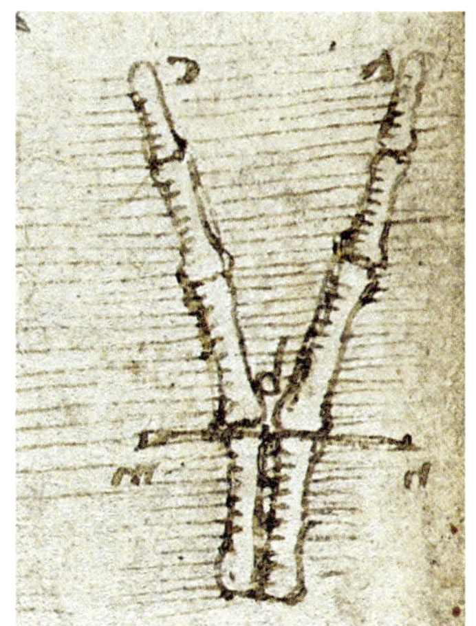

fig. 4 a—Finger spread,
detail from plate
Windsor, RL 19009r / 1510

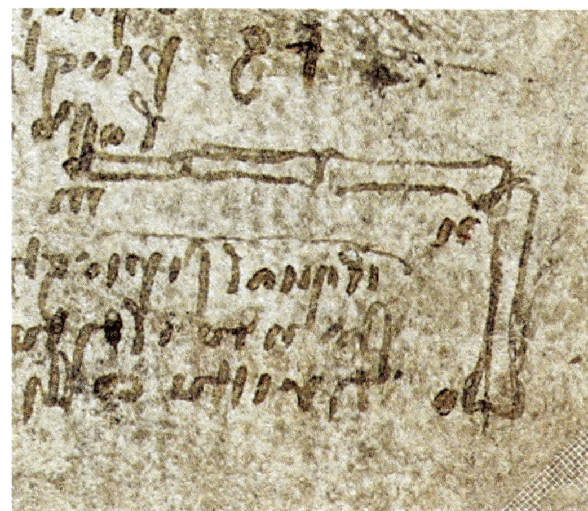

fig. 4 b—Metacarpophalangeal flexion,
detail from plate
Windsor, RL 19009r / 1510

From Anatomy to Functions

In a major plate devoted entirely to the hand (Windsor, RL 19009 r/c.1510, p. 94), a few small drawings, sometimes barely visible, are no less significant because they provide information on the hand's functions. Accompanying his descriptive drawings with simple explanatory diagrams was one of the virtues of Leonardo's work.

For example, two diagrams concern the function of certain small muscles of the hand, whose action he describes in a precise manner (today they are called 'interossci muscles'), in particular the spreading and bringing together of the fingers [fig. 4]: "Remember to draw the cause of the widening movement of the fingers a b and b c, and by the same rule, describe all the widenings of the other fingers and of the other members...".

Here, as elsewhere, Leonardo tells himself or a pupil to investigate further a point of detail observed.

The Body as a Machine

Leonardo was above all an engineer. It is no surprise that he took a 'mechanical' view of the human body, breaking it down into its component parts in order to represent its functions.

In a plate devoted to the muscles of the lower limb, a drawing describes the 'balance' mechanism of the ankle (Windsor, RL 19143 - 19144/c.1506–8). He likens the tibia to a boat's mast forming the axis of a set of scales, whose beam consists of the anterior tarsus on one side, into which the extensor tendons of the ankle are inserted, and the posterior tarsus, on the other side, into which the Achilles tendon is inserted.

Also applied today in the design of certain bridges, shrouds did not escape Leonardo's attention, who adopted the principle in anatomy, applying it masterfully, for example, to the costo-vertebral muscles of the neck [fig. 5b].

Modelling the Body

In some of the plates, Leonardo da Vinci models the muscles in 3D using copper or brass rods heated in the fire in order to explain the muscles' respective positions, their interactions and their mechanical principles: "Before you represent the muscles make, in place of these, threads which may serve to show the positions of these muscles, which should abut with their extremities in the centre of the attachment of the muscles above their bones. And this will supply a speedier conception when you wish to represent all the muscles one above the other...". In doing this, Leonardo simplified a complex anatomy in order to make it understandable. In several folios, by breaking down a muscular region into linear structures, he offers a simplified representation, recreating volume using multiple 'cords' passing over or under one another. One of the most beautiful examples of a body model is a drawing of a shoulder [fig. 6a]. The muscles are identifiable by their insertions and their paths; their representation is simplified to the extreme in the form of one, two or even three 'cords'. By modelling the body,

fig. 5 a—Anatomy of the neck

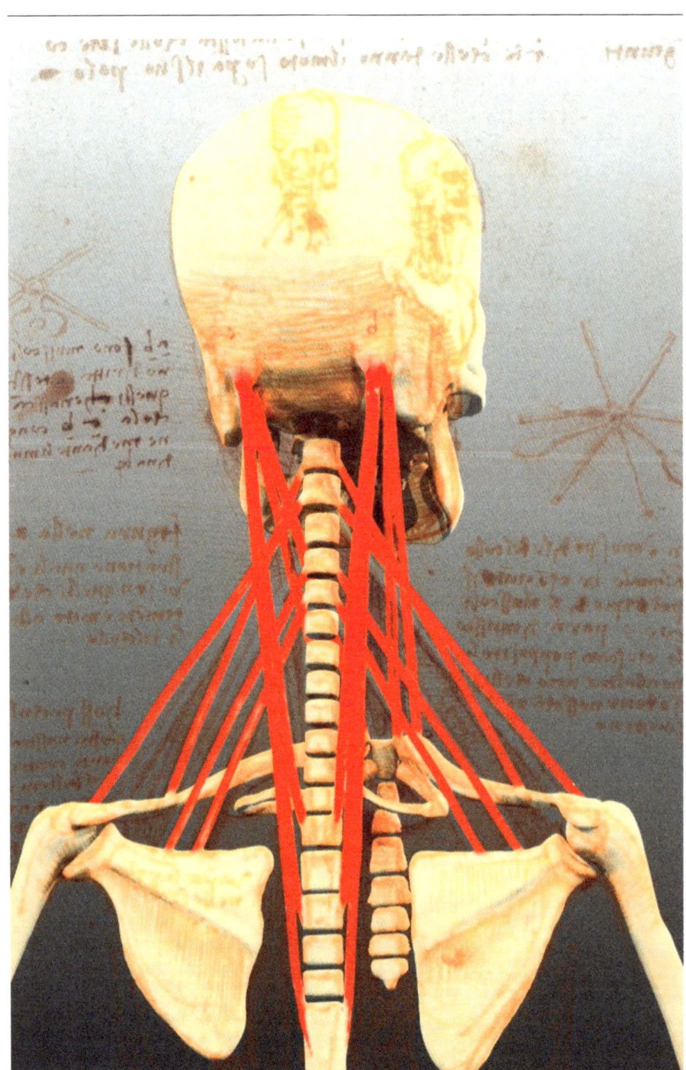

3D Modelling

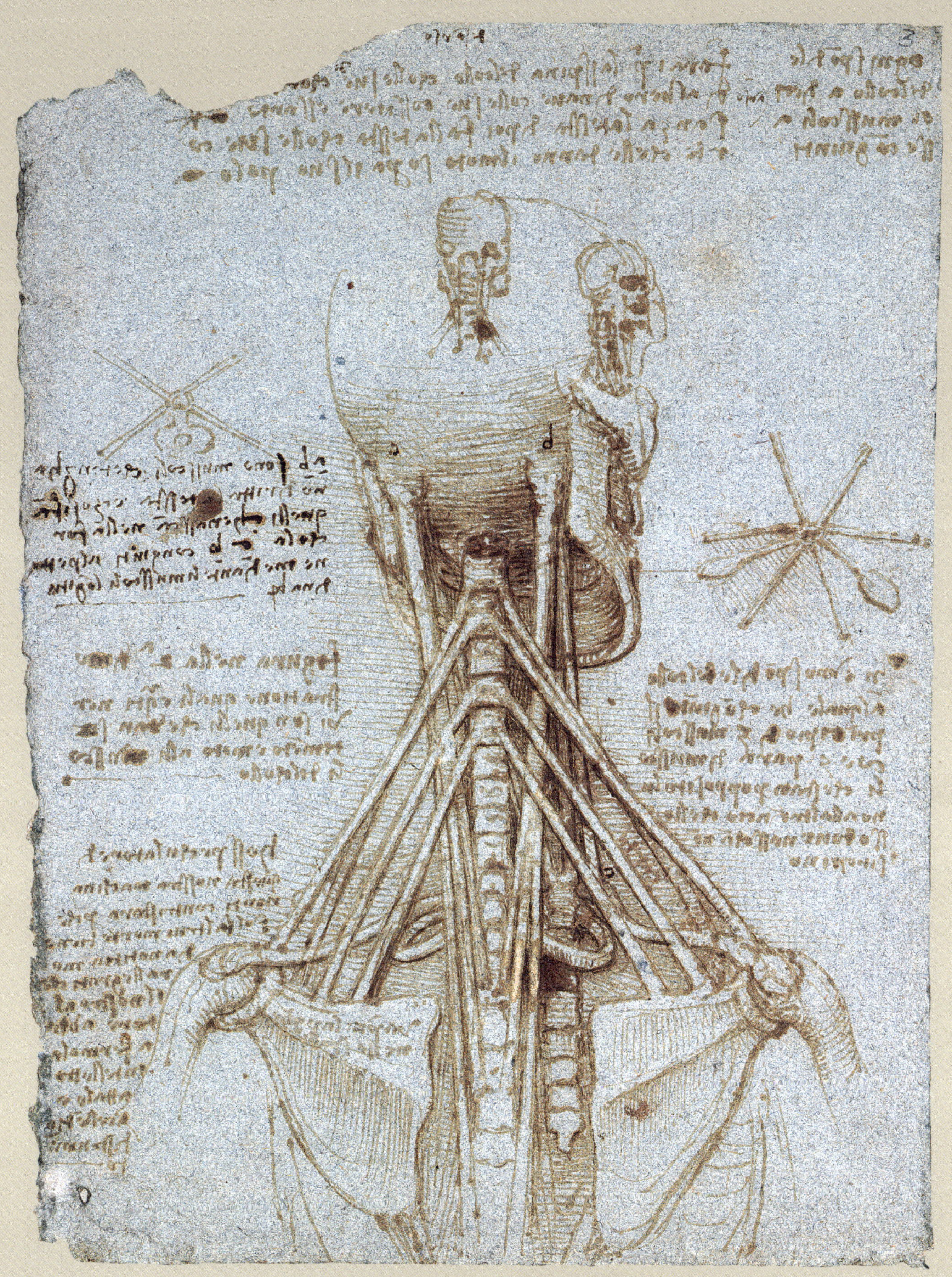

fig. 5 b — *The anatomy of the neck*, c.1512–13, pen and ink on blue paper, 27.6 × 20.7 cm

Windsor, Royal Collection Trust, RL 19075 v

fig. 6—The shoulder

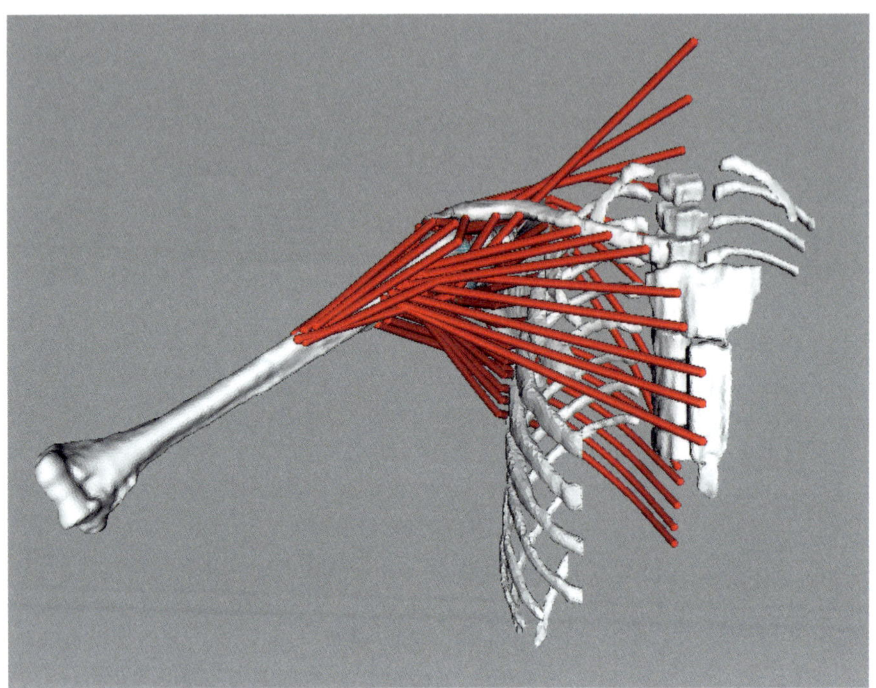

fig. 6 b—From: Asma Salhi, *Towards a combined statistical shape and musculoskeletal modeling framework for pediatric shoulder joint*
Doctoral thesis, École nationale supérieure Mines-Télécom Atlantique – Brittany Pays de la Loire, June 2019

his aim was to represent the muscles and their attachments to bones; and to create, with copper rods arranged on a skeleton model, a 3D vision of the area being studied. These days, some ingenious researchers are doing the same thing using computer modelling [fig. 6b].

Conclusion

Can it be said that Leonardo da Vinci is still considered to be pioneering and innovative in the field of dissection? It is difficult to answer this with certainty. What can be said, however, is that his methods of representing dissections and the principles that we have just looked at are certainly his own. His powers of observation and his unrivalled skill as an engineer and artist came together in an unprecedented way.

A visionary anatomist, Leonardo da Vinci astonishes us and will continue to do so. In his approach to the anatomy of the human body, at least, he is, without question, a forerunner in this field.

*

Leon Battista Alberti, *De pictura*, Paris, Allia, 2007.
Pascal Brioist, Edward Maccurdy, Louise Servicen, *Carnets de Léonard de Vinci*, Paris, Gallimard, 2019.
Benedetto Varchi, Vincenzo Borghini, *Pittura e Scultura nel Cinquecento*, edited by Paola Barocchi, Livorno, Sillabe, 1998.
Dominique Le Nen, *Leonardo da Vinci, L'Aventure Anatomique*, Paris, Éditions E/P/A, Hachette, 2019.
Charles Donald O'Malley, John Bertrand de Cusance Morant Saunders, *Leonardo da Vinci on the Human Body*, New York, Gramercy Books, 1982.

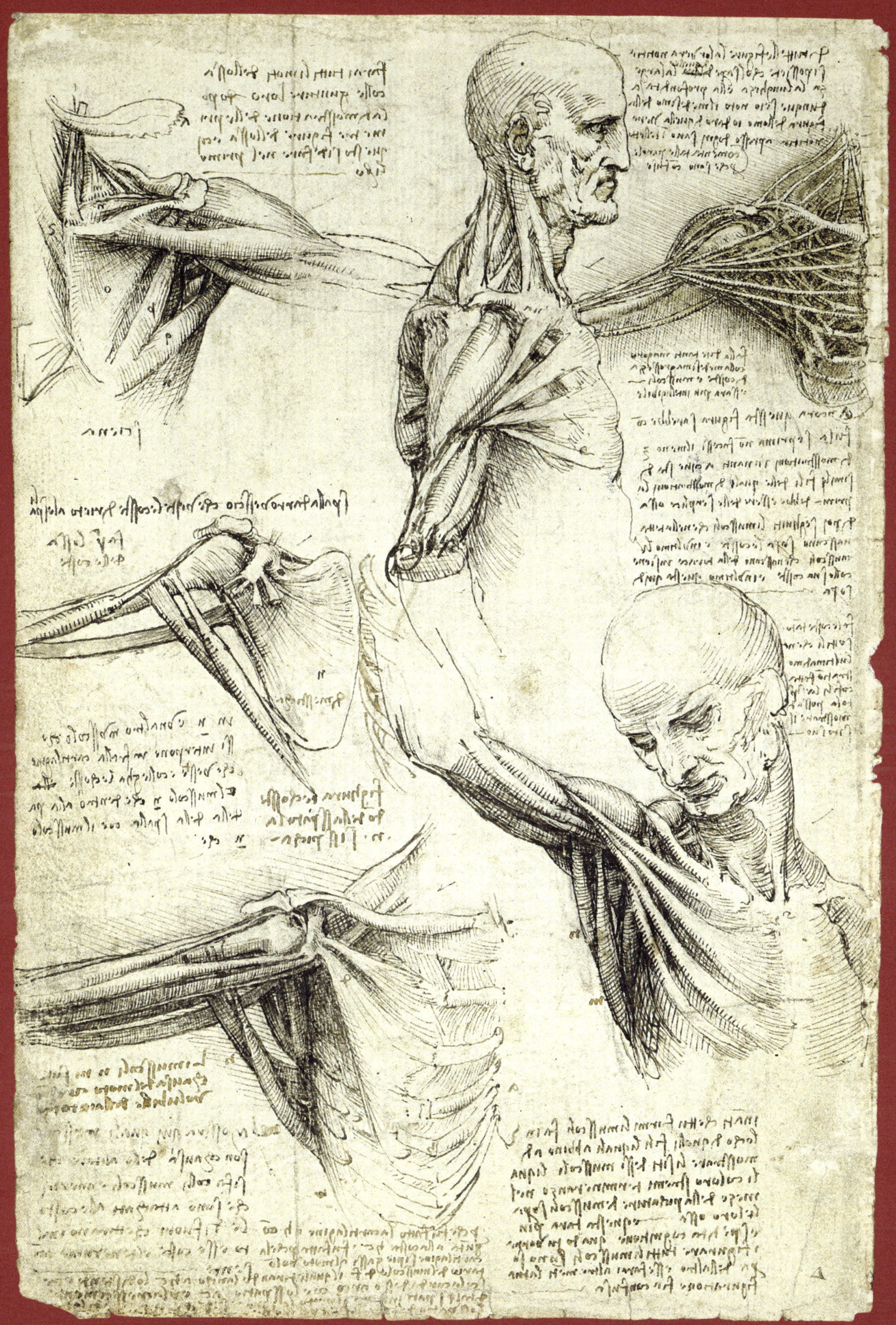

fig. 6 a — *The muscles of the shoulder*, c.1510–11,
pen and ink with wash, over black chalk, 29.2 × 19.8 cm
Windsor, Royal Collection Trust, RL 19003 v

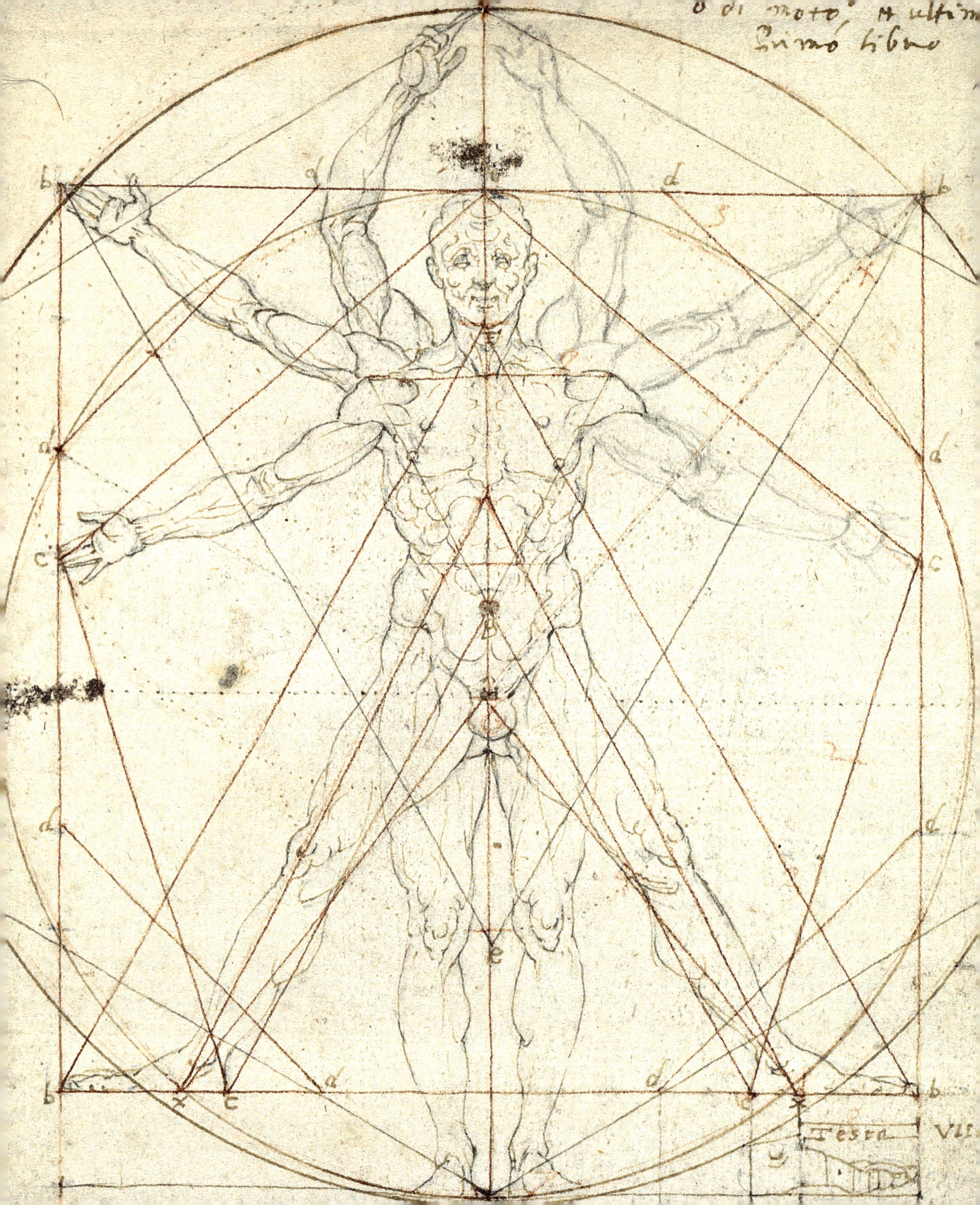
Testa

Leonardo and the Mechanics of the Human Body

Matthew Landrus
Researcher at Wolfson College, Oxford University, specialist in the history of art and science in Italy

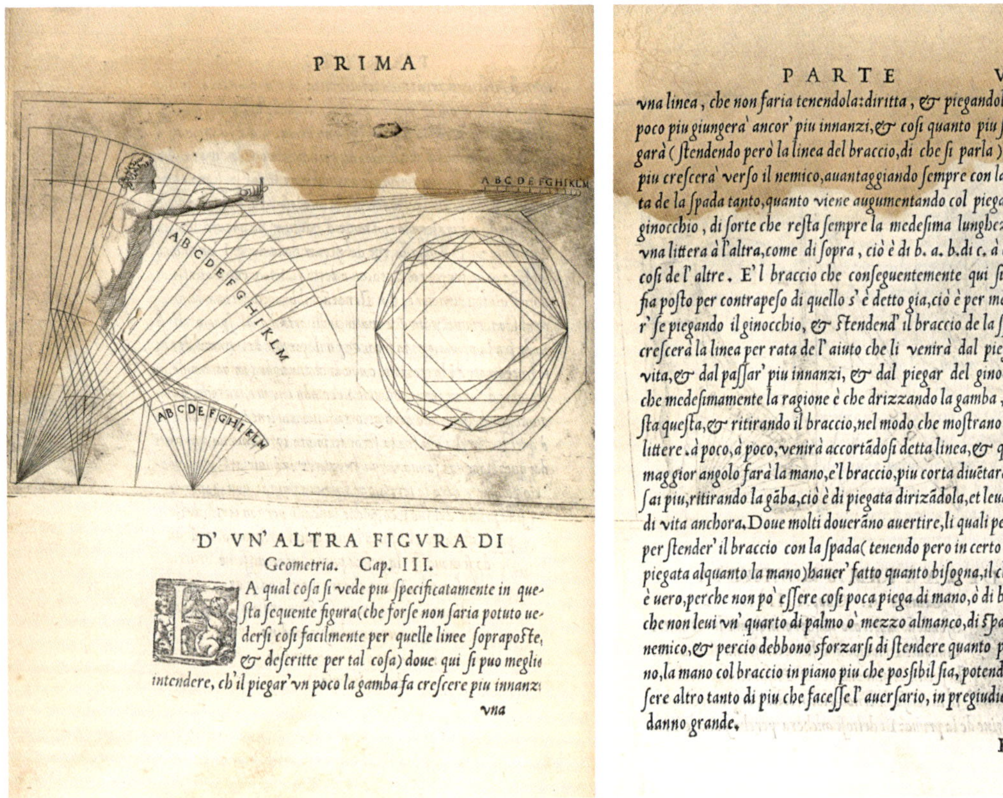

PRIMA

D' VN' ALTRA FIGVRA DI Geometria. Cap. III.

LA qual coſa ſi vede piu ſpecificatamente in queſta ſequente figura (che forſe non ſaria potuto vederſi coſi facilmente per quelle linee ſopraposte, & deſcritte per tal coſa) doue qui ſi puo meglio intendere, ch'il piegar' vn poco la gamba fa creſcere piu innanzi

vna

PARTE V

vna linea, che non faria tenendola: diritta, & piegandola vn' poco piu giungerà ancor' piu innanzi, & coſi quanto piu ſi piegarà (ſtendendo però la linea del braccio, di che ſi parla) tanto piu creſcerà verſo il nemico, auantaggiando ſempre con la punta de la ſpada tanto, quanto viene augumentando col piegar' del ginocchio, di ſorte che reſta ſempre la medeſima lunghezza d' vna littera à l'altra, come di ſopra, ciò è di b. a. b. di c. à c. & coſi de l' altre. E'l braccio che conſeguentemente qui ſi vede ſia poſto per contrapeſo di quello s' è detto gia, ciò è per moſtrar' ſe piegando il ginocchio, & ſtendend' il braccio de la ſpada, creſcerà la linea per rata de l' aiuto che li venirà dal piegar di vita, & dal paſſar' piu innanzi, & dal piegar del ginocchio, che medeſimamente la ragione è che drizzando la gamba, come ſta queſta, & ritirando il braccio, nel modo che moſtrano le ſue littere. à poco, à poco, venirà accortãdoſi detta linea, & quanto maggior angolo farà la mano, e'l braccio, piu corta diuẽtarà, et aſſai piu, ritirando la gãba, ciò è di piegata dirizãdola, et leuandoſi di vita anchora. Doue molti doueràno auertire, li quali penſano per ſtender' il braccio con la ſpada (tenendo pero in certo modo piegata alquanto la mano) hauer' fatto quanto biſogna, il che non è uero, perche non pò eſſere coſi poca piega di mano, ò di braccio che non leui vn' quarto di palmo ò mezzo almanco, di ſpada dal nemico, & percio debbono sforzarſi di ſtendere quanto piu ponno, la mano col braccio in piano piu che poſſibil ſia, potendoli eſſere altro tanto di piu che faceſſe l' auerſario, in pregiudicio, & danno grande.

B

fig. 1 — Camillo Agrippa, *Trattato di scientia d'arme, con un dialogo di filosofia di Camillo Aggrippa Milanese*, illustrated by Carlo Urbino, Rome, 1553 – folios 4 v and 5 – Shelf number: RC_01a
Bibliothèques virtuelles humanistes, CESR, Tours – private collection

Previous page:

Carlo Urbino, *Quinta figura et principio di moto et ultima del primo libro*, Codex Huygens, folio 7, c.1560–1570, black chalk, red chalk, pen and brown ink on laid paper, 13.3 × 18.8 cm (detail)
New York, The Morgan Library, 2006

According to Luca Pacioli (c.1447–1517) in 1498, Leonardo wrote "an inestimable work on local motion, percussion, weights and all the forces, that is, accidental weights, having already with great diligence finished a worthy book on painting and human movements" (Pacioli, folio 12r [2r]). This 'inestimable work' – today known partially as *Codex Madrid I* – addresses the science of mechanics, which includes studies of statics and dynamics (science of weights and motion). Among Leonardo's first tasks when he joined Ludovico Sforza's Court in Milan as an official full-time courtier around 1489 was this book 'on painting and human movements', as well as a book 'on mechanics', both of which were at an initial stage of completion as presentable manuscripts around 1493. They were part of a much larger project Leonardo planned around 1488–89, of several treatises 'on man', addressing human growth, form, movements, senses, emotions, etc. Common to these projects (on man, painting and mechanics) were studies of the mechanics of the human body.

Rather ambitious for its time, but not unexpected at a princely court, this collection of dozens of treatises would develop as an early form of encyclopaedic text on the human condition and the liberal arts. Thus began a project of thousands of interdisciplinary notes and drawings that would make Leonardo famous as a 'genius' in the centuries to follow. Around 1508, he reconsidered the order of this project, to start with mechanics and useful inventions, presumably including or followed by the other books he wrote – as lessons for himself and demonstrations for others – on geometry, painting, military arts, flight, water, the earth, and anatomy. Fundamental for all of these approaches were two natural laws: mechanical functions that would obey the science of statics and dynamics, and

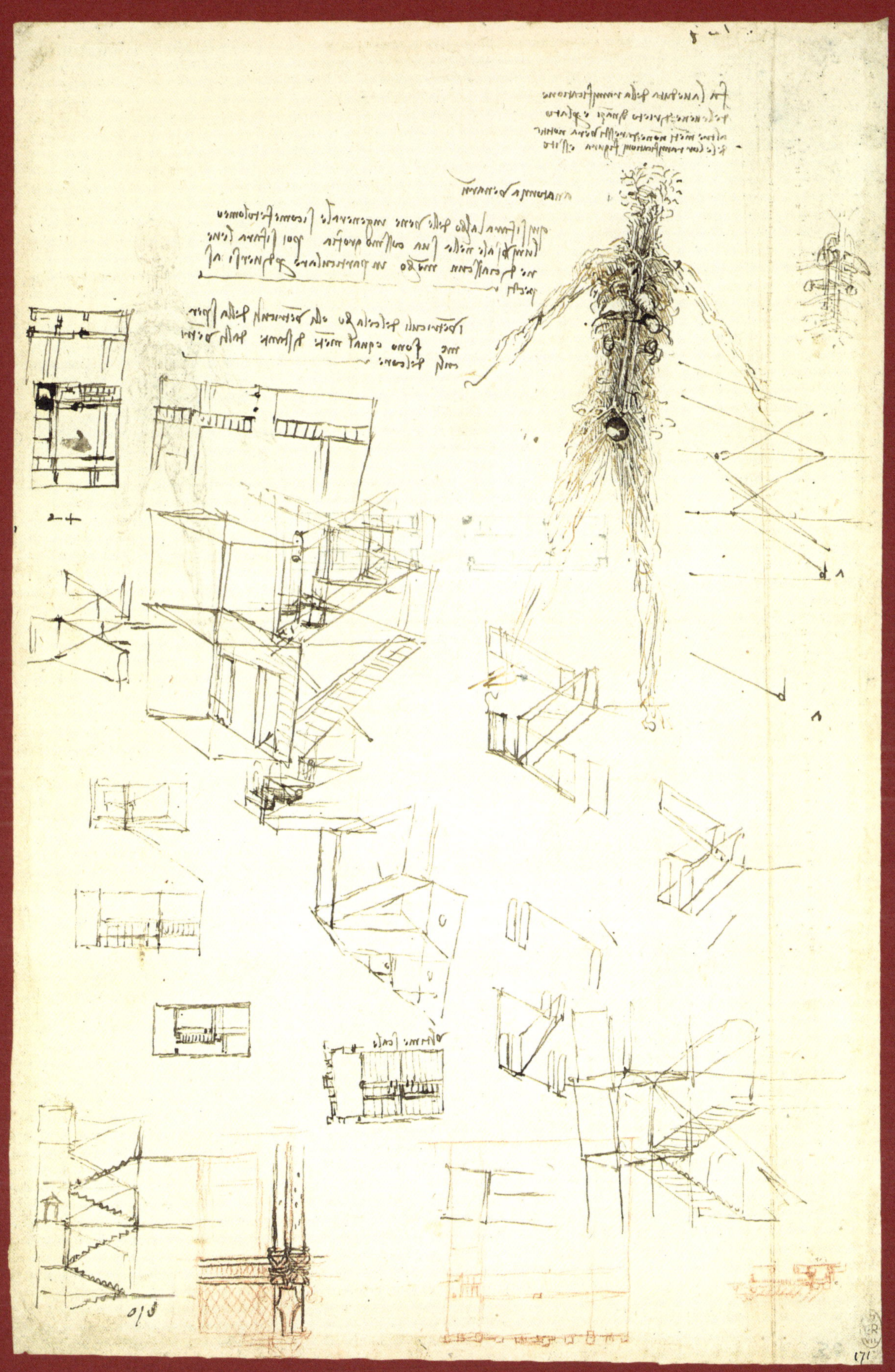

fig. 2—*Studies of the vessels of the body, and of staircases*, c.1506–10, pen and ink and red chalk, 29.5 × 19.8 cm
Windsor, Royal Collection Trust, RL 12592 r

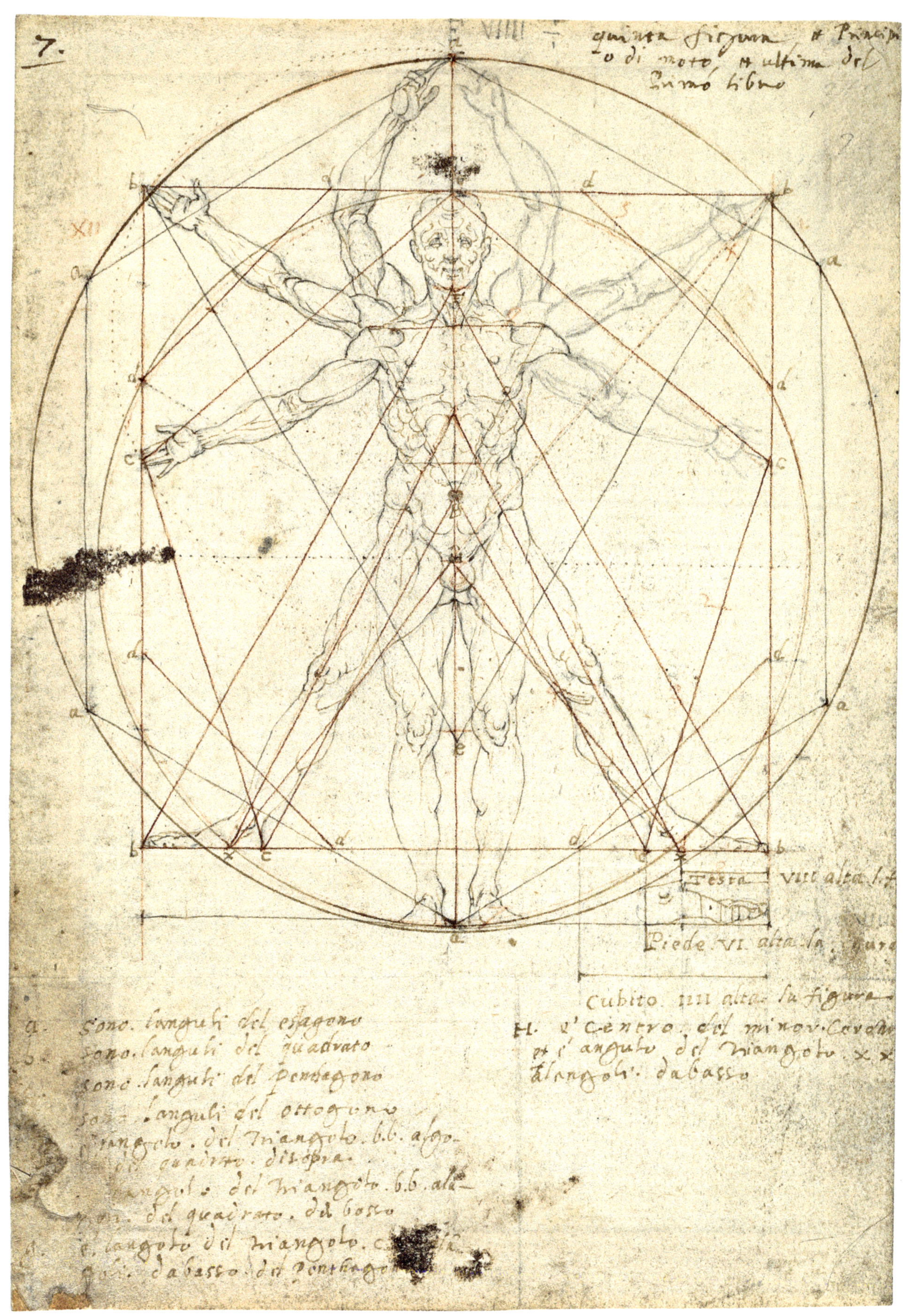

fig. 3—Carlo Urbino, *Quinta figura et principio di moto et ultima del primo libro*, Codex Huygens, folio 7, c.1560–1570, black chalk, red chalk, pen and brown ink on laid paper, 13.3 × 18.8 cm
New York, The Morgan Library, 2006

the geometry of physical quantities governed by a 'pyramidal law' of proportional expansion and/or diminution. This law, which assumes a linear mathematical relationship between cause and effect, and which can grow from nothing to infinity by equal degrees, is described by Leonardo as "pyramidal", because it reminds one of a pyramid or an isosceles triangle when represented. These basic principles – or theories of everything – helped Leonardo develop relatively consistent systematic demonstrations of his work. From c.1488 to c.1513, he focused on the mechanics of the human body, from the highly reductive abstract form of it, to the in-depth, detailed anatomical studies.

At age 36 or 37 (1488–89), Leonardo embarked on a new career plan to work as an engineer, sculptor and painter at the Sforza Court, making numerous notes on the advice he could gather for sculpting an equestrian monument for the Sforza family, on festival planning, on architectural projects, on maps, on Euclidean geometry, on the military arts, on Latin language studies and much more. He also planned an innovative treatise 'on man', noting for "the order of the book... begin with the conception of man, and describe the form of the womb... also its growth... then you will describe which parts grow more than others... then describe the grown man and woman... describe how they are composed of veins, nerves, muscles, and bones... depict the four universal conditions of man... describe attitudes and movement... the function of the eye; on hearing... of music... then describe the nature of the five senses" (Windsor, RL 19037 v).

A work like this could have modernised medical treatises, from the many copies of Galen's second century notes on basic diagrams of arteries, veins, nerves, muscles and bones, to a comprehensive study of human anatomy and development. Indeed, many of Leonardo's anatomical studies of c.1508–13 were substantial innovations, though it is not likely that they were known to physicians thereafter. Whereas he too would begin with Galenic and medieval assessments of the body, Leonardo's novel approach combined naturalistic illustrations with diagrammatic analogies, comparing the human body with examples in ancient literature (e.g. Galen) and examples in the natural world. For example, the Windsor demonstration, RL 12603 r (c.1990–92) offers an analogy between layers of an onion and layers of the scalp and cranial cavity, while offering diagrams of cerebral ventricles that oversimplify them as three round vessels, much the same way medieval illustrations of Galenic medical texts had done. This kind of diagrammatic illustration is arguably part of the proposal for the treatise, 'on man', which is to demonstrate in a new manner the natural appearances of the body (rather than rudimentary diagrams of it) and diagrams of its significant aspects, in this case an *imprensiva* (ventricle 1), which receives images from the eyes – the *sensus communis* (ventricle 2), which received all sensory stimuli, governed the person and contained the soul – and *memorativa* (ventricle 3), memory. An early presentation drawing of a sectioned cranium (Windsor, RL 19058 r), of c.1489, demonstrates the gravitational centre of the cranium, directly above the spinal column, later identified by Leonardo as the position of the *sensus communis*. As a natural start to an innovative book 'on man', this *sensus communis*, the master organ of the senses that contains the soul, governs the mechanics of the body.

Another purpose of the treatise 'on man' demonstrations was for a book 'on painting' around 1490–93, for which Leonardo produced dozens of human proportion diagrams. During this period, he also assessed human proportions for architectural design with the now famous 'Vitruvian Man' diagram (Gallerie dell'Accademia, Venice, no. 228), which was likely one of a series of similar systematic, diagrammatic analogies of figural geometry, mechanics, movement and proportion, as diagrammed by Carlo Urbino da Crema (1525/30–1585) in c.1560–80 for his manuscript, *Regole del disegno* (rules of design). Forty-three pages of his *Regole* compare directly with autograph Leonardo drawings and with three drawings by Francesco Melzi (1491–1568/70), indicating that Urbino had access to these drawings in Melzi's collection, potentially copying examples that are now lost, of human diagrams inscribed in polygons. An example similar to Leonardo's 'Vitruvian Man' is on page 7 of the *Regole* [fig. 3].

However, much more important for Urbino and Leonardo were systematic diagrams of the mechanics of man, which they used as examples in their manuscripts, that the discipline of painting is a science, a potentially noble, systematic, mathematical demonstration of every mechanism and mechanical movement of the human body. For Camillo Agrippa's 1553 *Treatise on the Science of Arms*, Urbino provided geometrical diagrams of the numerous possible movements of a man while fencing [fig. 1]. By 1508–10 Leonardo was committed to emphasising the mechanical basis of his various projects, noting that "the book 'on the science of mechanics' should precede the book 'on utilities' [and that] the book on the elements of mechanics and their practice should precede the demonstration of the movement and force of man and other animals, and by means of these you will be able to prove all of your propositions" (Windsor, RL 19009 r). These comments are somewhat marginal on pages with extensive discussions on the anatomy of the cardiovascular system (Windsor, RL 19070 v) and on bones and tendons of the hand (Windsor, RL 19009 r), where he is apparently concerned with the reader's understanding of mechanics, statics and dynamics before reading the anatomical studies. While demonstrating the myology of the leg and torso on Windsor, RL 19014 v, he alludes to the mechanism of the human body and to an Aristotelian prime mover by praising "the first composer of such a machine" (Windsor, RL 19014 v).

Leonardo's anatomical studies in 1508 prompted his return to the twenty-year-old treatise project, 'on man' with an expansion of anatomical studies and a reordering of books, most of which were at that point, "a collection without order, taken from many papers that I have copied here, hoping hereafter to arrange them in their proper order" (*Codex Arundel* 1r). He planned to arrange the collection according to the arrangement of the human body, of earth, and of the universe. On Windsor, RL 12592 r, next to the drawing of a man's veins, titled in Latin *anatomia venarum* (venous anatomy), he states: "here shall be a general depiction of the vessels, as Ptolemy did with the universe in his *Cosmographia*; then the vessels of each particular member will be represented separately, from different views" (Windsor, RL 12592, [fig.2]).

He possessed a copy of Ptolemy's impressively illustrated *Cosmographia*, along with Latin books that addressed medicine, anatomy and surgery, listing them in a collection of 164 books that he put in storage in 1503–4 (this booklist appears on folios 2v–3r of *Codex Madrid II*); and he actively sought books on anatomy and medicine in private collections. Expanding plans for his book, 'on man', Leonardo clarifies on Windsor, RL 19061 r that "in twelve figures you will have set before you the cosmography of this lesser world on the same plan as, before me, was adopted by Ptolemy in his *Cosmographia*; and so I will afterwards divide them into limbs as he divided the whole world into provinces; then I will speak of the function of each part in every direction, putting before your eyes a description of the whole form and substance of man."

One of those sections would have included the proportional, somewhat mechanical ordering of the brachial plexus, as seen in Windsor, RL 19040 r [fig. 4]. The plan at this point was relatively holistic and Aristotelian, a modelling of the proportional mechanisms of the body in a manner consistent with the harmony of the spheres in the heavens.

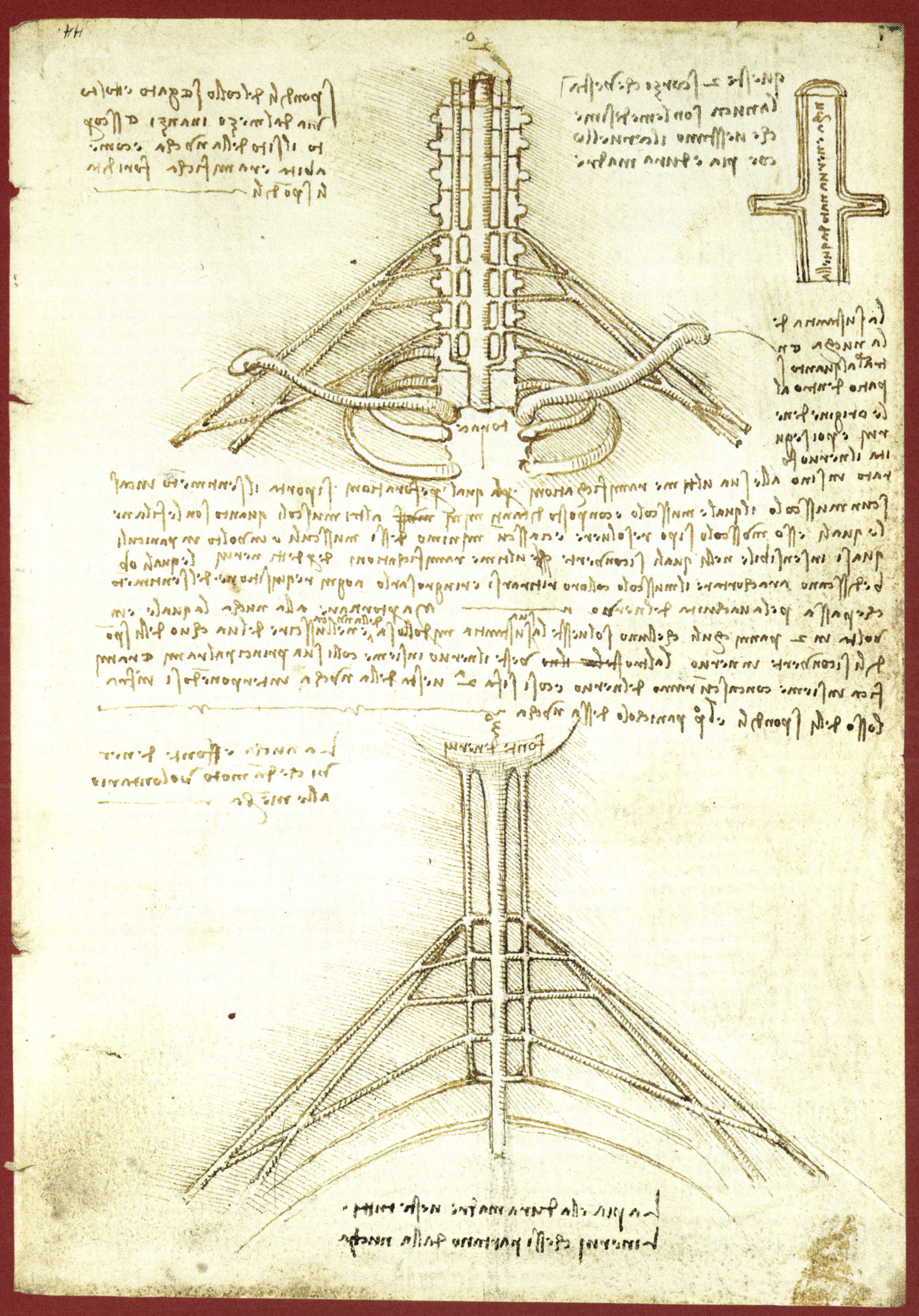

fig. 4 — *The brachial plexus*, c.1508,
pen and ink over black chalk, 19.1 × 13.7 cm
Windsor, Royal Collection Trust, RL 19040 r

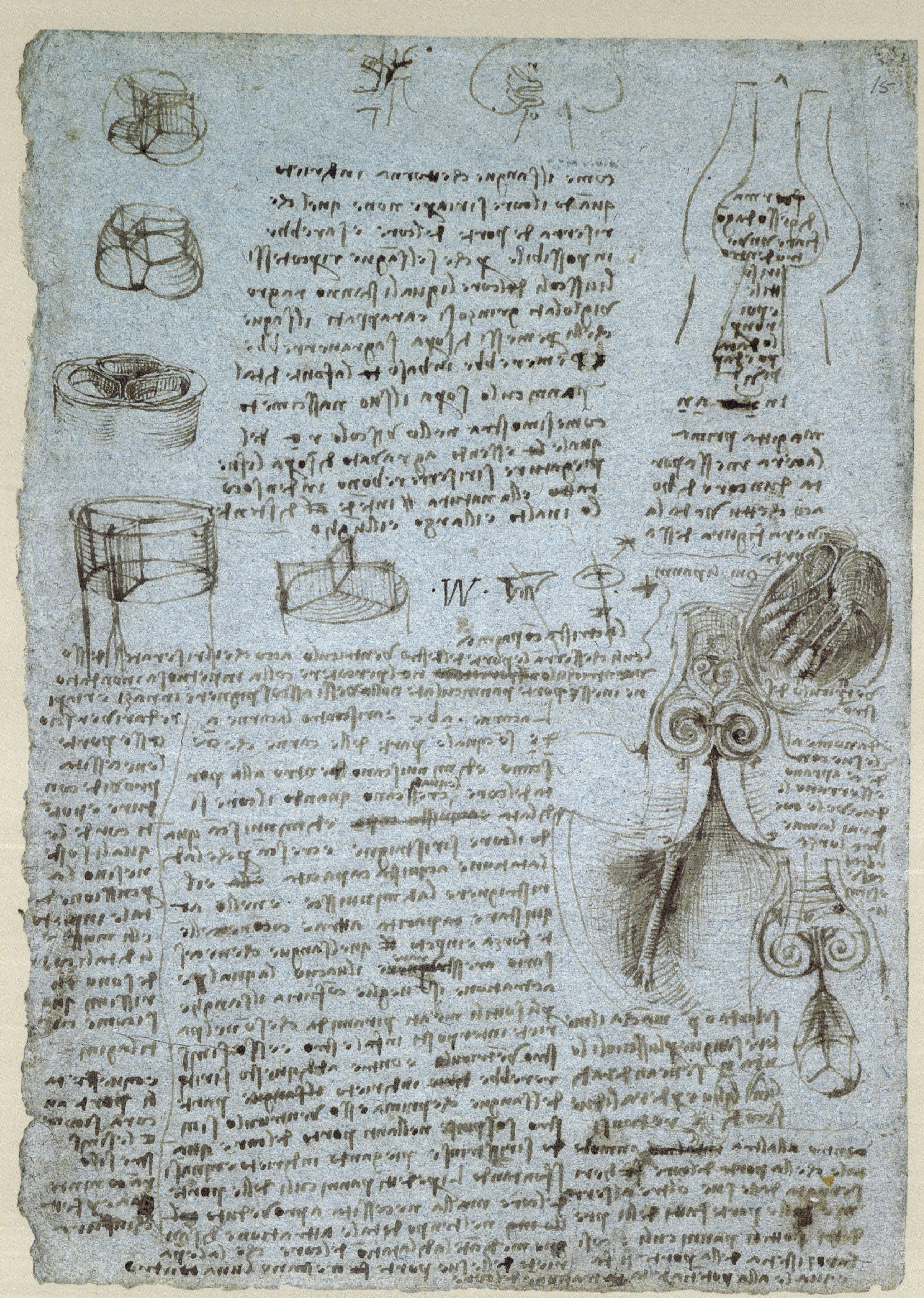

fig. 5—*The aortic valve*, c.1512–13,
pen and ink on blue paper, 28.3 × 20.4 cm

Windsor, Royal Collection Trust, RL 19082 r

Leonardo's most sophisticated and innovative approaches to anatomical studies concerned the mechanical properties of the heart, especially the means by which it manages blood flow. Around 1512–13 he proposed an experiment [fig. 5] whereby vortices of blood flow through 'three valve-cusps' of the aortic root could be examined. He states, "make this test in the glass [vessel] and move inside it water and ... grass seed". One can see around the sheet the turbulence of water in the experimental vessel, which may in this case be a 'thought experiment' or an actual glass vessel Leonardo had produced for this study. In any event, it was proven with an experiment using a similar glass model in 2001 that Leonardo's design for the glass vessel was reliable for the observation of turbulence in the aortic root (Kremers et al., 2002). In 1991, the heart surgeon Francis Robicsek confirmed that Leonardo discovered the function of the sinus of Valsalva, in which eddy currents help close aortic valve leaflets. Leonardo referred to this dynamical function of the aortic valve, rather than assume that it was operated with pressure from above, as was the standard medical theory until the 'Bellhouse experiment' conducted by the medical engineer Brian Bellhouse in 1969. Leonardo could see with his own experiment that pressure from above would partially collapse the sinuses.

It would seem that Leonardo enjoyed writing and illustrating demonstrations that he intended to bind as books, on man, on mechanics, on painting, and on water, the earth, military arts, geometry, and other subjects. Fundamental to these projects were his analyses of proportional and mechanical principles, which helped with complicated projects. Although he produced a substantial body of notes and drawings, he lamented around 1510 that he had not completed his anatomical studies, noting "whether all these things [these skills as an anatomist] were found in me or not, the hundred and twenty books composed by me will give the verdict, yes or no. In these I have been impeded neither by avarice or negligence, but only by time. Farewell" (Windsor, RL 19070 v).

✷

Agrippa, Camillo. *Trattato di scientia d'arme, con un diologo di filosofia di Camillo Agrippa Milanese*, Rome, Andonio Blado, 1553.
Kremers, David and Martin Kemp et al., 'Leonardo's vision of flow visualisation', *Experiments in Fluids* 33 (2002): 219–23.
Landrus, Matthew. 'Leonardo's Lost Book on Painting and Human Movements', in: The Fabrication of Leonardo da Vinci's *Trattato della pittura*, With a Scholarly Edition of the Italian *editio princeps* (1651) and an Annotated English Translation, edited by Claire Farago, Leiden, Brill, 2017, pp. 183–212.
Pacioli, Luca. *De Divina Proportione*, 1498, Biblioteca Ambrosiana, Manuscript 170 sup.

Leonardo da Vinci and the Hand: From Anatomy to Function

Dominique Le Nen
University Professor and Surgeon
at Brest Regional University Hospital

Jacky Laulan
Hand Surgeon at the Regional University Hospital in Tours

Previous page:

The bones, muscles and tendons of the hand, c.1510–11, black chalk, pen and ink, wash, 28.8 × 20.2 cm (detail)
Windsor, Royal Collection Trust, RL 19009 r

Leonardo da Vinci was fascinated by the hand and the mechanisms that enable it to function. He was probably influenced by Claudius Galen, who devoted the first chapter of Book I of *De usu partium* to this subject.

In Leonardo's view, the hand and the rotational movement of the forearm (called 'pronation-supination') and the shoulder constituted a single functional entity. Any movement of the upper limb should, therefore, present the hand in the best possible way so as to introduce the appropriate movement. Thus, the number of plates that Leonardo devoted to the shoulder and the upper limb clearly indicates the importance he gave to their functions. He associated the action of the muscles with the stress exerted on the bones and joints, and he gave the hand the appropriate orientation according to the action of the muscles on the bones of the forearm and/or the arm. This correlation between movement and anatomy in painting was difficult to achieve at the beginning of the Renaissance movement, although this was overcome with the harmonious balance created by Leonardo and the other anatomist painters in the early 16th century.

The most beautiful illustration of this phenomenon can be seen in plate 19011 v/c.1510 [fig.1]. In the upper part, two upper limbs are firmly holding a cylindrical object. The first limb has the skin removed to show the veins. All the tendons used to flex the wrist are shown tensed in the extension position. In this drawing, Leonardo transferred his static observation of the cadaver to the dynamic reality of life. He dissected in order to draw reality more accurately, which in a way explains why he did not always represent what he observed. The drawing of the Windsor folio, therefore, combines an artistic vision with a functional approach to anatomy.

At the bottom of the plate, Leonardo writes: "No movement of the hand or of its fingers is caused by the muscles that lie above the elbow; and it is the same in birds, and thus they are so strong because all the [pectoral] muscles that lower the wings arise in the breast, and they have in themselves greater weight than all the rest of the bird." In this passage, the comparison with birds shows the serious attention he paid to the mechanics of flight.

The Mechanics of Pronation and Supination

Leonardo had a keen interest in pronation and supination. Given that the function of the hand is the natural end of the pronation-supination movement, Leonardo symbolised this by referring to the world in which man evolves: "The ordinary position of the palm of the hand is to be turned toward the horizon, and its ordinary extreme positions are to be turned toward the sky [supination] or toward the earth [pronation], that is to say, toward the head or the feet of the individual."

Leonardo accurately analysed this mechanism. He dissected, probably moving the muscles and tendons for this purpose, observing their action on the bones and joints; and ended by interpreting what he had observed.

In another plate, the bones of the upper limb are shown [fig.2]. The bones are in the extension position or in very slight flexion. He implicitly demonstrates the mechanism of pronation-supination, showing in some drawings the muscles involved in pronation, especially the *pronator teres*, but also the *biceps*, responsible for supination. In his notes, there is repeated mention of his intention to include transverse and longitudinal sections of the bones to reveal their relative thickness and internal structure.

The most detailed and revealing plate relating to the mechanism of pronation-supination contains two drawings [fig.3]: the drawing at the top

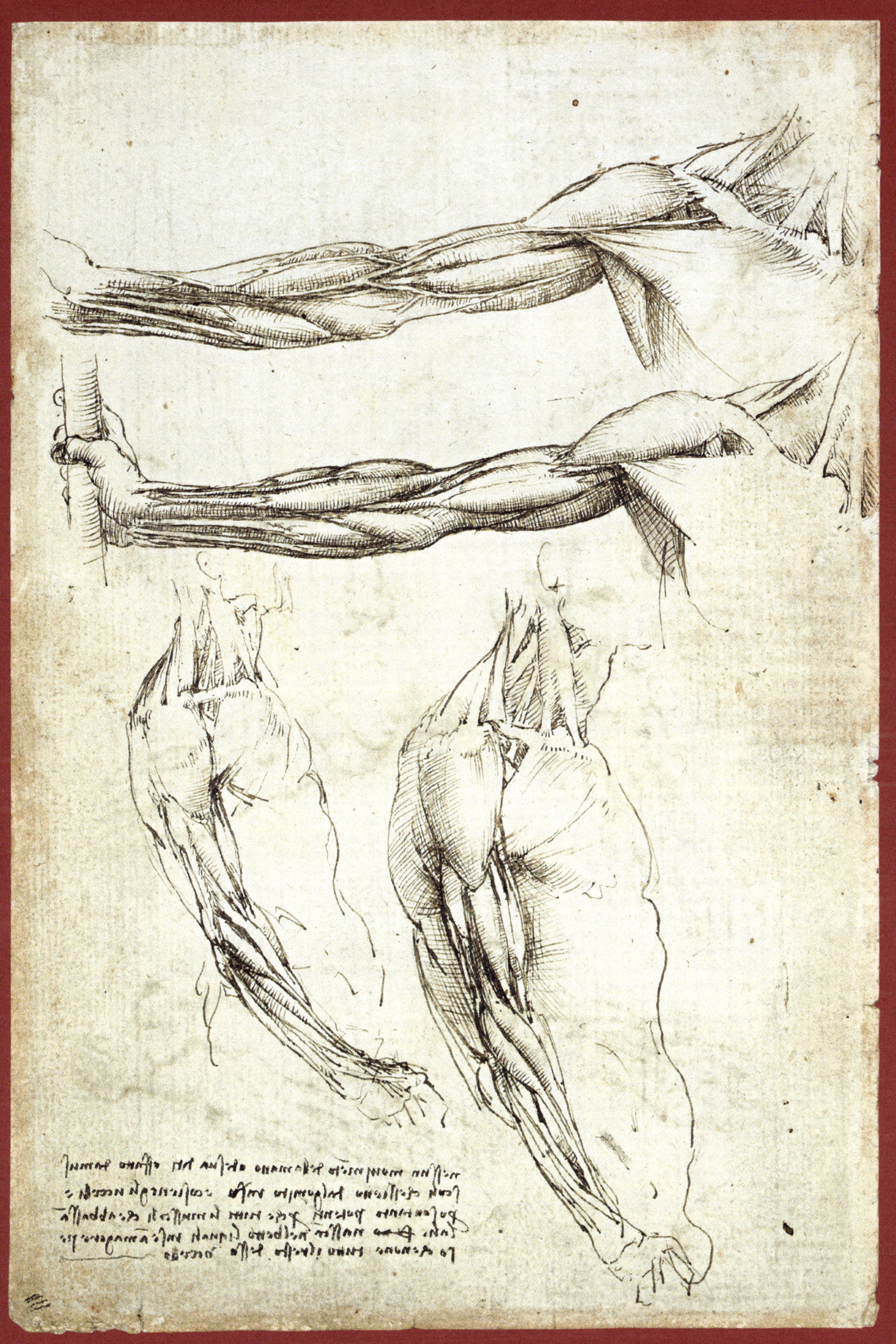

fig. 1 — *The veins and muscles of the arm*, c.1510–11,
pen and ink, over traces of black chalk, 28.7 × 19.8 cm
Windsor, Royal Collection Trust, RL 19011 v

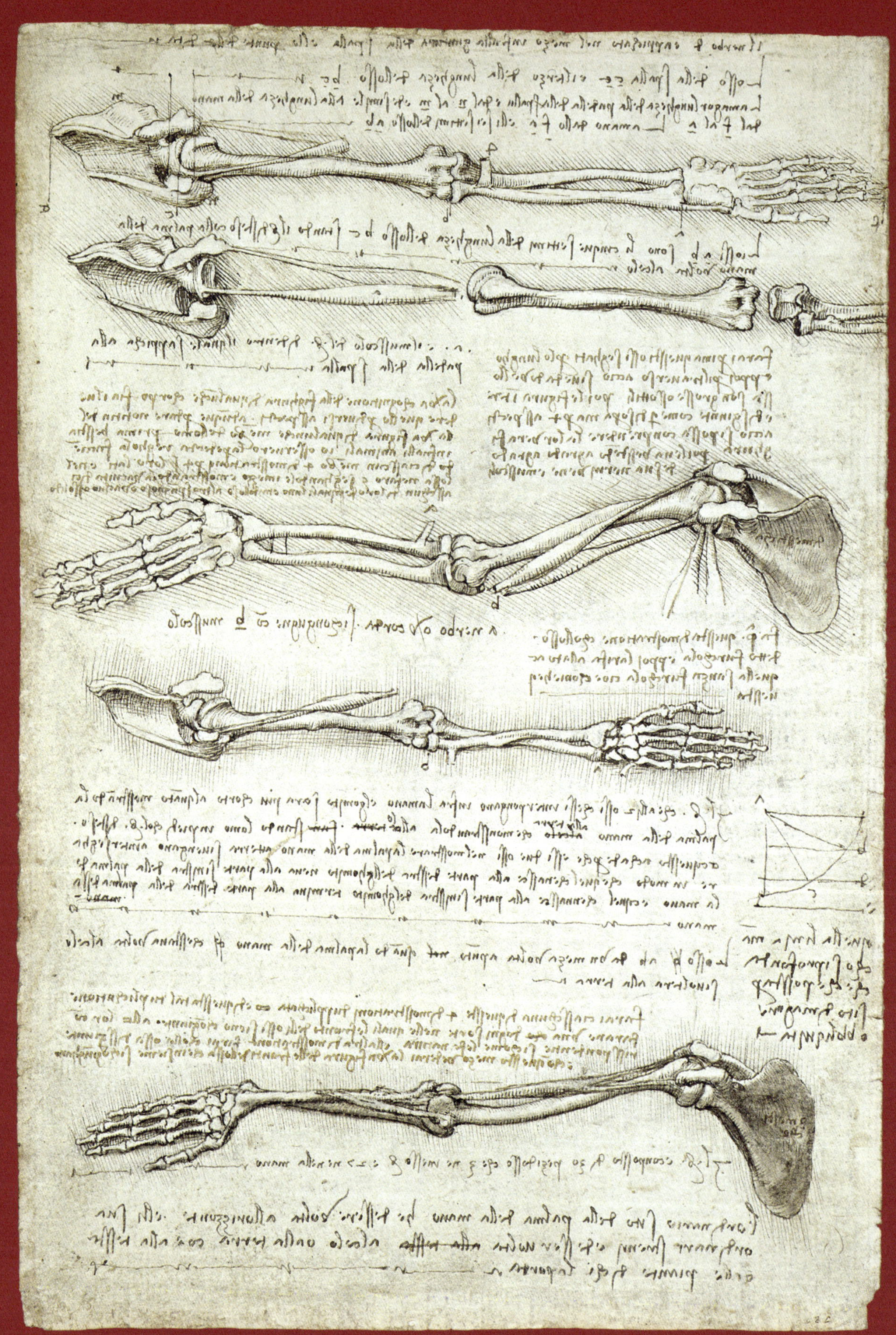

fig. 2 — *The bones and muscles of the arm*, c.1510–11, black chalk, pen and ink, wash, 29.3 × 20.1 cm
Windsor, Royal Collection Trust, RL 19000 v

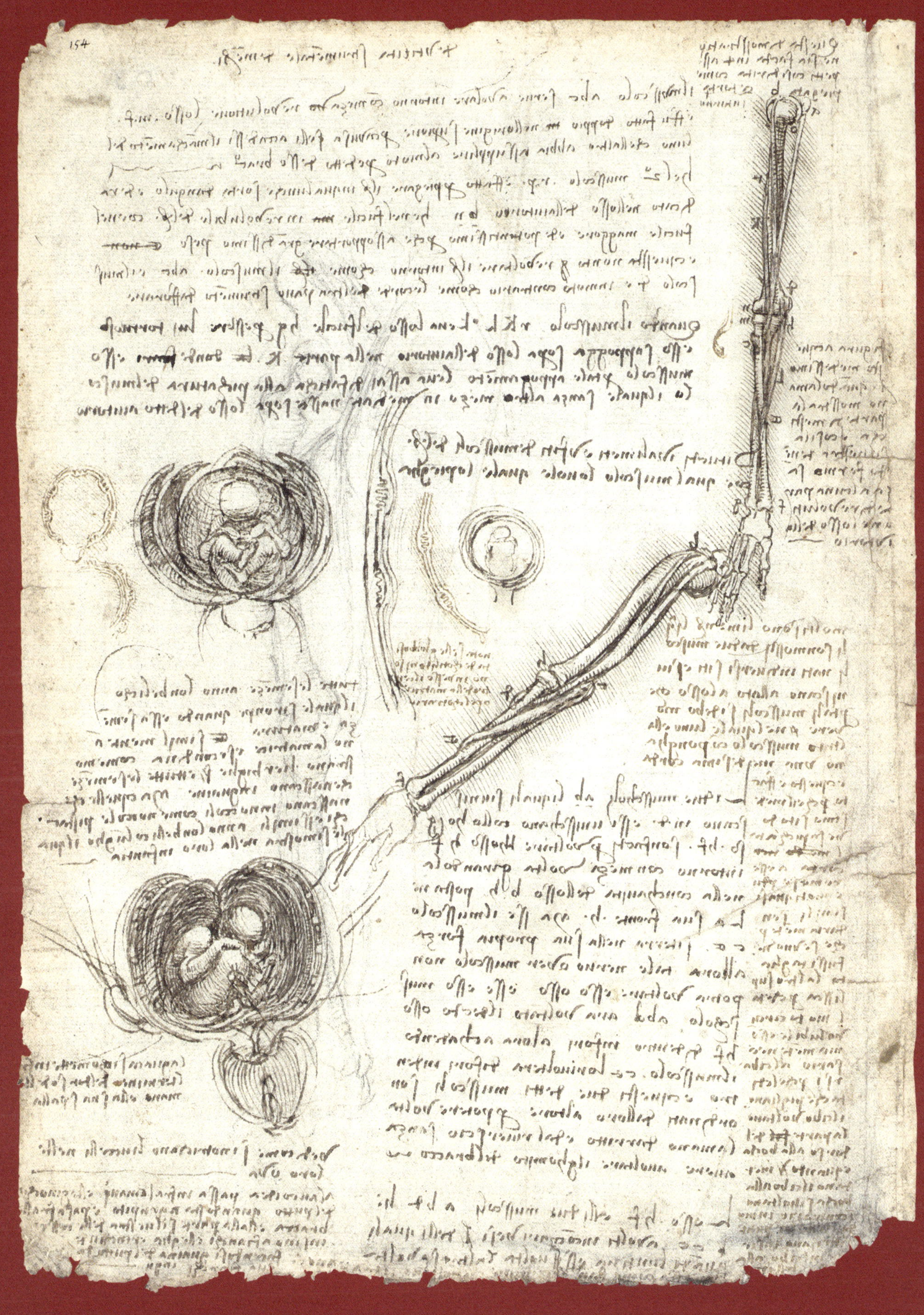

fig. 3 — *The rotation of the arm, and the foetus in the womb*, c.1505 (bones), c.1510–1512 (foetus), pen and ink over black chalk, 28.7 × 21.1 cm
Windsor, Royal Collection Trust, RL 19103 v

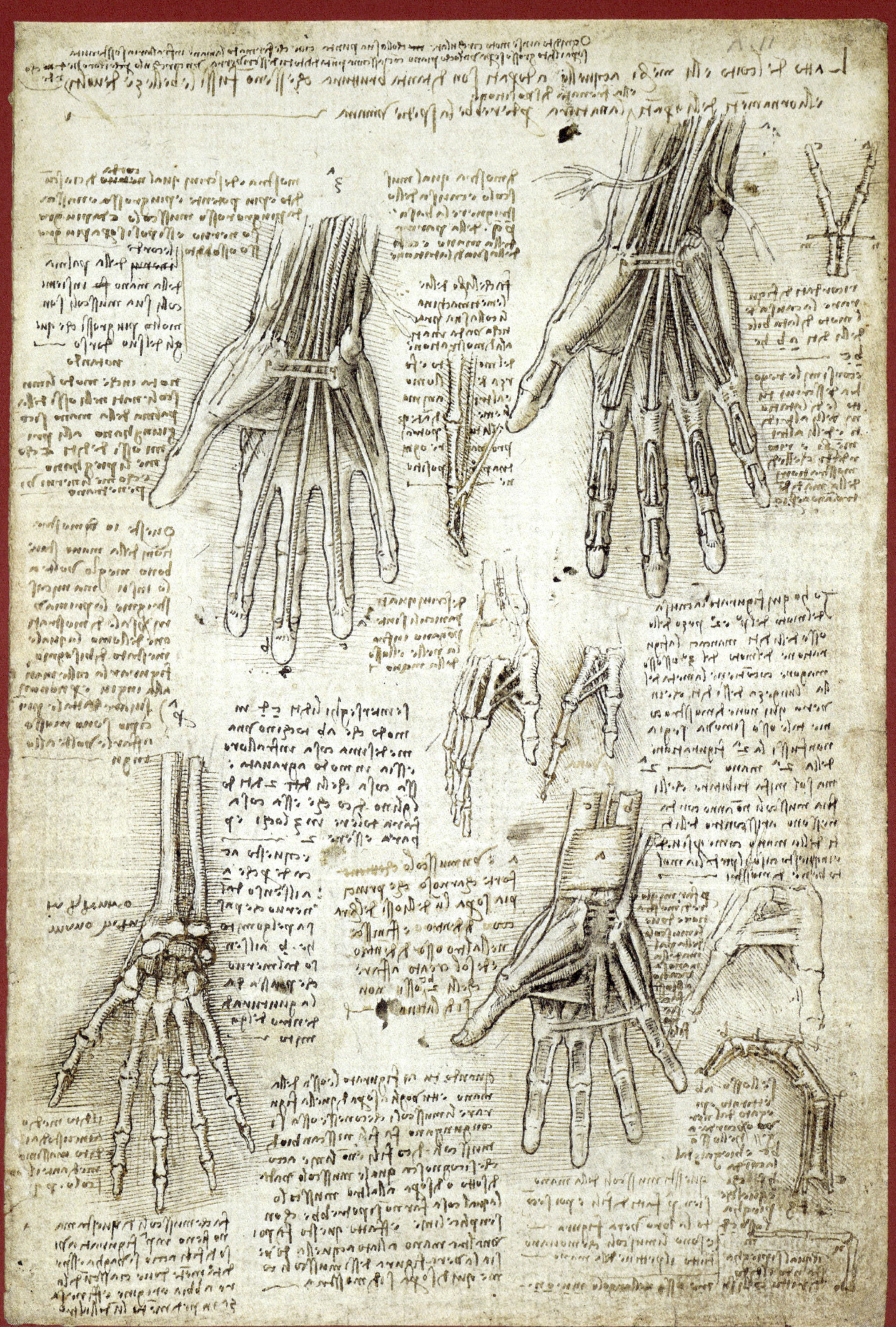

fig. 4 a —*The bones, muscles and tendons of the hand*, c.1510–11,
black chalk, pen and ink, wash, 28.8 × 20.2 cm
Windsor, Royal Collection Trust, RL 19009 r

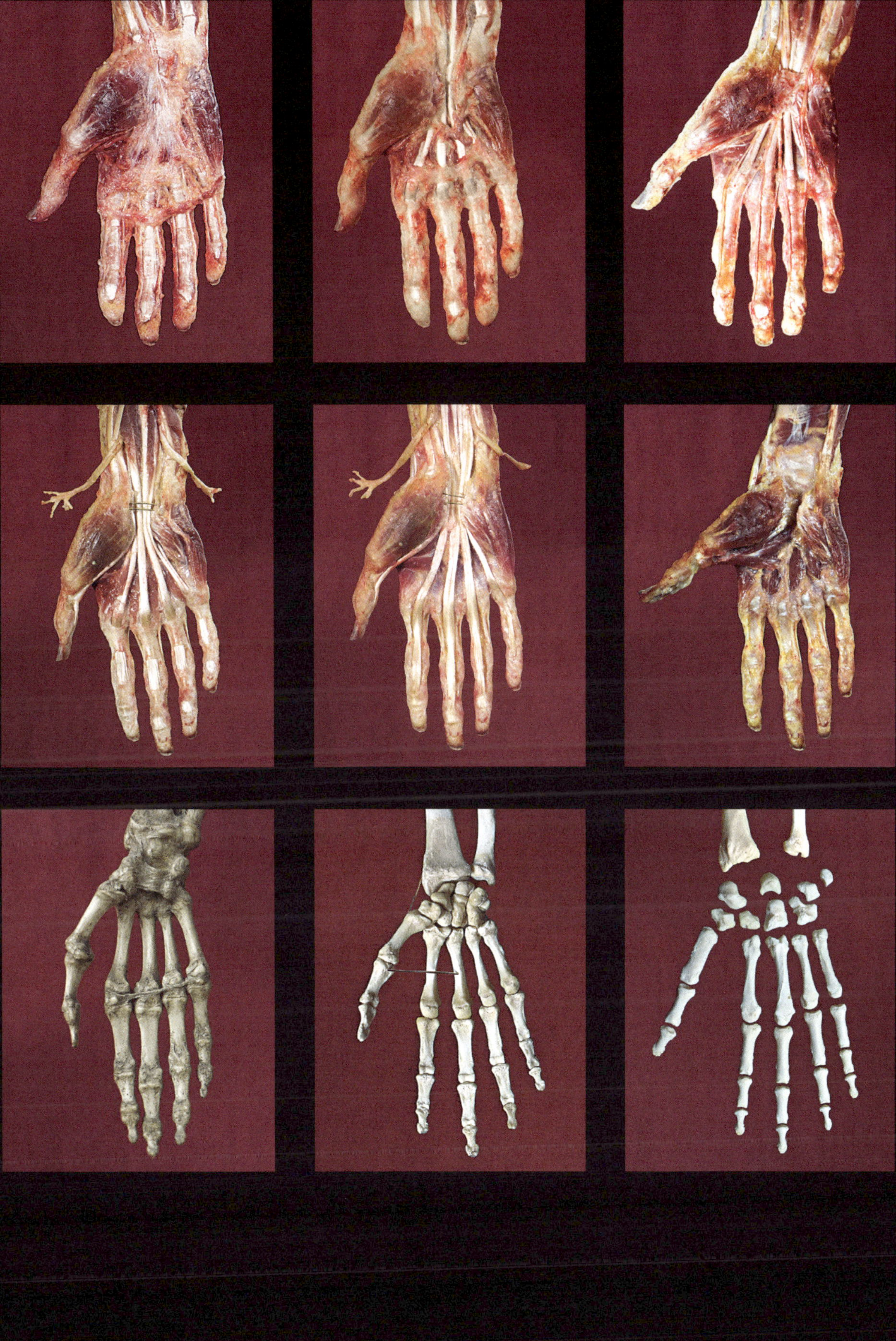

fig. 5—Finger pulleys

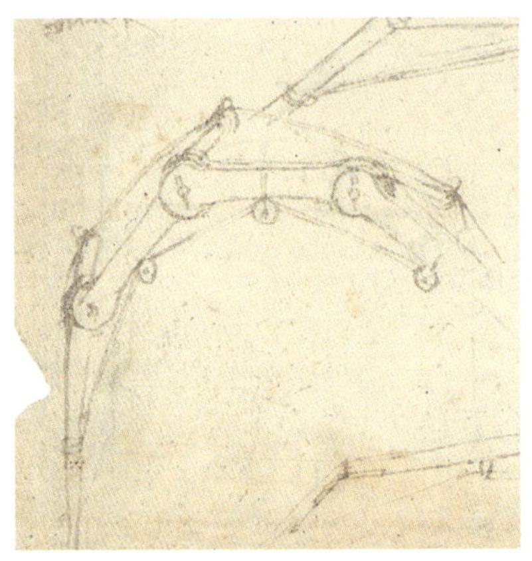

Study for artificial flight (detail), c.1486–1490, *Codex Atlanticus*, folios 747 r/276 r-b, Milan, Biblioteca Ambrosiana

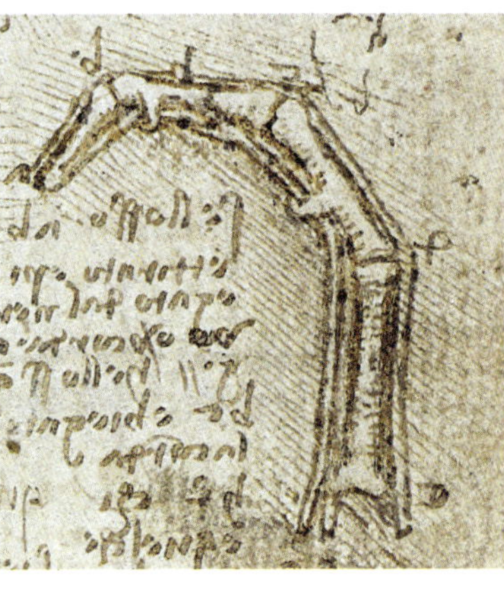

Detail from plate Windsor, RL 19009 r/c. 1510

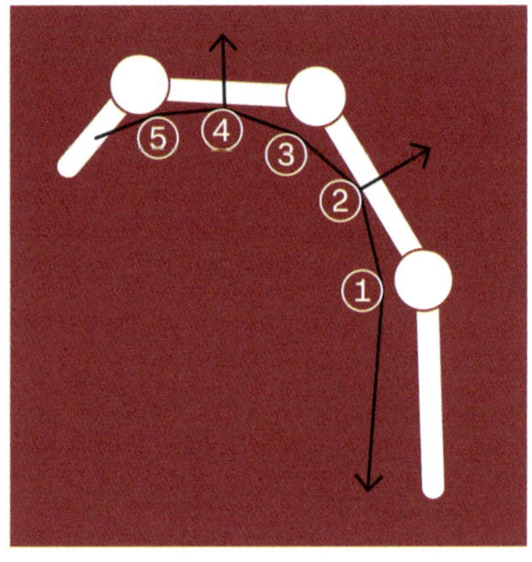

Diagram of Leonardo da Vinci's drawing with bones (white), flexor tendons (black), and pulleys from 1 to 5

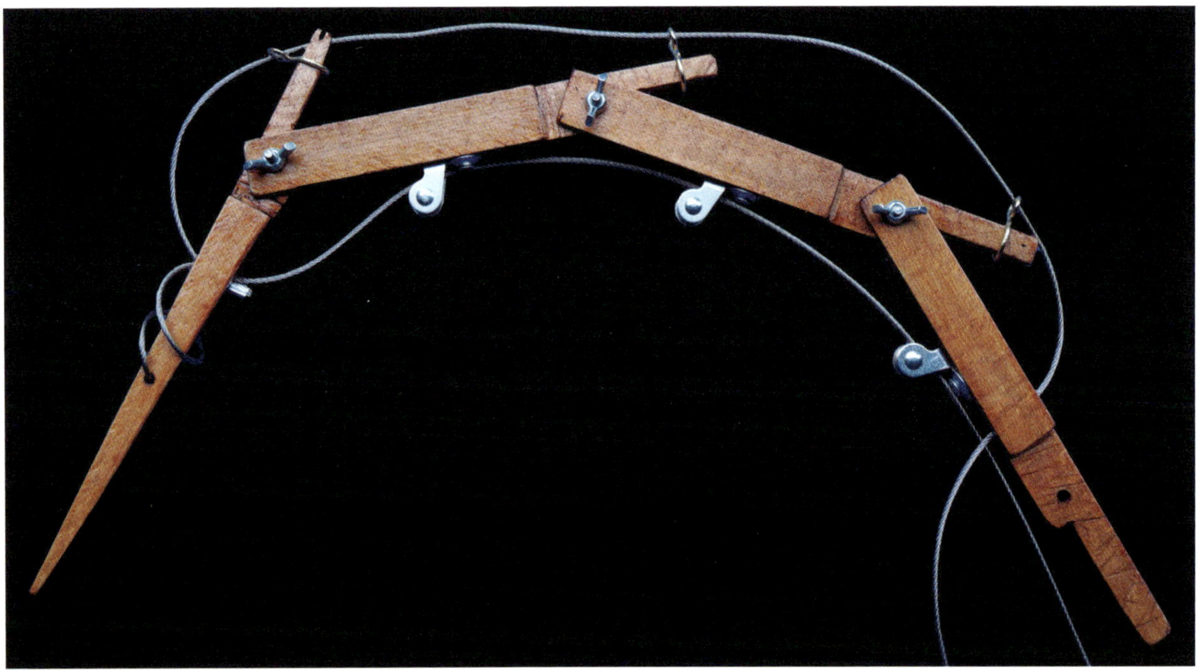

Model of an assembly with wooden parts, pulleys, and cables

of the plate shows an upper limb in extension and pronation; the one below it shows the same limb in supination.

The opposing actions of the *biceps* and *pronator teres* can be seen here, very clearly and unambiguously. As in the previous plate, Leonardo leaves only the two muscles studied on the forearm bones, which proves that after observation and dissection, he recognised the function of the muscles responsible for pronation.

How can one explain such an interest in this movement? Ought we not simply, like Leonardo, to marvel at the sophisticated nature of human mechanics, at this unique movement in man, a movement which directs and orients the hand in the best possible way, and whose observation was actually assessed with the eyes of an engineer and inventor of countless machines?

The Hand: From Anatomy to Prehension

There are four plates devoted to the hand. They are exceptionally beautiful and take the reader into the depths of an anatomy that no man had analysed this well since Galen.

The most detailed plate on the subject represents the muscles and tendons of the palm of the hand [fig.4 a-b].

It contains two types of drawings: 'anatomical' hands, four in number, representing stages of dissection that reveal the different planes; and interposed between these drawings are functional diagrams that are very understated, but whose importance in the physiology of prehension is, nevertheless, significant. The diagrams that represent the pulleys of the fingers on the one hand, and the muscles of the first commissure between the thumb and index finger on the other hand, are particularly commendable.

Finger Pulleys

Leonardo draws with great accuracy the pulleys which hold the flexor tendons against the phalanges. In a diagram of the bones of the finger in profile, he places the pulleys in front of the phalanges. Five in number, they hold these flexor tendons against the bone [fig. 5]. In a plate in the *Codex Atlanticus* devoted to the design of a flying machine [fig. 7], an earlier diagram of pulleys, joints and cables is strangely reminiscent of the anatomical diagram of the hand and shows how Leonardo oscillates between the inventiveness of an engineer and his observation of human nature.

The Muscles of the First Commissure

Three figures show schematically the muscles located in the first commissure of the hand, between the first and second metacarpal [fig. 6]. There are two of these muscles: the *first dorsal interosseous* muscle to the back; the *adductor pollicis* or *thumb adductor* in front. The *first dorsal interosseous* muscle, which appears in the foreground, is shown in the form of two, more or less parallel 'cords' whose direction crosses that of the deeper *adductor*, also represented by two cords. The role of these diagrams is to illustrate the 'scissor' movement of the thumb and index finger; and like the two blades of a pair of scissors, each of these fingers cannot work without the other, otherwise there will be a gap, a deficit, or a decrease in strength when holding objects. The three figures that address this issue, all close to each other, demonstrate Leonardo's interest in these two muscles which are essential to the functioning and strength of the pollici-digital pinch (functional pinch between the thumb and the other fingers, especially the index and middle fingers).

fig. 6—The muscles of the first commissure

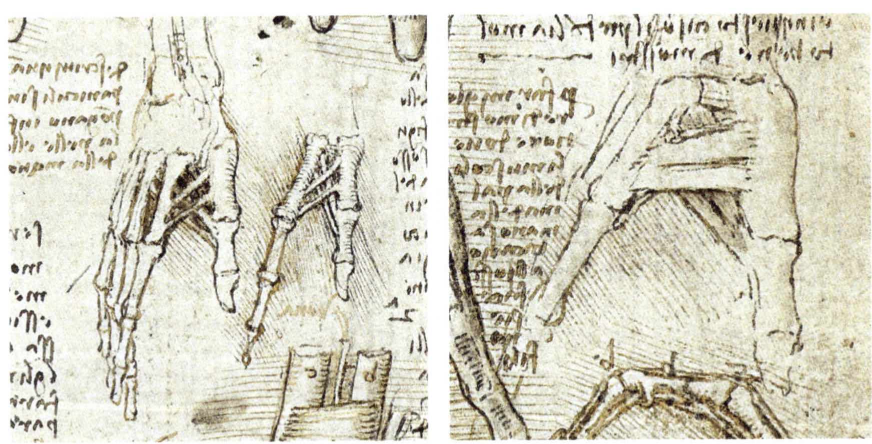

Detail from plate Windsor, RL 19009 r/c. 1510

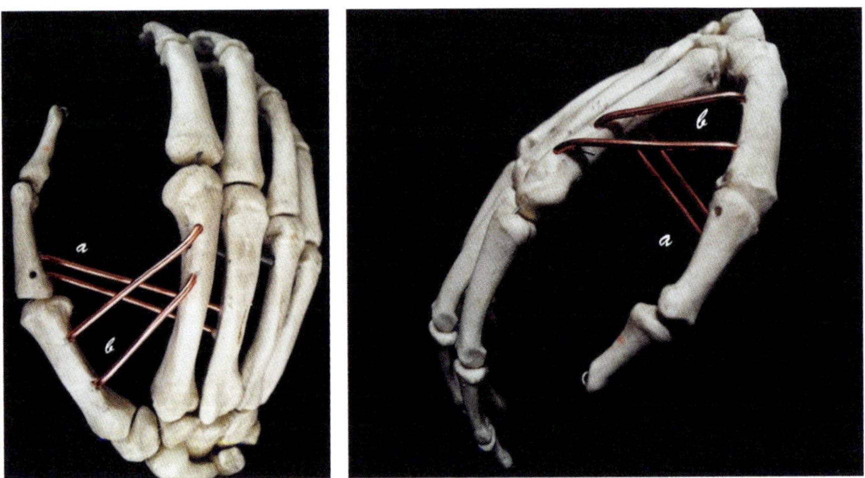

Model of the muscles of the first commissure represented by copper wires
a. *thumb adductor* muscle – b. *first dorsal interosseous* muscle

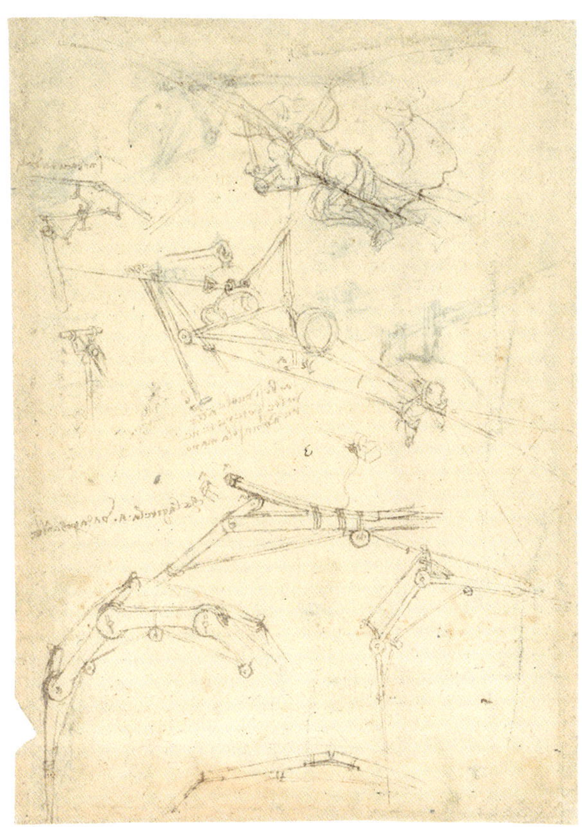

fig. 7—*Study for artificial flight*, c.1486–1490, *Codex Atlanticus*, folios 747 r/276 r-b
Milan, biblioteca Ambrosiana

Conclusion

In Leonardo's mind, the anatomy of the hand is obviously both a descriptive anatomy and an anatomy concerned with function. Although he performed his dissections with a mechanical view of the functions of the upper limb, the artistic aspect was never far away.

Throughout Leonardo's life, his skills as an engineer, anatomist and painter were closely connected, through the same scientific vision. The role that he attributed to drawing in the transfer of knowledge, of his work and of his observations, offers the most accurate expression of his thought. We can only, therefore, agree with Domenico Laurenza when he writes in the introduction to his book dedicated to Leonardo's machines: "... even though he used three-dimensional models in various aspects of his research (machines, painting, anatomy), he appears to have given drawing pre-eminence over models, recognising its value both in terms of design and as a means of expression."

Pascal Brioist, Edward Maccurdy, Louise Servicen, *Carnets de Léonard de Vinci*, Paris, Gallimard, 2019.
Claudius Galen, *Selected medical works – from the usefulness of the parts of the human body*, Volume I, trans. Charles Daremberg, André Pichot presentation, Paris, Gallimard, 1994.
Domenico Laurenza, Mario Taddei, Edoardo Zanon, *Les Machines de Léonard de Vinci*, trans. Emmanuel Pailler, Paris, Gründ, 2006.
Dominique Le Nen, Jacky Laulan, *La Main de Léonard de Vinci*, preface D. Laurenza, Paris, Springer, 2010.
Charles D. O'Malley, John Bertrand de Cusance Morant Saunders, *Leonardo da Vinci on the Human Body*, New York, Gramercy Books, 1982.

Dimostratione della vessicha dell'omo

prima dimostratione

Dimostrassi tre dimostrationi di vessicha · nella prima si figura
le vie orinali in che modo si partano dalle reni b b e come
si congiungano colla vessicha [illegible] altro che [illegible] del
collo della vessicha e questo è il vero modo della congiuntione e l'altre
le quali torceranno nella vessicha · a p b m [illegible] etc.
si figura in prima nel secondo · S · donde poi si mostra [illegible]

Leonardo da Vinci and the Urinary System: Mystery of the Missing Prostate

François Rozet
Senior Surgeon in the Department of Urology
at the Institut Mutualiste Montsouris in Paris

Previous page:

The bladder (detail), c.1508, black chalk, pen and ink, 19.4 × 14.2 cm

Windsor, Royal Collection Trust, RL 19054 r

Of the two hundred folios in the Windsor collection, only about ten relate to a description of genito-urinary anatomy [fig.4]. They are the result of anatomical explorations conducted around 1508 at the Santa Maria Nuova Hospital in Florence. While Leonardo produced descriptive anatomy, by applying the mechanical and hydrodynamic knowledge of the day, he also sought to understand how the organs he depicted functioned. He also drew on the ancient works and theories of Hippocrates, Aristotle and Galen.

Leonardo, 'Hydraulic' Engineer: The Limits of Physiological Understanding

Leonardo, a man of his time, produced both descriptive anatomical work, on the whole accurate, and physiopathological interpretations based on mechanical concepts that were not always relevant to the genito-urinary system. He could not have understood, for example, merely from dissection, that the ureter, a duct that transports urine from the kidneys to the bladder, is much more than a simple tube, and that it has involuntary muscles able to contract and relax (through peristalsis) allowing urine to drain, in a dynamic antegrade flow, from the kidneys to the bladder [fig.1].

Leonardo describes renal vascularisation and its relationship to the ureter in a convincing manner. In folio 19030 v from the Royal Library, one can recognise a left kidney with its artery, its vein, as well as a spermatic vein (previously described by Galen [fig.2]). It would have been impossible at that time, from simple analysis of the anatomy, to understand the filtration and purification capabilities of this organ, in the way we can analyse them today. The papillae of the kidney, the conical structures that transport urine from the kidney into the renal pelvis, were commonly thought to resemble small alembics for the distillation of urine. Leonardo writes: "Cut it down the middle and represent how the channels for the urine are constricted and how they distil it."

The Ureter

The ureter is described as a simple duct, whose physiological function the Tuscan explains by advancing a hydraulic hypothesis. He hypothesises that urine flows from the kidney to the bladder owing to a difference in pressure (Windsor, RL 19054 r [fig.3]).

"The urine having left the kidneys, enters the ureters and from there passes into the bladder near the middle of its height. It enters the bladder through multiple perforations made transversely between tunic and urethra. This oblique perforation was not made because nature doubted that the urine could return to the kidneys, for this is impossible from the 4th book on conduits where it is stated: water which descends from above through a narrow vessel and enters under the bottom of a pond cannot be opposed by reflux movement if the magnitude of the water in the pool is not as great as the magnitude of the vessel which descends, or the height of the water greater than the depth of the pool."

Current thinking holds that the transport of urine is not governed by gravity, but is the result of a relationship between propulsion and resistance forces. The transport of urine is actively ensured by the involuntary contractions (peristalsis) of the smooth muscles of the ureter. The anti-reflux mechanism from the bladder to the ureter is analysed in several illustrations (Windsor, RL 19054 r and 19031 r [fig.3 and 5]). With his knowledge of valve systems that he studied to make pumps, the engineer explains that the more the bladder is filled, the more it closes.

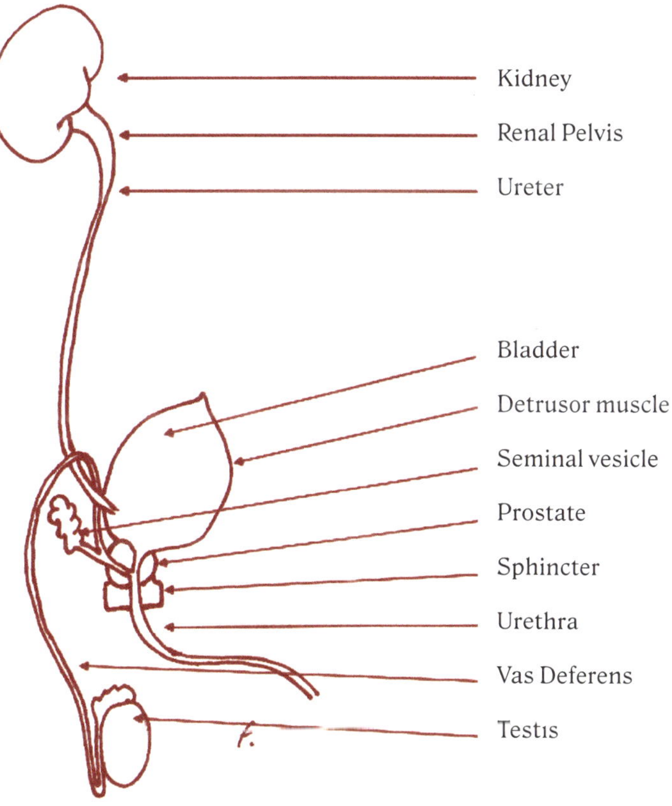

fig. 1—Anatomical diagram summarising the urinary system
© François Rozet

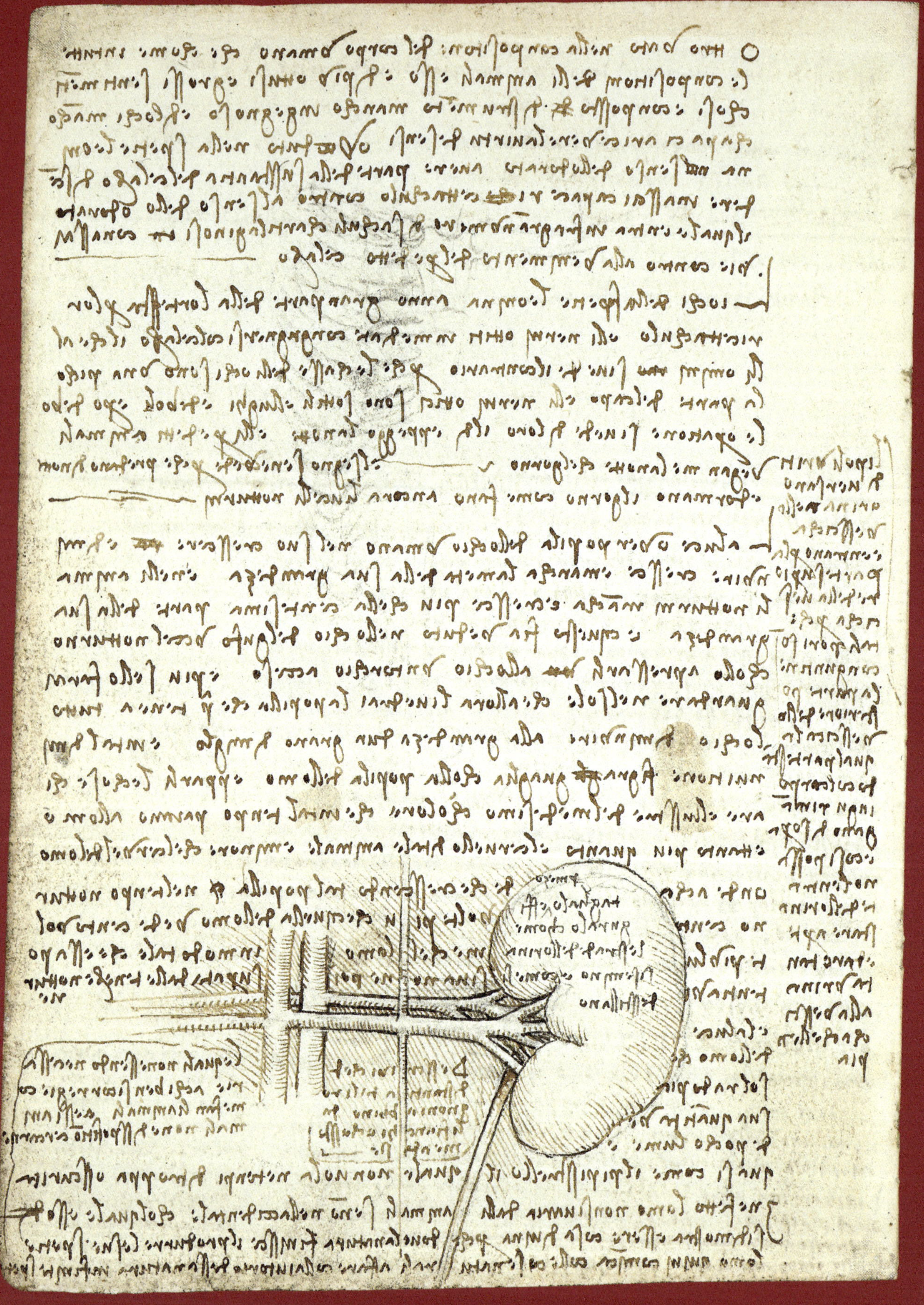

fig. 2 — *A kidney, with notes on the passage of urine, and notes on the sense organs of man compared with other animals*, c.1508, pen and ink over traces of black chalk, 19.1 × 13.9 cm

Windsor, Royal Collection Trust, RL 19030 v

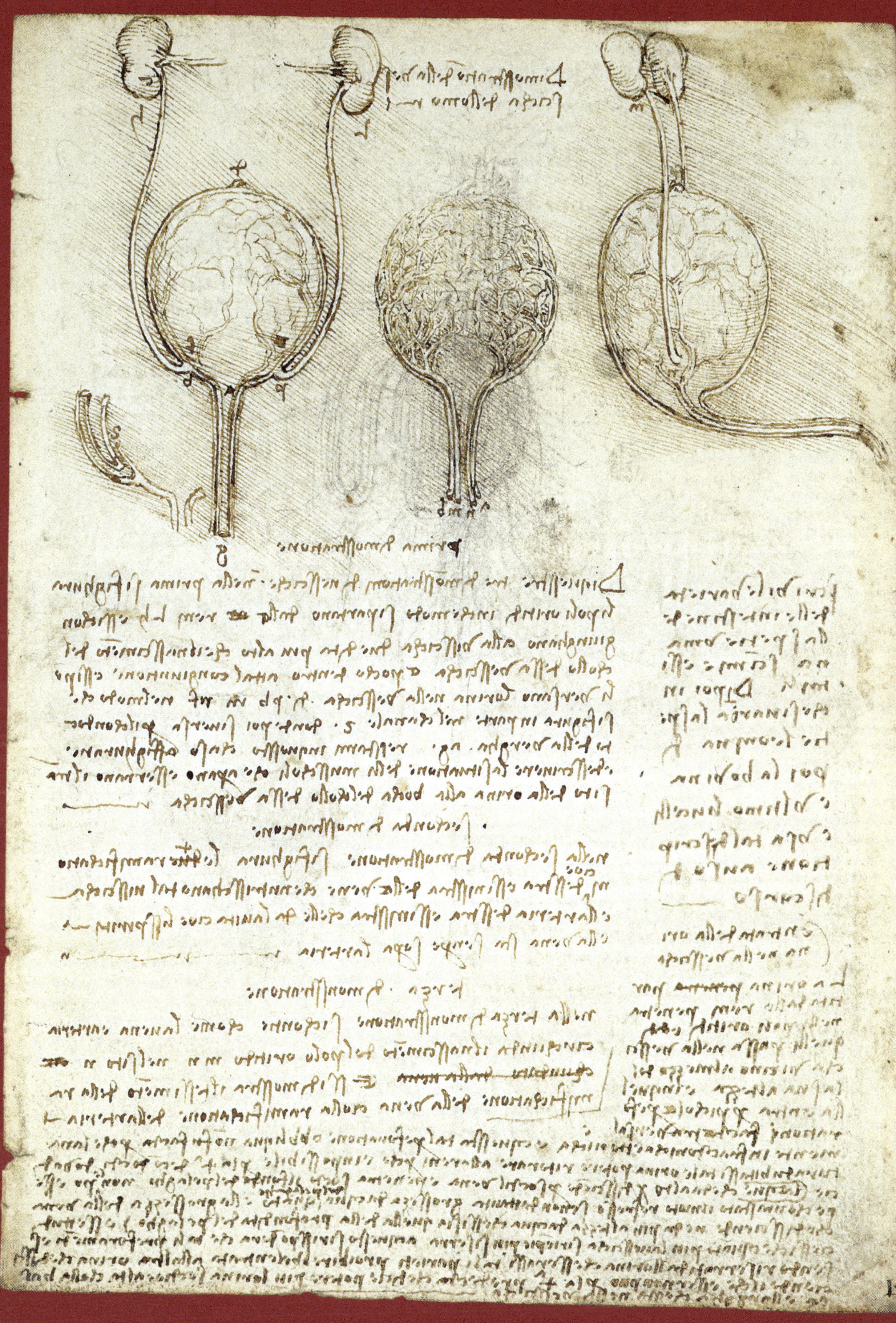

fig. 3 — *The bladder*, c.1508, black chalk, pen and ink, 19.4 × 14.2 cm
Windsor, Royal Collection Trust, RL 19054 r

We therefore have both an understanding of an anti-reflux system, but also a misinterpretation, as Leonardo thought that when the bladder was full, urine would be blocked in the ureter and could no longer fill the bladder. A mechanic at heart, the Tuscan developed a theory involving each ureter functioning independently depending on the position of the person: standing, on their side, or on their back (Windsor, RL 19031 r [fig. 5]). He writes:

"When a man lies upside down, the entrance for the urine is closed," then "We can establish therefore ... that the urine enters through a long and tortuous passage into the bladder, and then, when the bladder is full, the ducts of the ureters remain full of urine. The urine contained in the bladder cannot rise higher than their surfaces (of the intramural portion of the ureters, note taken from O'Malley and Saunders, 1952) when the man is standing erect. But if he is lying down, it can return back through the ureters, and even more so, if he places himself upside down, which occurs infrequently, although recumbency is common. Whereas, if a man lies upon his side, one of the ureters remains above, the other below, and the entrance of that above opens and discharges the urine into the bladder. The other duct below closes because of the weight of the urine. Hence, a single duct transfers its urine to the bladder."

On folio RL 19054 r [fig.3], the bladder is depicted as a simple rounded vessel opening into a funnel, named the 'bladder neck', on which Leonardo notes: "It remains for me in this case to represent and describe the position of the muscles (sphincters) which open and close the urinary passage at the mouth of the bladder neck." The sphincter is represented in detail on plate RL 19098 v [fig.6]. Leonardo understands it as the organ of continence that controls "how the door of the bladder is closed".

Circular muscular fibres surrounding the bladder neck are described here, but there is no description of the external sphincter in continuity with the pelvic floor muscles. Here again, the bladder is considered a hollow, passive emptying organ, like a Basque gourd made of soft skin. In reality, the *detrusor* ('muscle found in the wall of the bladder') is distended at low pressure during filling, thanks to its visco-elastic capabilities. This low pressure is fundamental, as it protects the upper urinary tract. As the bladder fills, urethral pressure is maintained by the reflex activity of the sphincter of the urethra. During micturition, the *detrusor* actively contracts and the sphincter relaxes, allowing the bladder to empty.

Today, however, we know that bladder and sphincter coordination relies on reflex loops involving the medullary and brainstem centres in linking the sympathetic, parasympathetic and somatic nervous systems. Such an understanding of the physiology of bladder filling and emptying is clearly not possible through the anatomical study of the urinary system alone.

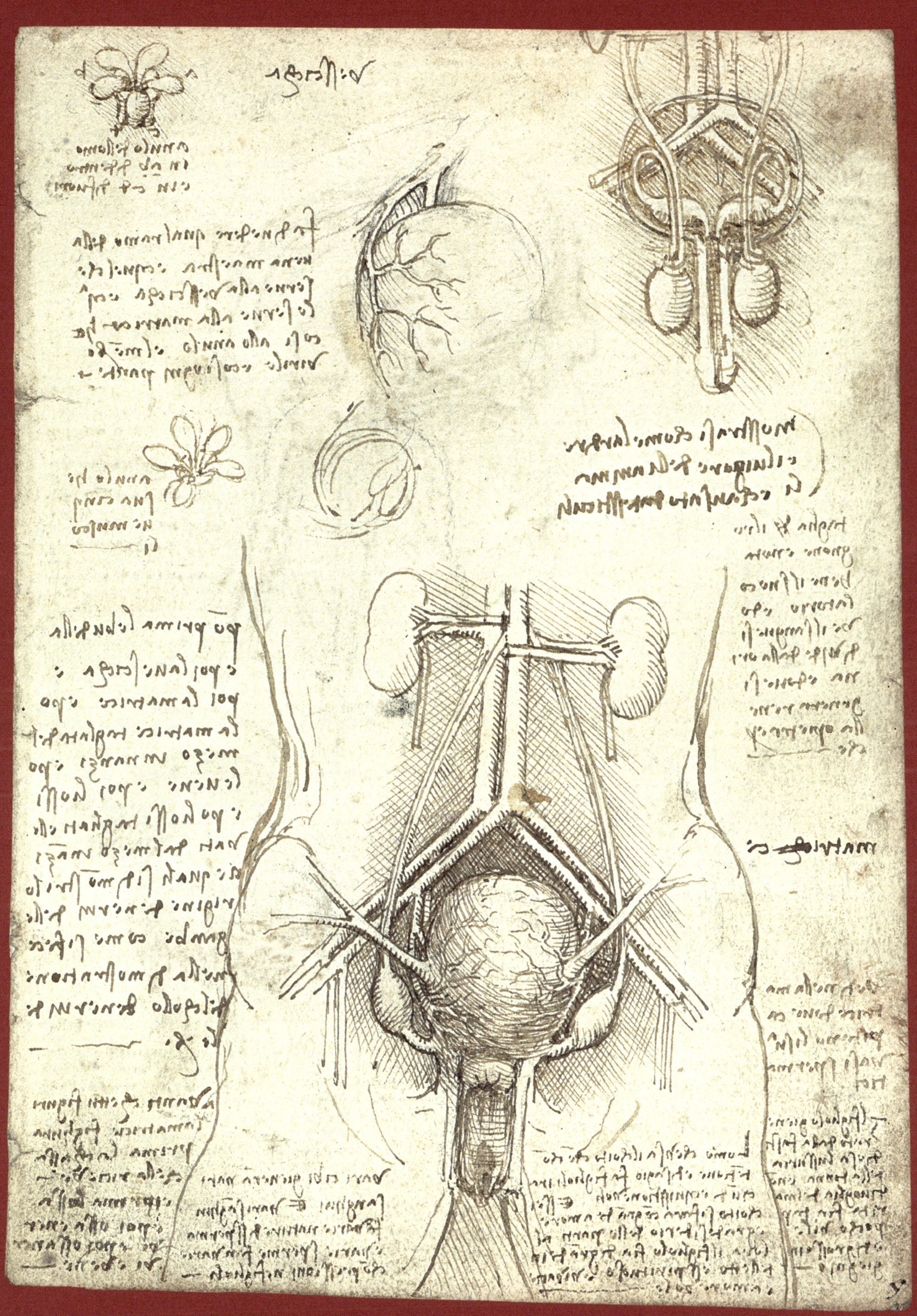

fig. 4 — *Studies of the male genito-urinary system*, c.1506–08, pen and brown ink, 19.3 × 14.1 cm

Klassik Stiftung Weimar KK 6287

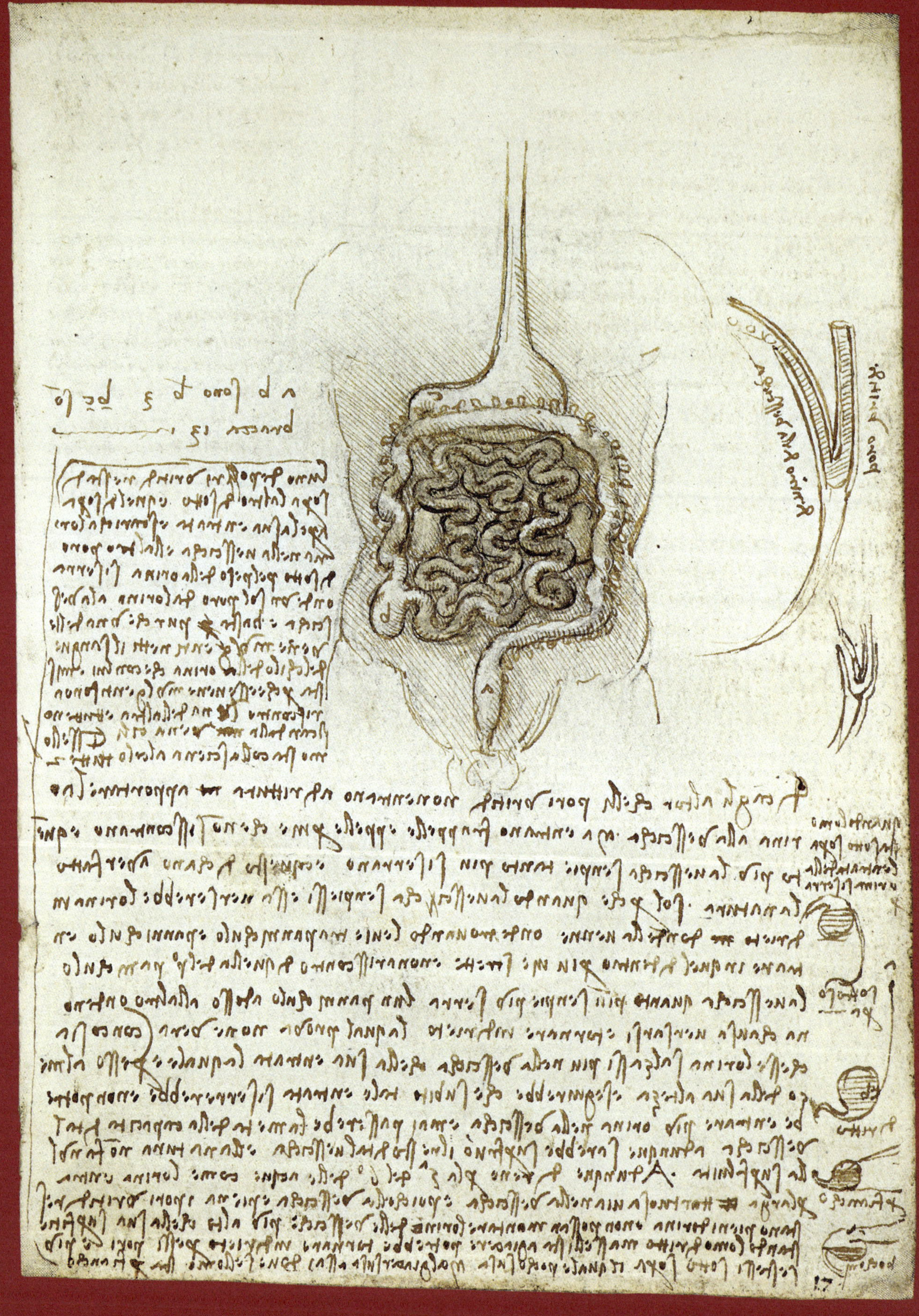

fig. 5 — *The gastrointestinal tract, and the bladder*, c.1508,
traces of black chalk, pen and ink, 19.2 × 13.8 cm
Windsor, Royal Collection Trust, RL 19031 r

Leonardo and the Mystery of the Missing Prostate

Initially, in 1508, Leonardo confuses seminal vesicles with vessels. For example, he writes: "In the second demonstration are represented four branches, that is, right and left veins which nourish the bladder and right and left arteries which give it life, that is, spirit. The vein is always above (i.e., superficial to) the artery." (Windsor, RL 19054 r [fig.3])

In another plate also dated 1508, he is nevertheless the first to describe accurately the seminal vesicles, namely the glands located on either side of the bladder, which produce sperm. It is impossible to say, from these two contradictory propositions, which was Leonardo's final version. His description in the second plate of the path of the *vas deferens* (which carries sperm from the testes to the ejaculatory ducts) and of the urogenital crossroads is also relevant:

"Note well the spermatic vessels ('*vas deferens*', note of O'Malley and Saunders) from their origin to termination, that is, from the artery and vein as far as the mouth of the penis, how near they are to the anus and how nothing is lacking for their movement and requirements, and for how many coitions their store of sperm is sufficient." (Windsor, RL 19098 v [fig. 6])

He thus locates the position of the ejaculatory ducts at the level of the urethra, below the smooth sphincter of the bladder neck. Again, in this functional interpretation, one recognises the engineer behind the anatomist, for example when he recommends to his readers:

"See which enters the urinary canal first, either the mouths of the spermatic vessels or the mouth of the urinary vessel. But I believe that that of the urine is first so that it can clean and wash out the sperm stuck in the urinary canal." (Windsor, RL 19095 v)

The prostate, however, is curiously absent from the description of the lower urinary tract, whereas the anatomy of the bladder neck is described in detail. Why this 'absence'? The anatomical location of the prostate is inferior to the bladder neck, wrapped around the urethra, posterior to the pubis, and anterior to the rectum. The portion of the urethra that traverses the prostate is called the prostatic urethra. In young men, the prostate has the shape and size of a chestnut. With age, under the influence of androgens, it increases in volume. An adenoma, a benign tumour in the prostate, can grow to the size of a tangerine, an orange or a grapefruit, leading to functional disorders common in older men. It is possible that the small number of dissections performed by Leonardo were on young men with no prostate hypertrophy, and therefore without sufficient deformation of the lower part of the bladder to be visible when examined.

The association of anatomical descriptions and physiological explanations today forms the basis of functional anatomy. Leonardo's descriptions were at the forefront of anatomical dissection. His incorporation of functional analysis into descriptive anatomy is nevertheless extremely modern, with this intuitive and comprehensive approach perhaps coming from his engineering background. His physiological misunderstandings arise from the ancient data on which he relied.

It is currently estimated that half of medical knowledge becomes obsolete within a decade; with the benefit of five centuries of hindsight, Leonardo's representations should be interpreted with the greatest of humility.

✷

Dirk Schultheiss, Domenico Laurenza, Barnett Götte, Udo Jonas, 'The Weimar Anatomical Sheet of Leonardo da Vinci (1452–1519): An Illustration of the Genitourinary Tract', *British Journal of Urology*, Oct. 1999, 84(6), p. 595–600.

Martin Kemp, 'William Hunter on the Windsor: Leonardo and his Volume of Drawings Attributed to Pietro da Cortona,' *The Burlington Magazine*, No. 118, 1976, p. 144–148.

Kenneth D. Keele, Carlo Pedretti, *Leonardo da Vinci: Corpus of the Anatomical Studies in the Collection of Her Majesty the Queen at Windsor Castle*, 3 vols., London, Johnson Reprint Company [New York], 1978–1980.

Charles Donald O'Malley, John Bertrand de Cusance Morant Saunders, *Leonardo da Vinci on the Human Body*, Dover Publications, 1952.

Dirk Schultheiss, Völker Grünewald, Udo Jonas, 'Urodynamics in the Anatomical Work of Leonardo da Vinci (1452–1519)', *World Journal of Urology*, June 1999, 17(3), p. 137–143.

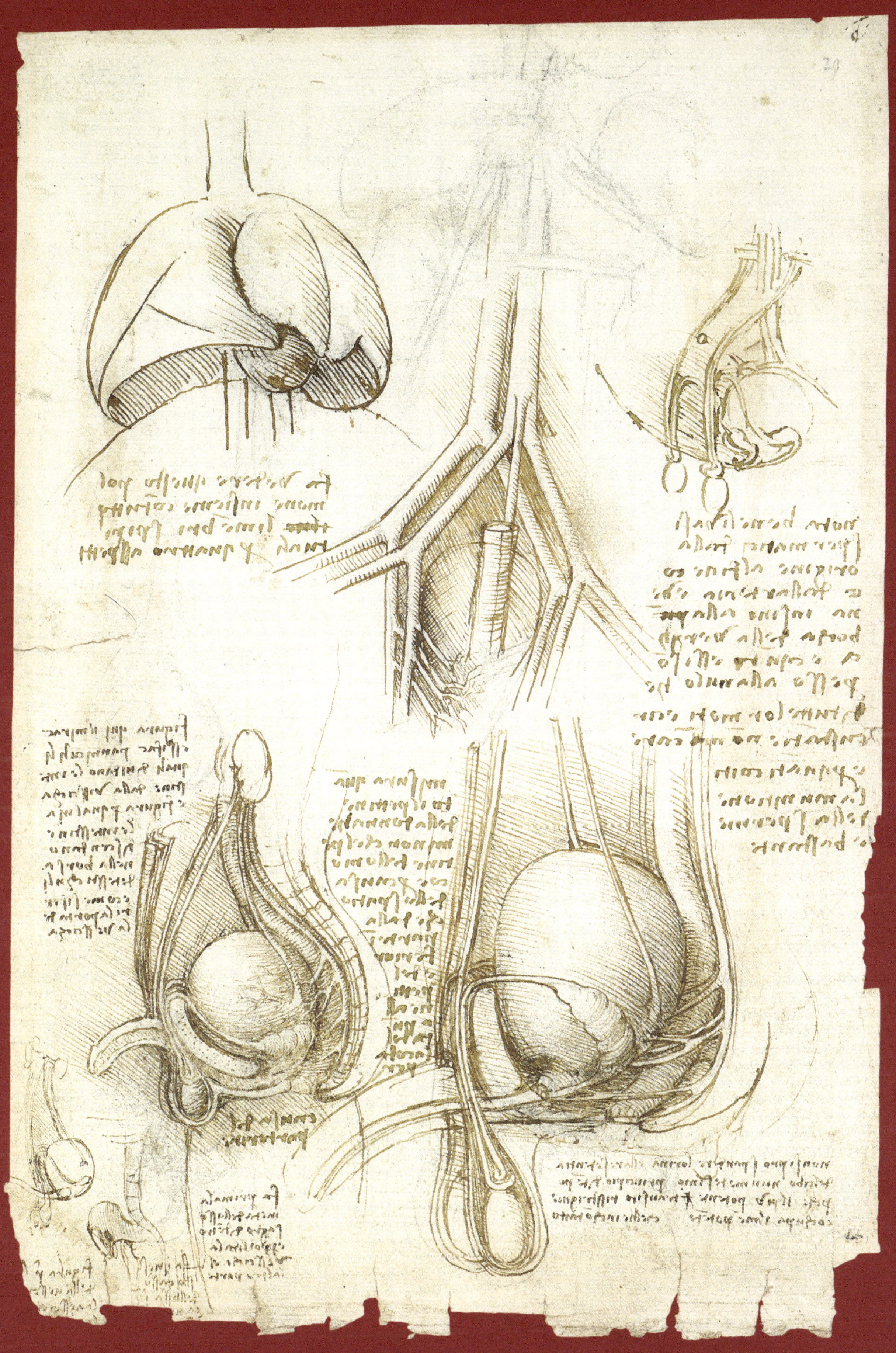

fig. 6 — *The male genito-urinary system*, c.1508, pen ink over black chalk, 27.2 × 19.2

Windsor, Royal Collection Trust, RL 19098 v

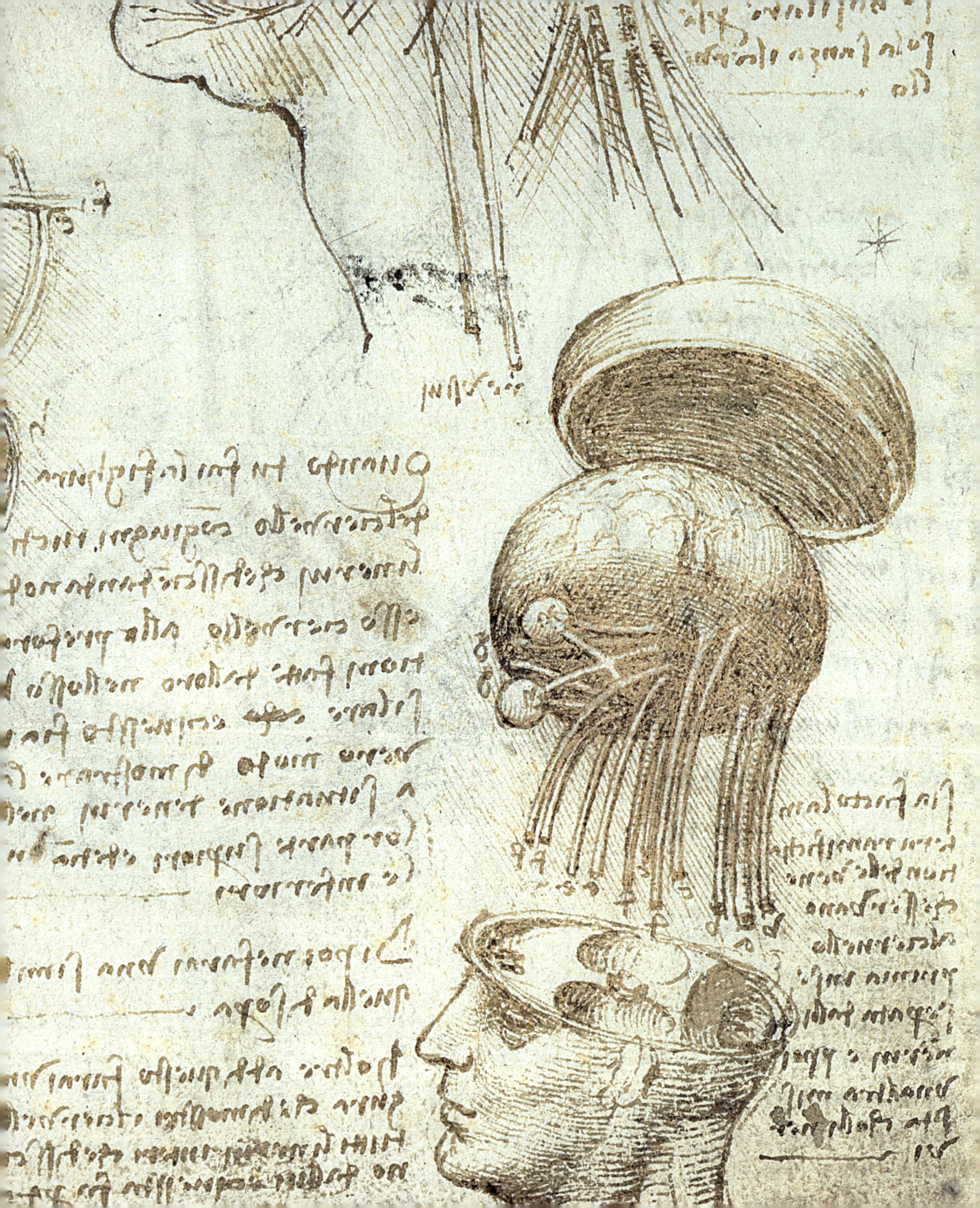

Leonardo da Vinci, Neuroanatomist of the Soul

Bertrand Debono
Neurosurgeon, Paris

Johann Peltier
Neurosurgeon and Professor of Anatomy, Amiens

Previous page:

Brain, cerebral ventricles and cranium nerves (detail), c.1508, pen and ink, 19.2 × 13.5 cm
Klassik Stiftung Weimar

Leonardo da Vinci described himself as an *Omo sanza lettere*, a "man without letters", owing to his lack of academic training, and saw himself more as a 'disciple of experience'. This early shortcoming may have allowed him to develop an atypical approach, free from the usual regurgitating of academic precepts. After gathering together ancient and contemporary texts and combining this with his knowledge of painting, sculpture, architecture and engineering, he experimented, analysing and assimilating his findings. A clear application of this can be seen in Leonardo's quest to find the *senso comune*, the anatomical location of the soul.

Common Sense: Aristotle, Galen, a Frog and an Elephant

According to the cephalocentric theory, supported by Plato, the 'breath of life' enters the body through respiration, passes through the heart, and finally takes its place in the cerebral ventricles, where it becomes the 'animal spirit' that controls the mental faculties. For Aristotle, the centre of psychic and sensory life (which he calls 'common sense', a term that Leonardo would take up as *senso comune*) is located in the heart.

Galen, who would influence Leonardo, located the mental functions in the 'substance' of the brain, although one of his translators transferred them to the ventricles. At his death, the Aristotelian cardiocentric view of the soul imposed itself on Western thought for nearly 2,000 years until the Renaissance.

In 1487, Leonardo had developed an experiment that prefigured much research in neurophysiology. Perhaps inspired by Livy (who tells us that the Carthaginians could quickly sacrifice an elephant by thrusting a blade into its neck at the level of the spinal cord), he transposed this action using an awl on a frog, causing its immediate death. Leonardo notes: "The frog retains a semblance of life for a few hours without its heart and all its intestines. And if you pierce the nerve in question (the spinal cord), it immediately twitches and dies." One can imagine that this observation strengthened Leonardo's cephalocentric hypothesis about the soul; the exact location of the *senso comune* remained to be determined!

An Architect Faced with the Anatomy of the Skull (1489)

Leonardo's exploration of the nervous system stemmed from his research on the anatomy of the eye ("window of the soul") and the optic nerves, and then on the orbital cavities. He proposed innovative, three-dimensional representations of the skull in which his artistic and architectural skills combined to produce masterful cross-sectional and transparent views. His drawings, which emphasise mathematical proportions, are reminiscent of a series of sketches of the domes of Milan Cathedral created through the influence of his friend the architect Francesco di Giorgio Martini (1439–1501). In a frontal view allowing comparison of the normal anatomy with the underlying structures, he reveals the frontal and maxillary sinuses, and accurately represents the structures of the orbits [fig.1]. Below this drawing, he notes: "The cavity of the eye socket and the cavity of the bone... terminate in a perpendicular line below the *senso comune*."

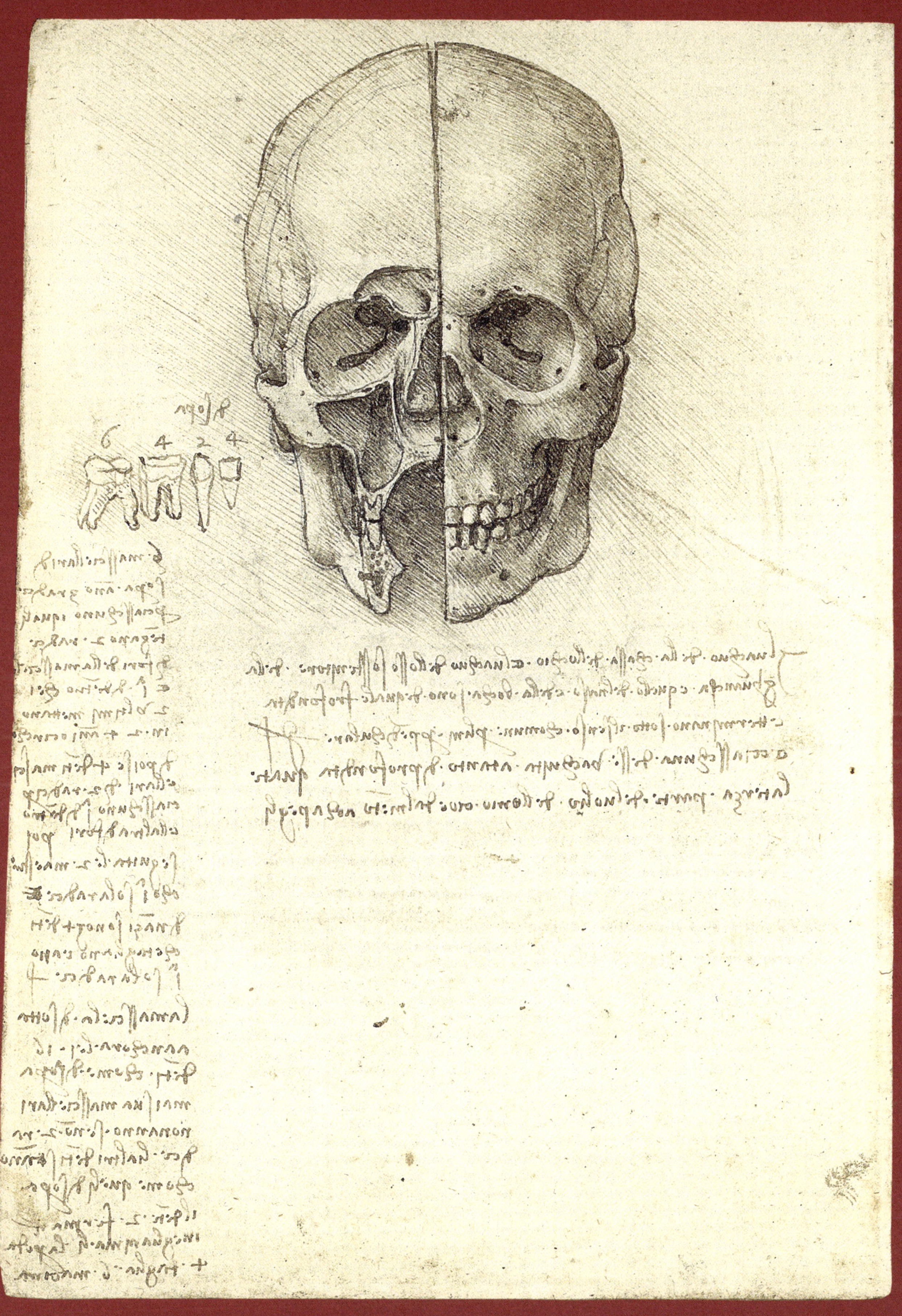

fig. 1 — *The skull sectioned*, 1489,
traces of black chalk, pen and ink, 19 × 13.7 cm
Windsor, Royal Collection Trust, RL 19058 v

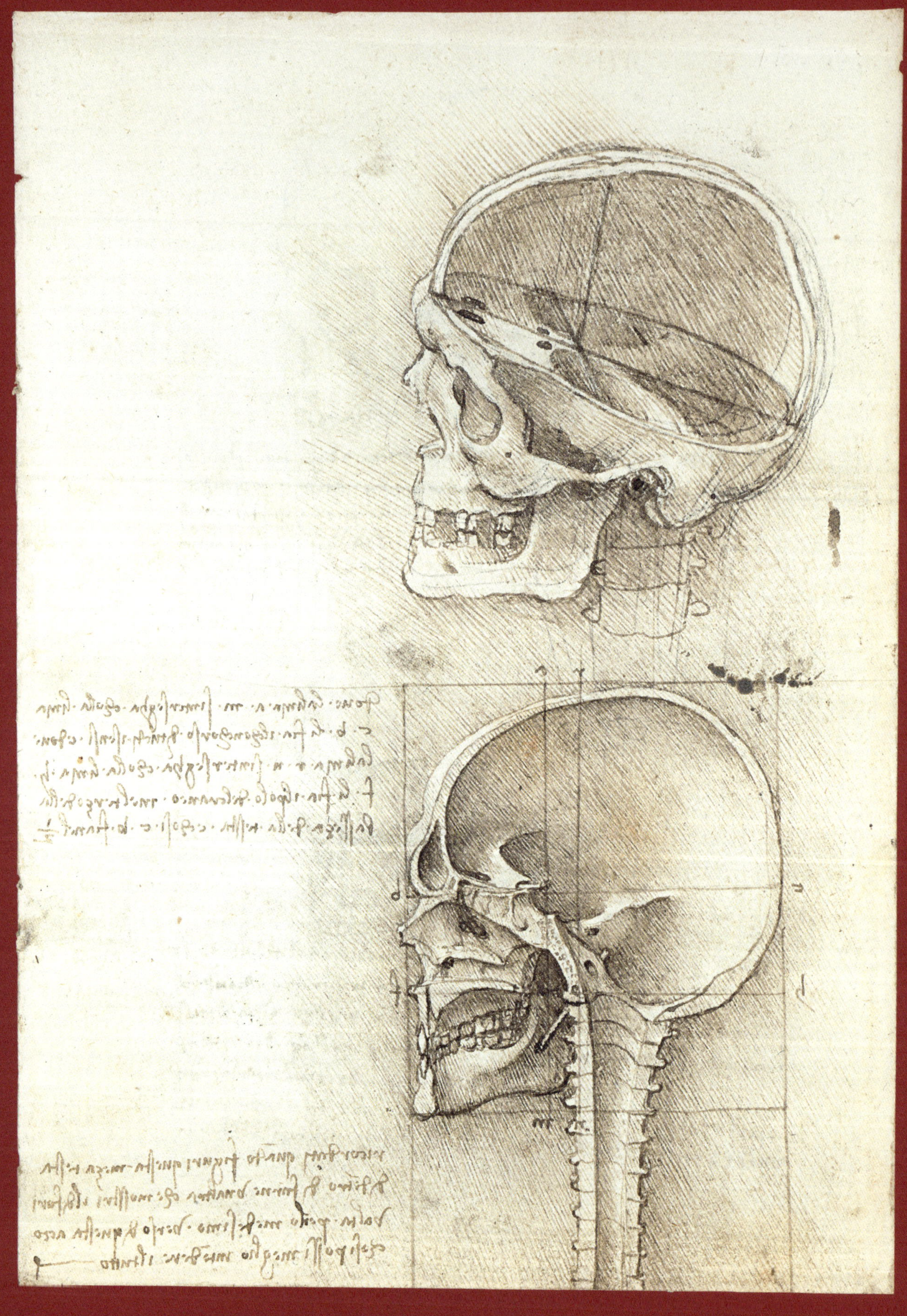

fig. 2 — *The skull sectioned*, 1489,
traces of black chalk, pen and ink, 18.8 × 13.4 cm
Windsor, Royal Collection Trust, RL 19057 r

Two longitudinal views of the skull use orthogonal lines to determine the position of this strategic area [fig.2], at the intersection of an anterior-posterior axis, which runs along the anterior level of the skull base; a vertical axis, which runs through the upper part of the skull; and a transverse axis, which follows the pituitary gland. This method of orthogonal localisation recalls the neurosurgical concept of stereotaxis, an intracranial localisation method used in the 19th century to improve functional neuroanatomy, and in the 20th century as a diagnostic and therapeutic technique.

In a more complex view where he integrates the arteries of the meninges and several nerves, he gives a new orthonormal representation of the 'common sense', which is located just above the optic chiasm and corresponds in our modern anatomy to the hypothalamus, located in the anterior region of our third ventricle [fig.3]. In fact, lesions in this area cause a profound change in the way patients perceive not only their external world, but also their internal world: a disturbance of common sense if ever there was one.

Drawings Subject to Past Influences (1490–1492)

In the early stages of his anatomical studies, Leonardo seems to have wanted to formalise in images the information available in books at that time. For example, the first illustrated version of Albert the Great's *Philosophia pauperum*, containing the first drawing of the cellular doctrine of the cerebral ventricles, was not published until 1490. Leonardo takes up the concept of three spherical ventricles that he represents in the brain based on writings from the past, without having yet conducted any experiments or dissections on this subject. The optic nerves converge towards the anterior ventricle which he calls *imprensiva*, seat of the intellect with its afferent nerves of the visual senses. The olfactory and auditory nerves go to the middle ventricle, labelled *senso comune*, confluence of sensory data where he located will and action. The last ventricle is referred to as *memoria*.

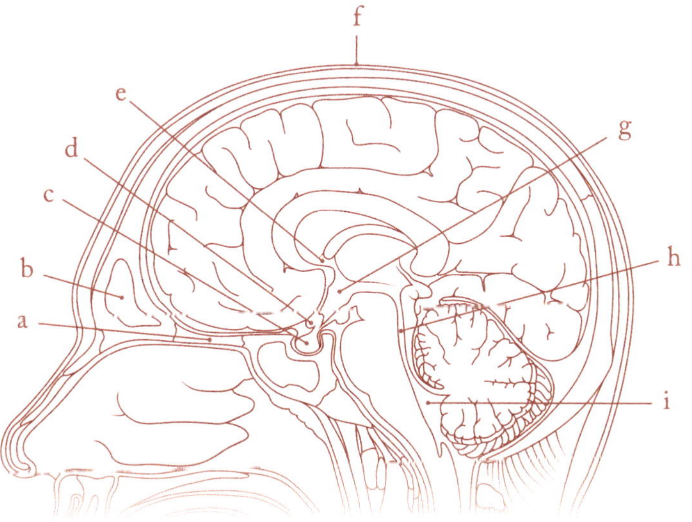

a: Base of the skull (anterior layer)

b: Frontal sinus

c: Pituitary gland and pituitary cavity

d: Optic chiasm

e: Interventricular foramen (Foramen of Monro)

f: Vertex

g: Third ventricle

h: Cerebral aqueduct

i: Fourth ventricle

Cross-sectional diagram summarising the main anatomical terms related to the skull

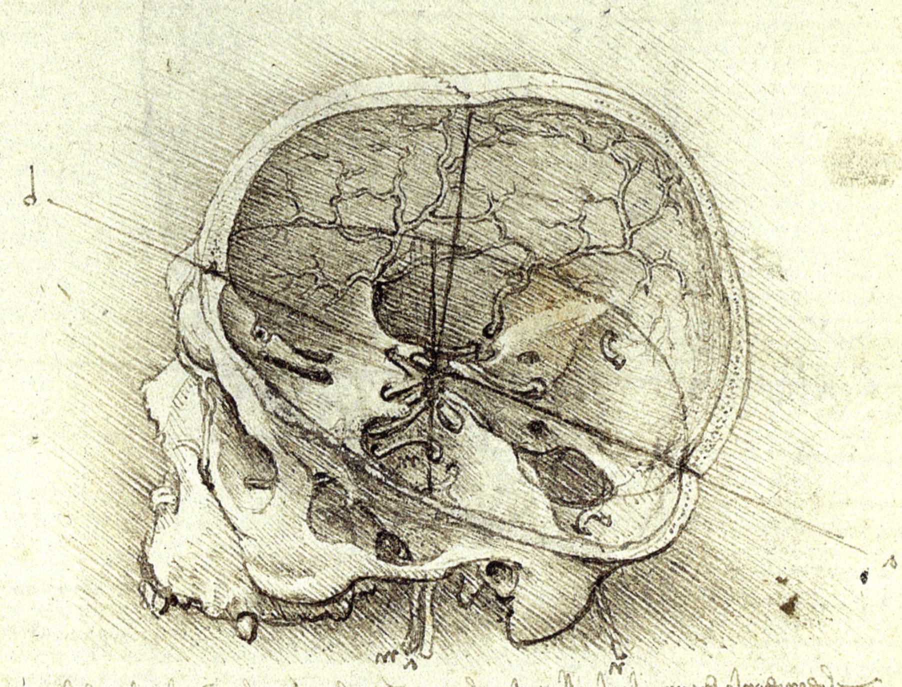

fig. 3 — *The cranium sectioned*, 1489, pen and ink, 19 × 13.7 cm
Windsor, Royal Collection Trust, RL 19058 r

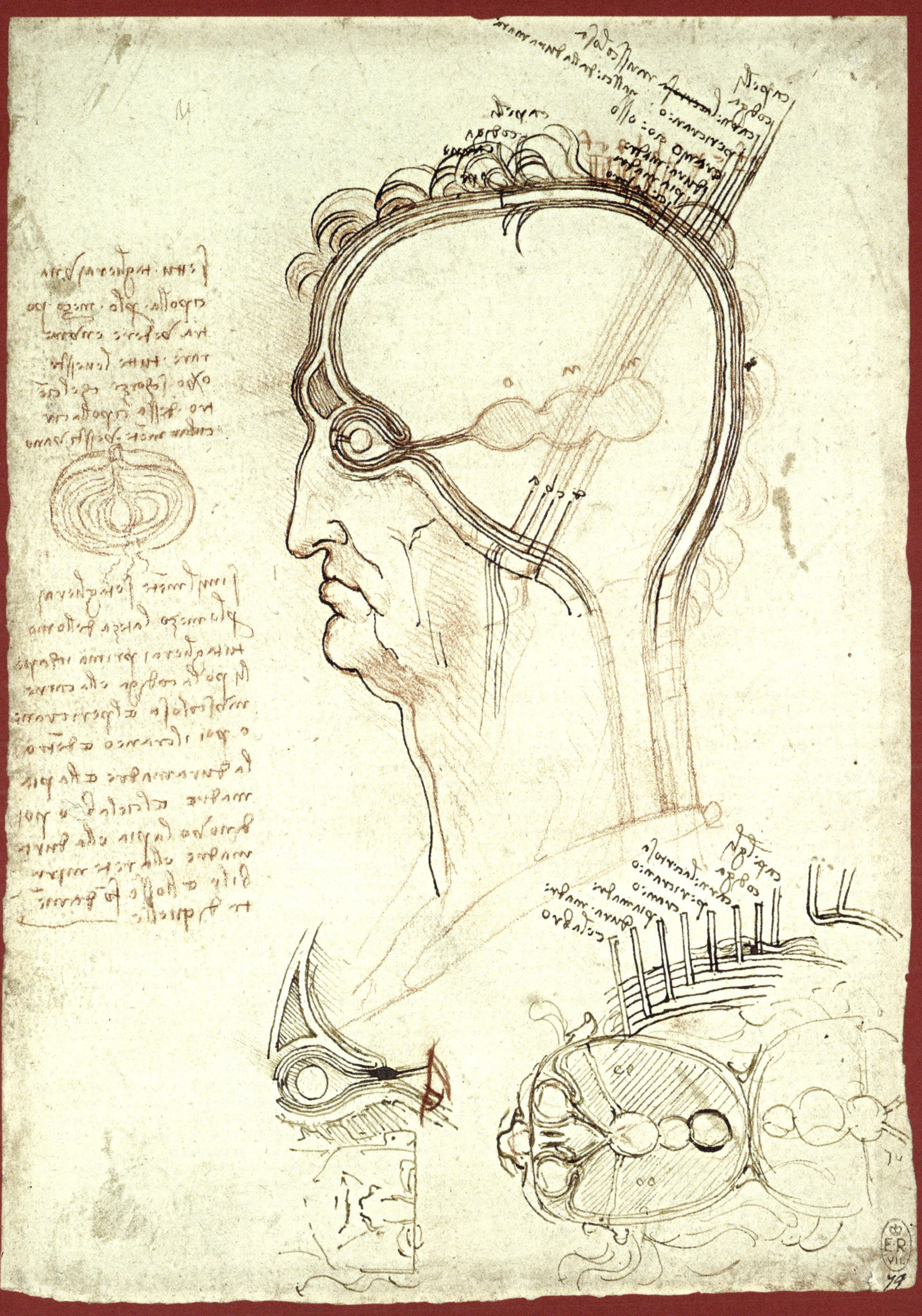

fig. 4 — *The layers of the scalp, and the cerebral ventricles*, c.1490–92, red chalk, pen and ink, 20.3 × 15.3 cm

Windsor, Royal Collection Trust, RL 12603 r

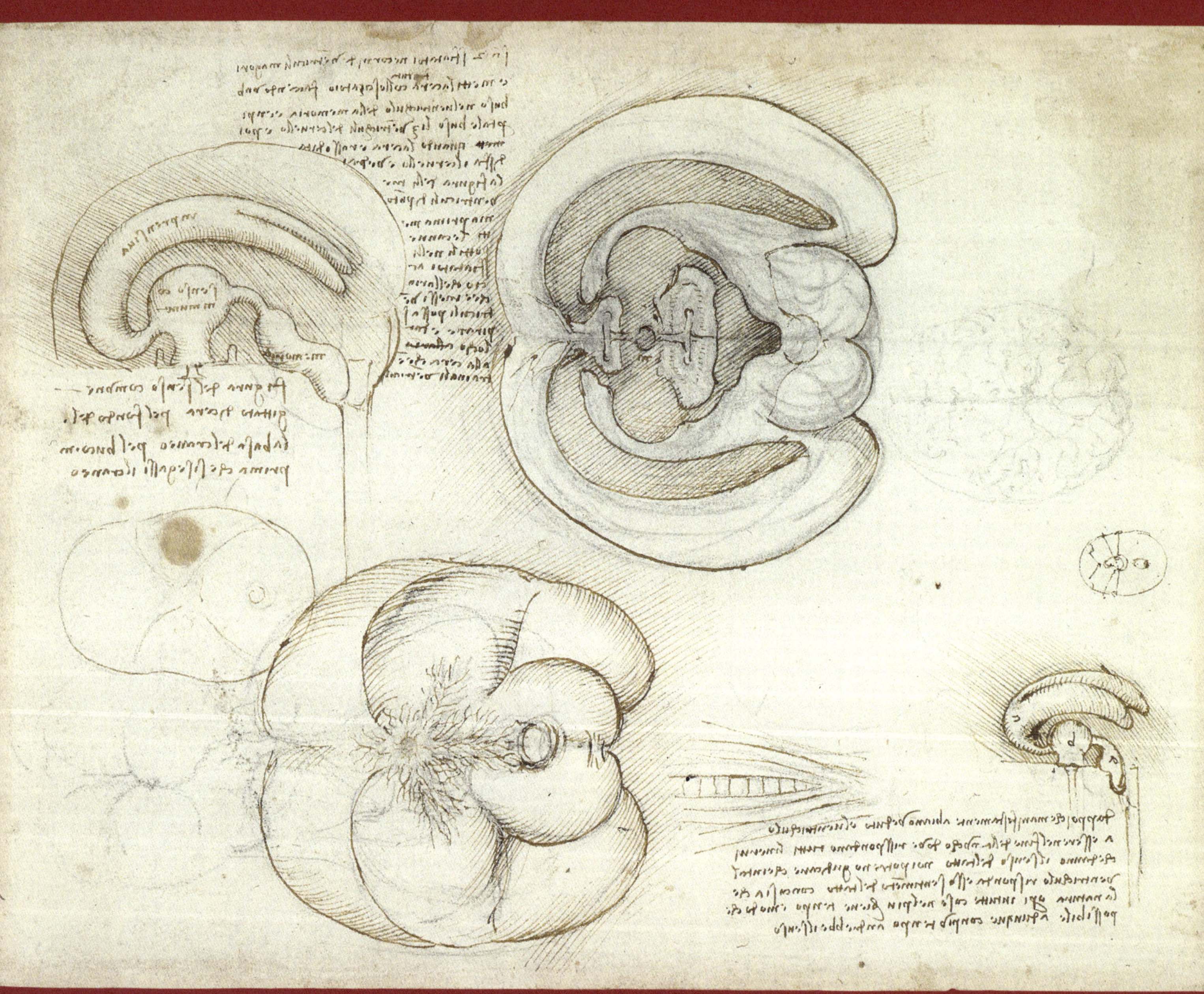

fig. 5 — *The brain*, c.1508–9,
black chalk, pen and ink, 20 × 26.2 cm
Windsor, Royal Collection Trust, RL 19127 r

Leonardo's first model, therefore, assumed that sensations and actions were derived from the middle ventricle (*senso commune*), and modulated by both the afferent nerves of the intellect of the anterior ventricle and of the memory in the third ventricle. A drawing summarises this model, in which he positions the three ventricles on the sagittal section of a human head and describes the different anatomical structures in order, from superficial to deep (scalp, bones, meninges, brain), ending with the ventricular system, in an amusing analogy with the layers of an onion [fig.4]. Leonardo displays his talents and innovation, but at this point, despite flashes of insight that foreshadow his later work, he is still relying on the traditional accounts of past anatomists.

A Sculptor of the Cerebral Ventricles

Around 1506–1508, Leonardo went deeper into his anatomical research on the location of the *senso comune* by mobilising all his artistic and technical skills combined with the results of his previous research. More than ten years earlier, he had drawn the cerebral ventricles inspired by ancient authors, without having been able to dissect brains. It is likely that obtaining human brains was not an easy task and that their preservation without anatomical preparation made the analysis of their internal structure almost impossible. Leonardo made a wax cast of the ventricles of a bovine brain, using a technique similar to the moulds used in sculpture, which existed years before wax became a widely used tool for research and teaching anatomy. Once the brain tissue was removed, the finished cast provided him with a three-dimensional representation of the bovine ventricular system that he extrapolated to humans [fig.5]. Leonardo derived the drawings of the interventricular foramen (now named after Alexander Monro [1697–1767]) from his casting experiments. He again named the lateral ventricles, of anterior disposition, *imprensiva*, which were for the first time represented as a pair. The third ventricle – the *senso comune* – appears enlarged (an artefact?), but the aqueduct of the midbrain is depicted and leads to the fourth ventricle (called *memoria*), which is contiguous to the spinal cord.

Leonardo progressed in his understanding of the complex structures, which he synthesised in three-dimensional views and exploded architectural projections in the Weimar folio [fig.6]. At this point, he broke free from the authoritative concepts asserting that the cranial nerves converge towards the geometrical centre of the brain, represented by the *senso comune*; he drew their routes as they naturally appeared, with their entry points into the skull. He gathered together his research over two decades, describing the brain and its ventricles with their afferent nerves; the optical system with one of the first natural representations of the optic chiasm; the connection with the spinal cord; and the relationships with the bone structures of the skull base and top of the skull – with a genius for 3D visualisation that would not reappear in anatomical books for centuries.

Between Neuroscience and Mystery

Our short presentation of Leonardo's work in the field of neuroanatomy has deliberately focused on the research of the *senso comune*, an archetypal structure that concentrated the many facets of his talents, linking the anatomists of the past with the foundations of modern concepts. But he also worked on the peripheral nerves, on their relationship with the spinal cord, on the brachial plexuses, the chain of sympathetic nerves, not to mention his research on the eye and sight, a sense that as a painter he prioritised above all others.

Through our own limitations, we are not able to rank Leonardo da Vinci according to our contemporary paradigms: he took a holistic approach to understanding nature and its mysteries, in search of a rational explanation using systemic thinking. By immersing ourselves in his anatomical drawings – which are of great interest to both beginners and experienced anatomists to art lovers and brain surgeons – and by contrasting them with his varied research and contemporaneous paintings, we can touch on how the mental processes of the fascinating mind of a polymath were constructed, element by element. We can see the artist in the marvellous skull sections or the exploded views of the base of the brain, but by looking at the *Mona Lisa*, the *Saint John the Baptist* or the *Saint Anne*, painted after the seat of the soul had been located, we can see hints of the budding scientist, in a 15th century where sciences and humanities coexisted happily.

✷

Kenneth Clark, *Leonardo da Vinci: An Account of his Development as an Artist*, 2nd ed., London, Cambridge University Press, 1952, p. 16.
Martin Clayton, *Leonardo da Vinci Anatomist*, London, Royal Collection Trust, 2017.
Dr Rolando F. del Maestro, 'Leonardo da Vinci: The search for the soul', *Journal of Neurosurgery*, 1998, Nov; 89(5): 874–87.
Kenneth D. Keele, Carlo Pedretti, *Leonardo da Vinci: Corpus of the anatomical studies in the collection of Her Majesty the Queen at Windsor Castle*, 3 vols., London, Johnson Reprint Company, 1978–1980.
Martin Kemp, *Leonardo da Vinci: The Marvellous Works of Nature and Man*, Oxford, Oxford University Press, 1981.
Jonathan Pevsner, 'Leonardo da Vinci's studies of the brain', *The Lancet*, 6 April 2019; 393(10179): 1465–1472.
Dr Patricio Sandoval Rubio, 'Leonardo da Vinci and neuroscience: A theory of everything', *Neurosciences and History*, 2019, 7(4): 146–162.
Giuseppe Santoro, et al., 'The anatomic location of the soul from the heart, through the brain, to the whole body, and beyond: A journey through Western history, science, and philosophy', *Neurosurgery*, 2009, Oct; 65(4)): 633–43.

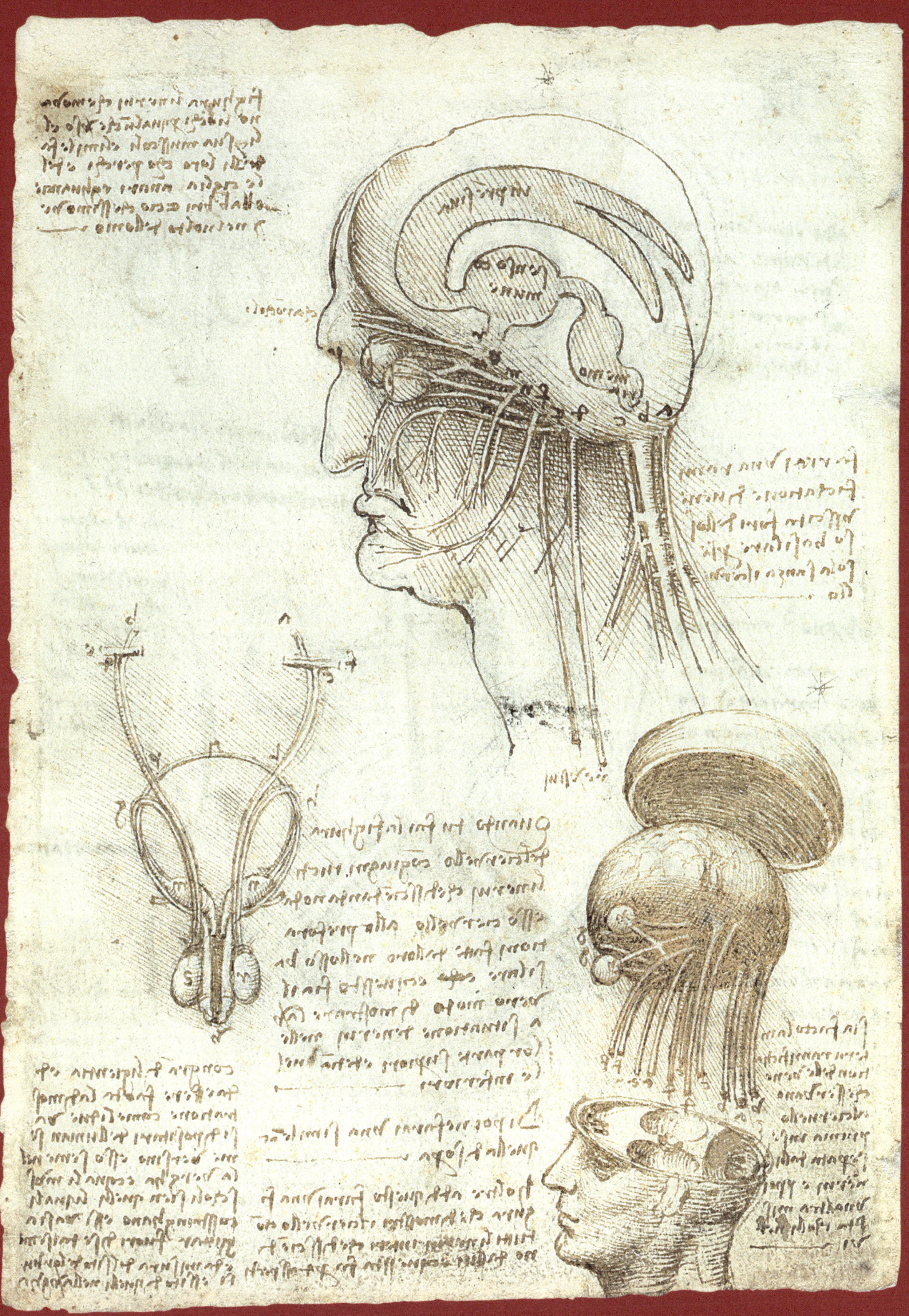

fig. 6 — *Brain, cerebral ventricles and cranium nerves*, c.1508, pen and ink, 19.2 × 13.5 cm
Klassik Stiftung Weimar

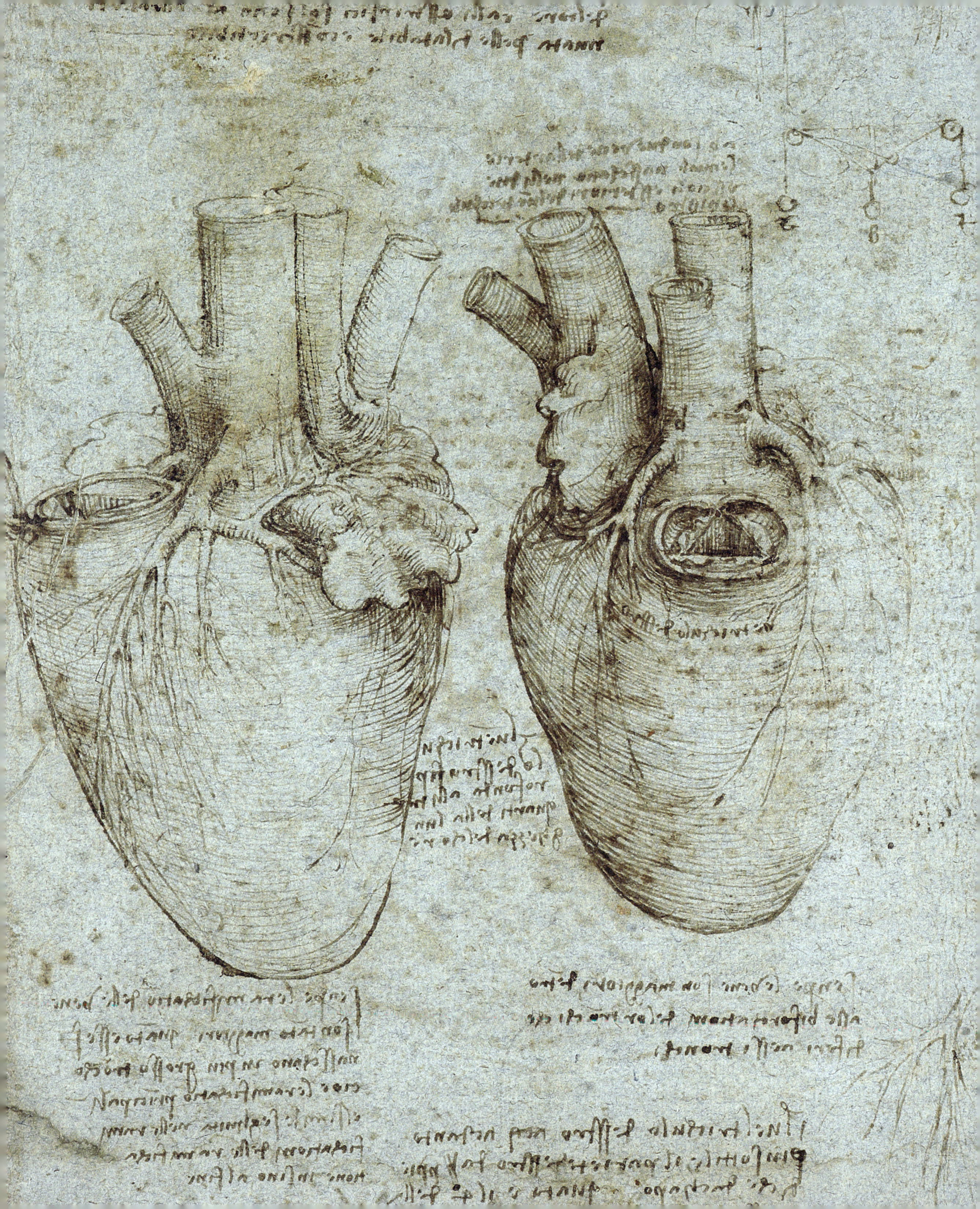

Leonardo da Vinci's Cardiovascular Anatomy

Jean-Jacques Monsuez
Cardiologist at René-Muret AP-HP Hospital

Previous page:

The heart and coronary vessels (detail), c.1511–13, pen and ink on blue paper, 28.8 × 41.3 cm
Windsor, Royal Collection Trust, RL 19073 v

Leonardo da Vinci's work on the cardiovascular system is not merely an artistic transcription of anatomy, but can be seen as part of a scientific approach, as we understand it today. Comparing the notebooks and the annotations provided with the drawings of the anatomical plates allows us to recognise several modern investigative procedures, used to understand the cardiovascular dynamics of the time.

Methodological Features

Under this current heading, several aspects of Leonardo's cardiovascular exploration are to be found. The first concerns the keenness of his observations. This keenness is all the more impressive when one considers the material conditions of dissections, in a basement, by candlelight, on bodies or organs that had had no preserving treatment, and whose tissues decomposed rapidly. "In order to have an exact and complete understanding, I dissected more than ten human bodies ... and as a single body does not last as long as is necessary, I had to proceed in stages on as many bodies as were needed, in order to arrive at a complete understanding, and I often repeated the process twice to discover any differences." This verification procedure, which reveals the rigorous thinking of its author, confirms the gap between observation and hypothesis and interpretation. And one can only admire the observations in his notebooks: "Experience is not at fault; it is only our judgement that is in error in promising itself from experience things which are not within her power."

Leonardo's drawings are as precise and conclusive as his thinking. "How in words can you describe this heart without filling a whole book? ... With what words can you, with a like perfection, describe the whole arrangement of that of which the design is here?" To this precision can be added an incomparable aesthetic, but also, in particular for the cardiovascular system, the introduction of movement, which in this case, can be regarded almost as haemodynamics. "Movement is the cause of all life."

Cardiac Contraction

Contraction is analysed in an approach that considers the four chambers of the heart. "The heart has four ventricles, that is two lower in the substance of the heart [the ventricles], and two upper [the atria] outside the substance of the heart, and of these, two are on the right and two are on the left ... The upper ones are separated by little doors or gateways of the heart [the atrioventricular valves, mitral on the left and tricuspid on the right] from the lower ventricles, and the lower ventricles are separated by a porous wall through which the blood of the right ventricle penetrates into the left ventricle." The porous wall between the ventricles refers to Galen's inaccurate understanding, although as Leonardo was unable to examine it, he could not confirm the inaccuracy [fig.1].

Cardiac contraction is described with its deformations in length and width: "N, the solid muscle, is drawn back, and this is the primary cause of the movement of the heart, for thus drawn, it enlarges, and on enlarging, it shortens." This is demonstrated by observing the movements of a spile, an instrument used to pierce the heart muscle of pigs at abattoirs; the satellite diagram confirms this interpretation [fig.2].

The role of the atria is described for the first time. "The auricles [atria] of the heart are the antechambers of this heart which receive the blood from the heart when it escapes from its ventricle from the beginning to the end of the pressure." The blood flow between the chambers is listed here as well, from a dynamic perspective, but which retains the inaccuracy of the flux and reflux interpretation, which Leonardo did not confirm for himself. "The upper ventricles are continuously causing blood to flow in and out, which is continuously being drawn in and pumped out through the lower ventricles by those above ...".

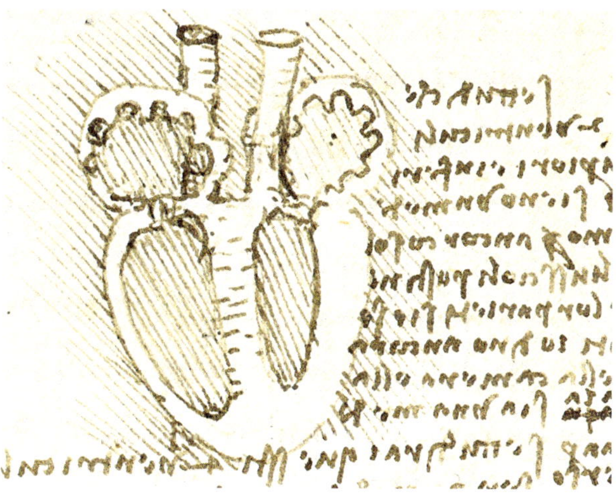

fig. 1 — The four heart chambers with the first representation of the atria and their function; and the pores between the ventricles, which are inaccurate
detail from plate RL 19062 r/c.1513

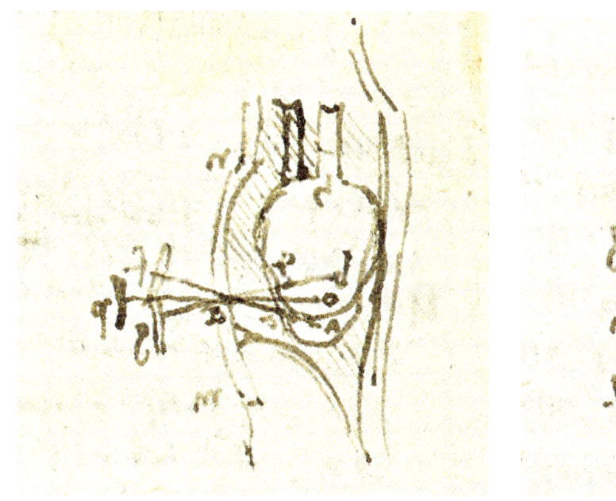

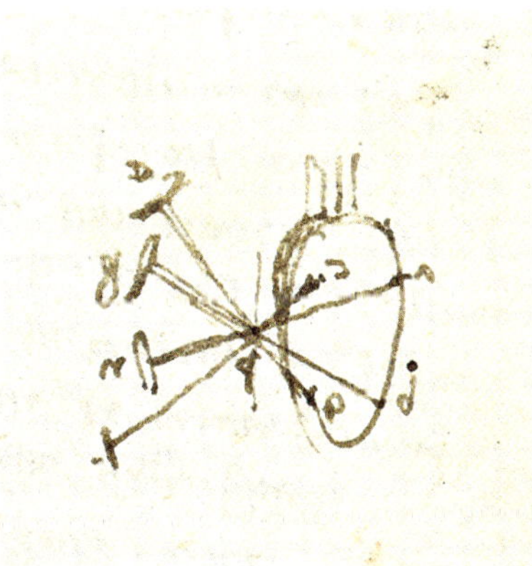

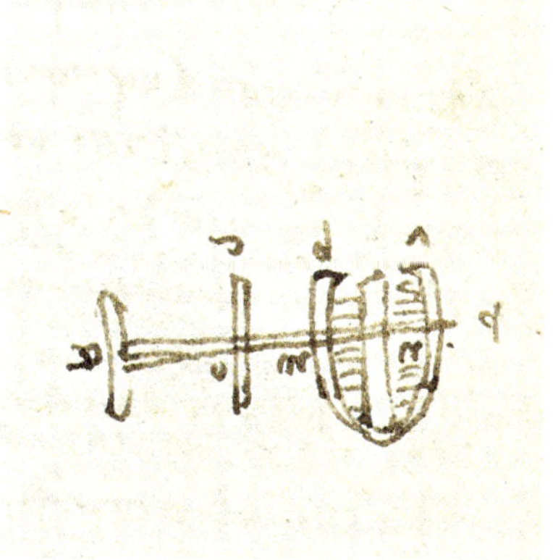

fig. 2 — Longitudinal and circumferential deformations of cardiac contraction analysed with the spile used for pigs
detail from plate RL 19065 r/c.1513

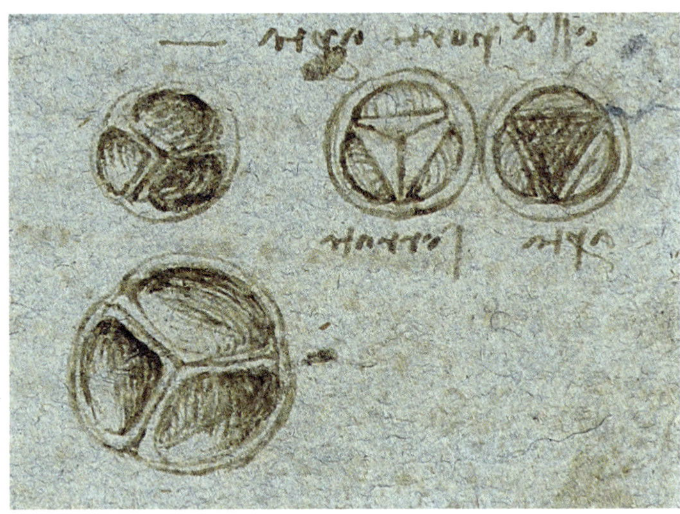

fig. 3 — The aortic valve and its three cusps: closed (left diagram) and open (right diagram)
detail from plate RL 19073 v/c.1513

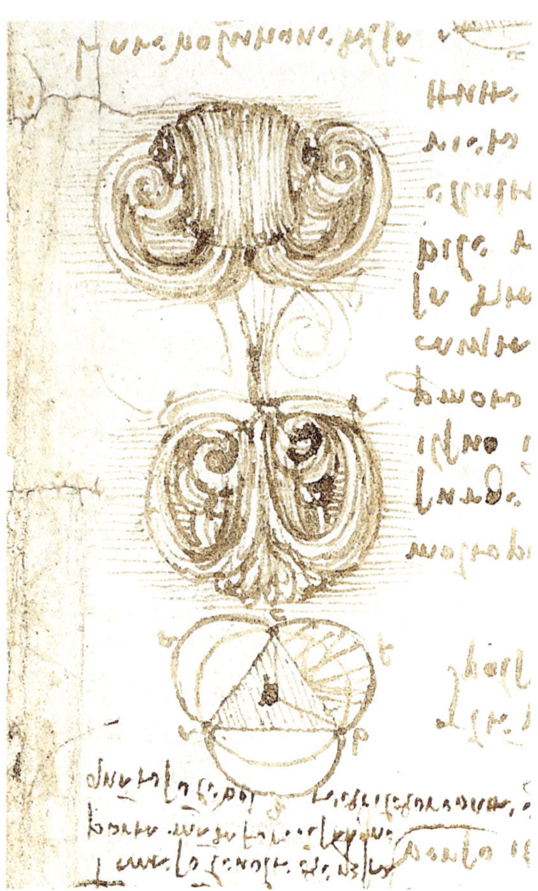

fig. 4 — The aortic transvalvular flow (bottom, with its different velocities and orientations; centre; and sides) and cusp closure (top)
detail from plate RL 19117 r/c.1513

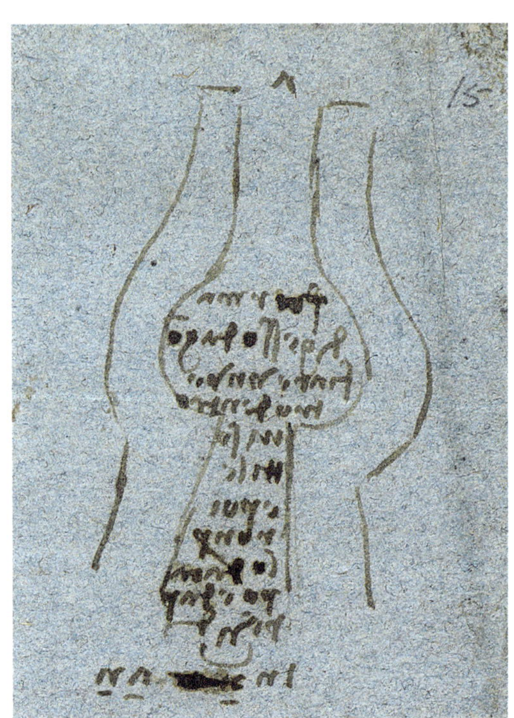

fig. 5 — The glass model reproducing the aortic bulb (the sinuses of Valsalva that Leonardo highlighted with a wax casting). The thick walls of the drawing correspond to the thickness of the plaster used to cast the glass
detail from plate RL 19082 r/c.1513
See p. 86

Valves of the Heart

The accuracy of the description of the aortic valve (through which the left ventricle pumps blood into the aorta and the bloodstream) is impressive, considering that in a normal subject its surface is about 3 cm^2. Its three semilunar cusps, or leaflets, are shown in both open and closed position [fig.3].

But it is in its dynamic aspect that the study of the aortic valve offers the most astonishing concepts of modernity. The left ventricular contraction opens the aortic leaflets and "the blood in the middle of the triangle directs its impetus straight upwards ... and that which surges along the sides distributes its impetus by lateral motion, and percusses against the front of the arches of the hemicycles ... and against the concavity at the base of this hemicycle ... this [valve] remains open as long as the small quantity of blood escaping from the heart keeps it free ... the constant impulse of the blood which had opened the valves closes them again in reflux."

Leonardo da Vinci draws the sequence of the opening of the valve with the progression of the blood flow, which surges higher in the central part of the aorta than along its walls, where the turbulence noted leads him to assume that it is this that closes the aortic orifice [fig.4]. "... the flow of blood that is pushed into the aorta through the orifice percusses and dilates the membranous valves and surges upwards with impulse ... it then divides in the narrow area of impact, to flow back in the opposite direction along the wall ... in a circular movement generated by the wall and comes to percuss the wall of the valve ... which closes under the action of the flow."

To complete his demonstration, he used a real experimental model by following the flow and turbulence of a suspension of millet seeds that he injected into a glass tube with a bulge, replicating the sinuses of Valsalva [fig.5]. The drawing illustrating this visionary description was recently superimposed on the 4D flow MRI scan by Professor Choudhury's team at Oxford University, which shows the same aspect as that described by Leonardo da Vinci [fig.6].

Heart Vascularisation

One of the most famous plates depicts the heart in perspective with its blood vessels running on its surface. "The heart itself is not the origin of life, but simply a vessel made up of dense muscle, vivified and nourished by arteries and veins ...". As for the drawing of the network of arteries and veins, one can only be impressed by the accuracy of its arrangement. The coronary arteries and the satellite venous network are almost as easily identifiable as in a modern anatomy treatise or on a 3D reconstruction of a coronary scan [fig.7].

This description is also the first to have been made of the circular, crown-like aspect of the coronary vessels. "The heart has its surface divided into three parts by three veins which descend from its base, of which veins two terminate the extremities of the right ventricle and have two arteries in contact below them ... The surface space of the heart enclosed within its arteries occupies half the circular surface area ...".

Conclusion

Leonardo's cardiovascular anatomy, with its quasi-physiological analysis of haemodynamics, remained unknown for a long time. Had this not been the case, it is likely that it would have had a significant influence on the subsequent advancement of knowledge of the cardiovascular system. It can also be assumed that it would have had an even more decisive influence if this unfinished work had been continued by Leonardo himself before his death.

✷

Leonardo da Vinci, *Carnets*, edited by Pascal Brioist, Paris, Gallimard, 2019.
Anatomical plates, Royal Collection Trust and Quaderni d'Anatomia, Royal Library, Windsor.
Dominique Le Nen, *Leonardo da Vinci, L'Aventure Anatomique*, Paris, Éditions E/P/A, Hachette, 2019.
Malenka M. Bissel, Erika Dall'Armellina, Robin P. Choudhury, 'Flow vortices in the aortic root: in vivo 4D-MRI confirms predictions of Leonardo da Vinci', *European Heart Journal*, Oxford, Oxford University Press, 2014, p. 1344.

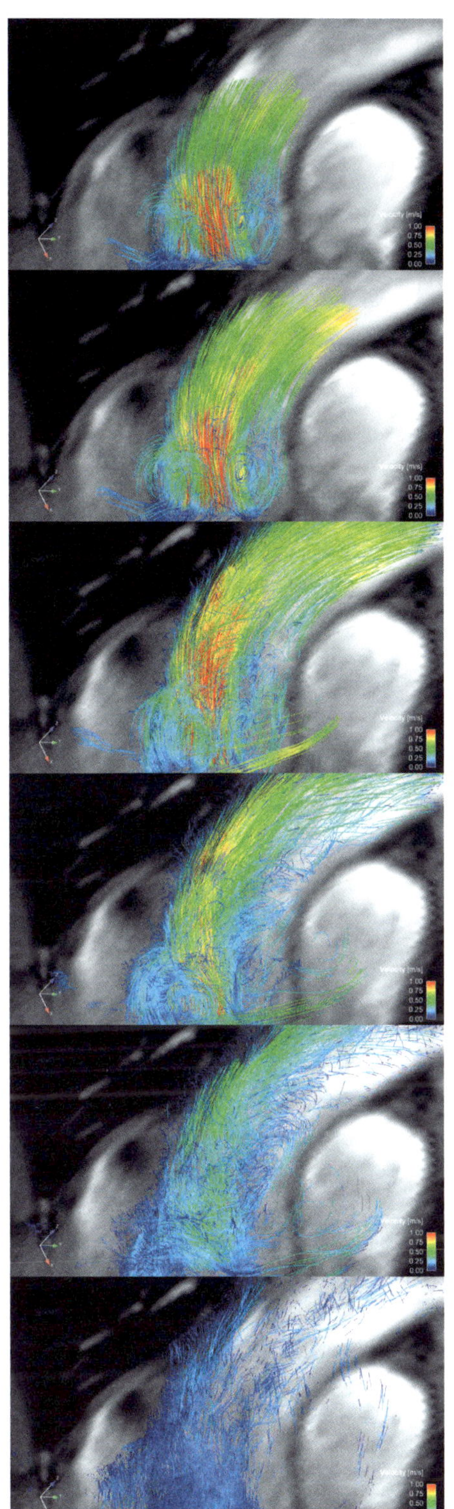

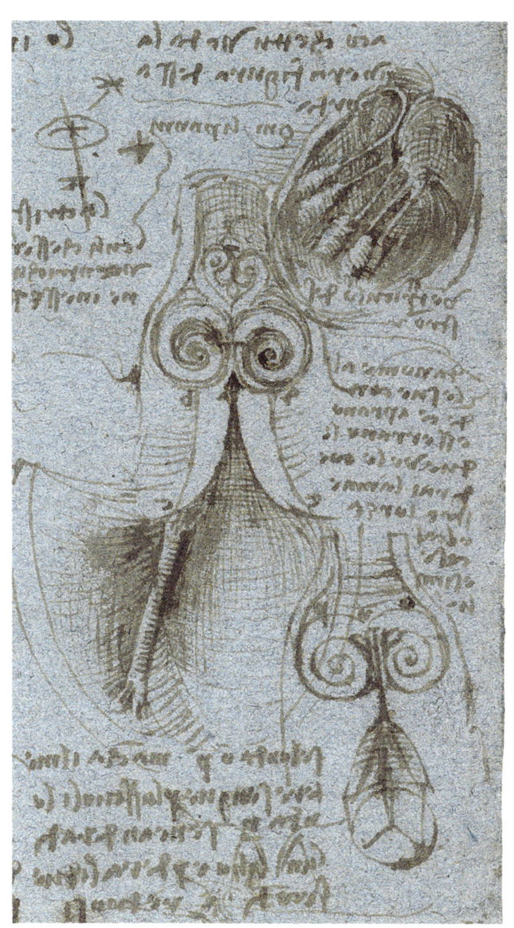

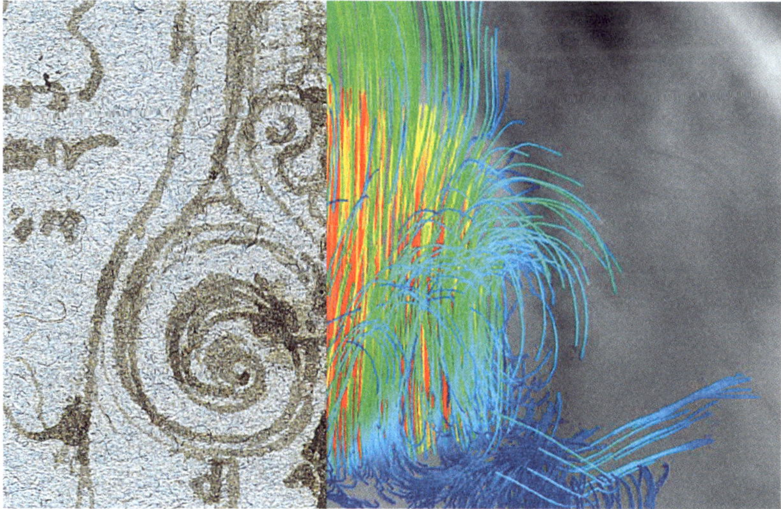

fig. 6 —Aortic flow as represented by Leonardo alongside a 4D flow MRI image
(courtesy of Professor Robin P. Choudhury)

Notes and diagrams on the atria and ventricles of the heart,
c.1511–12, pen and ink, 28.8 × 21.5 cm

Windsor, Royal Collection Trust, RL 19062 r

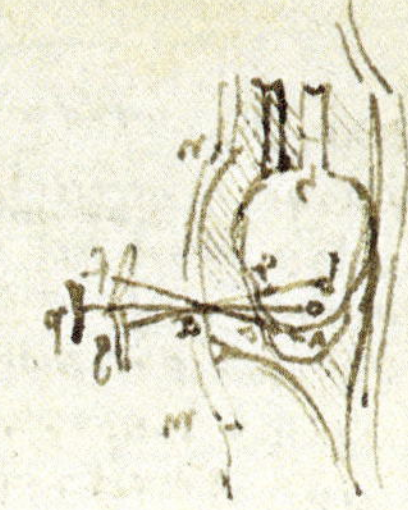

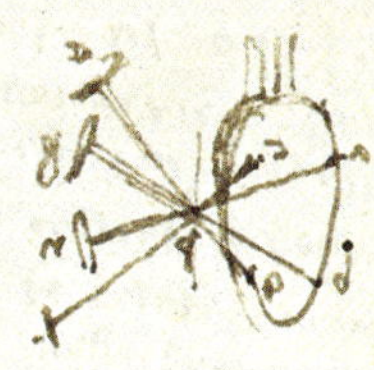

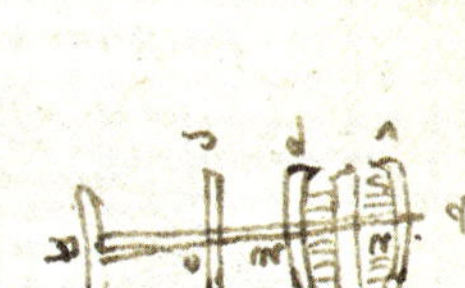

The movement of the heart, c.1511–12, pen and ink, 29.1 × 21.1 cm

Windsor, Royal Collection Trust, RL 19065 r

Studies of the nerves and muscles, the heart, and optics, c.1511–13,
pen and ink, 30.7 × 43.8 cm

Windsor, Royal Collection Trust, RL 19117 r

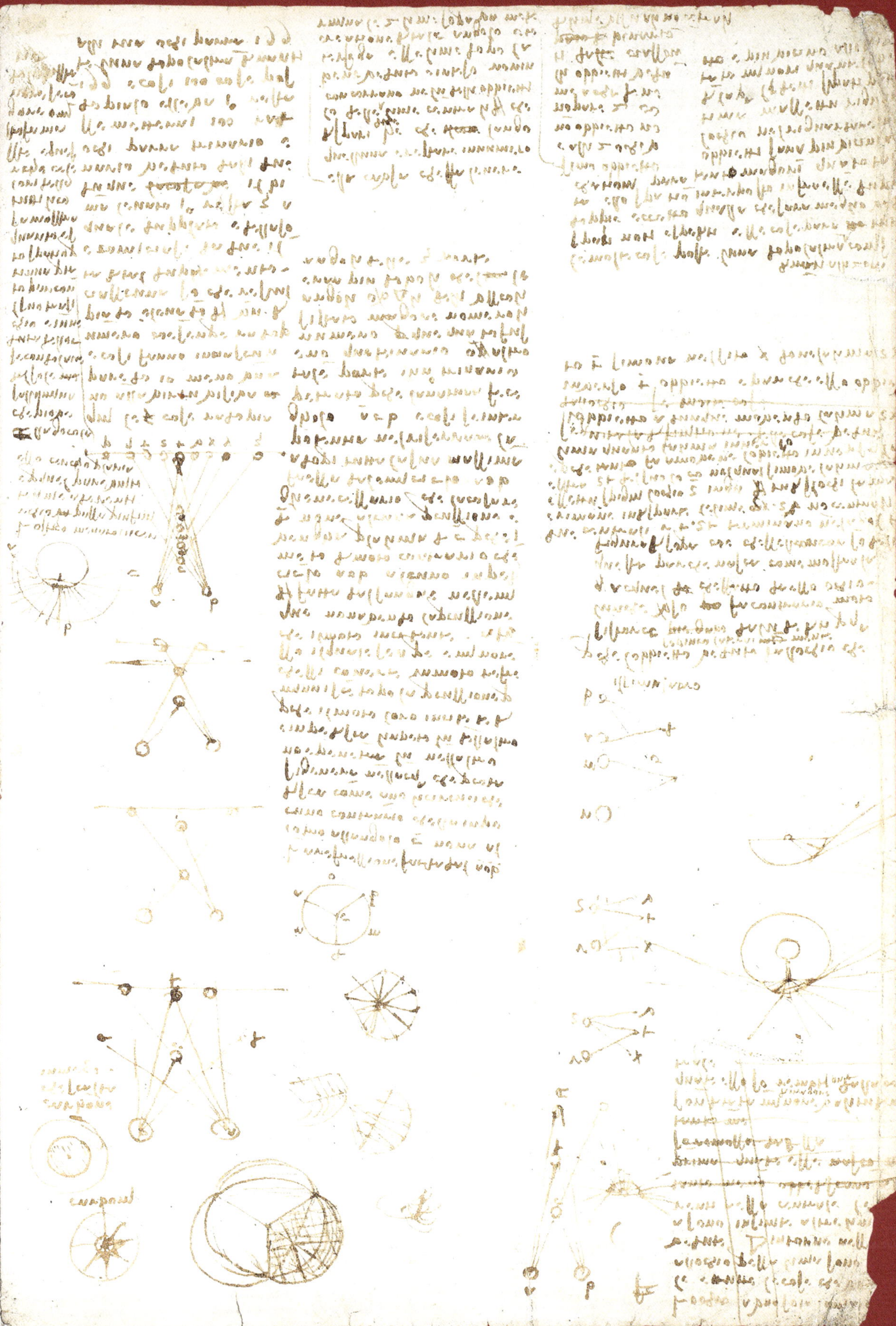

Studies of the nerves and muscles, the heart, and optics, c.1511–13, pen and ink, 30.7 × 43.8 cm

Windsor, Royal Collection Trust, RL 19117 r

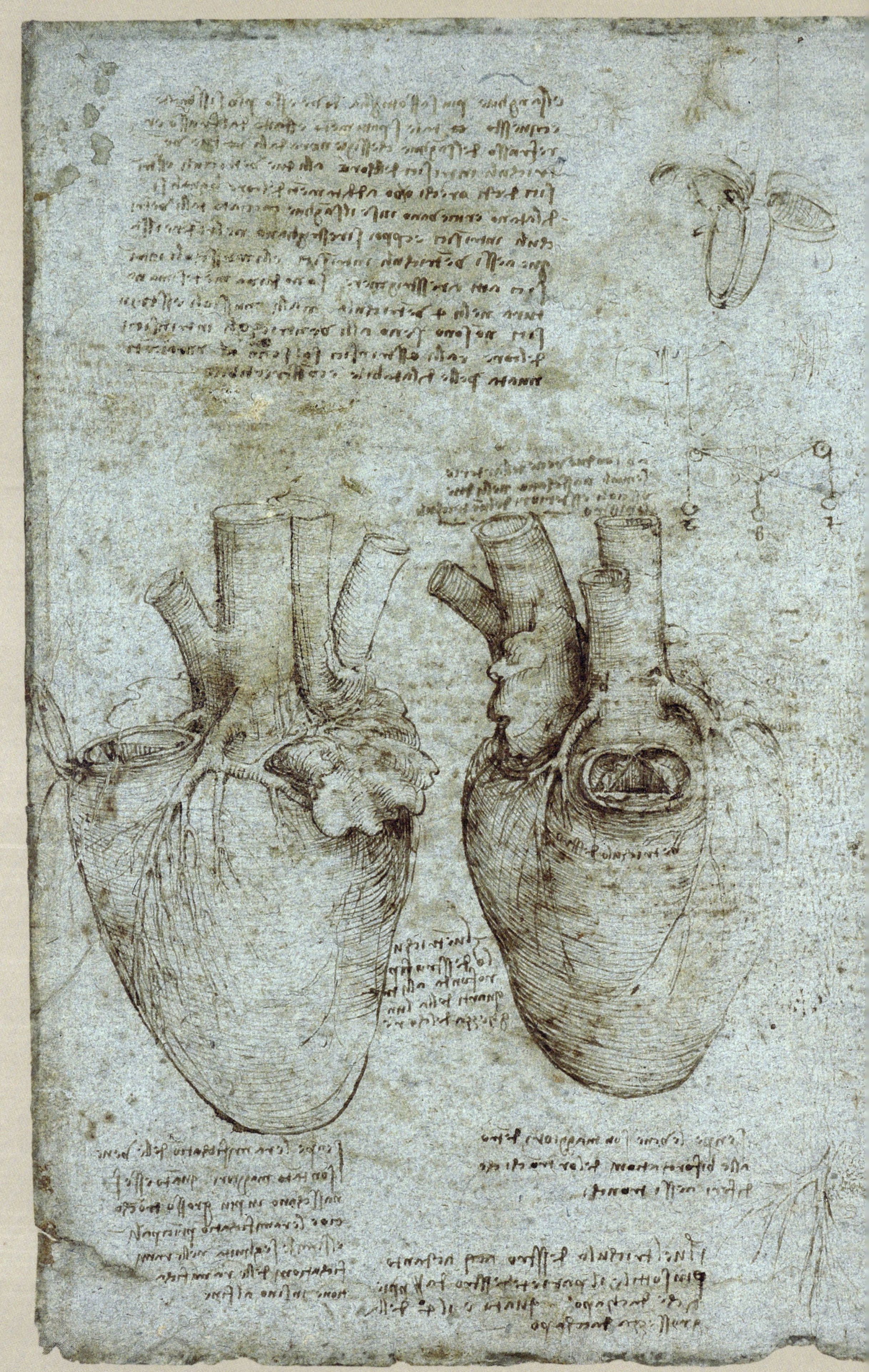

fig. 7
The heart and coronary vessels, c.1511–13, pen and ink on blue paper, 28.8 × 41.3 cm
Windsor, Royal Collection Trust, RL 19073 v

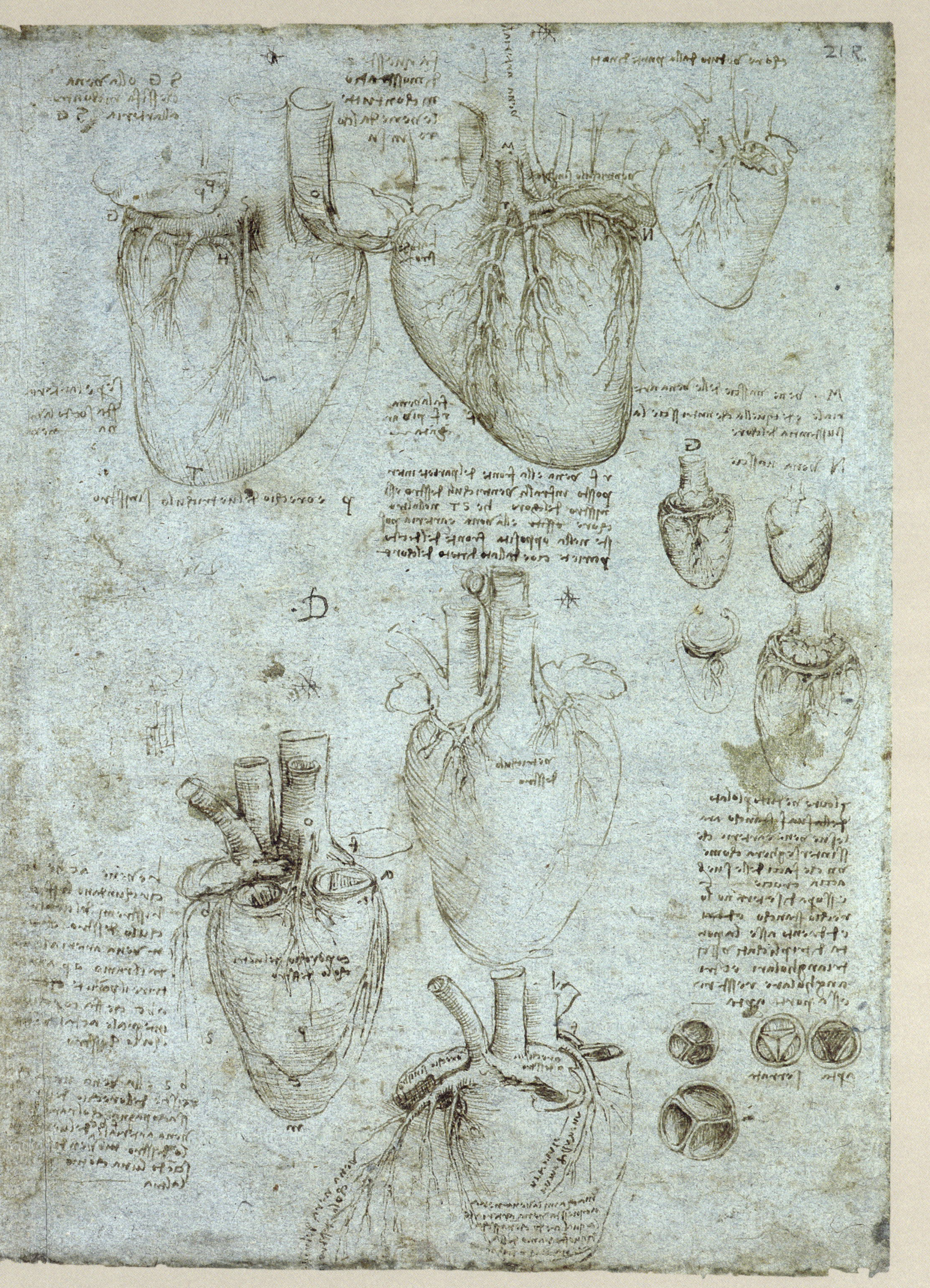
21 R.

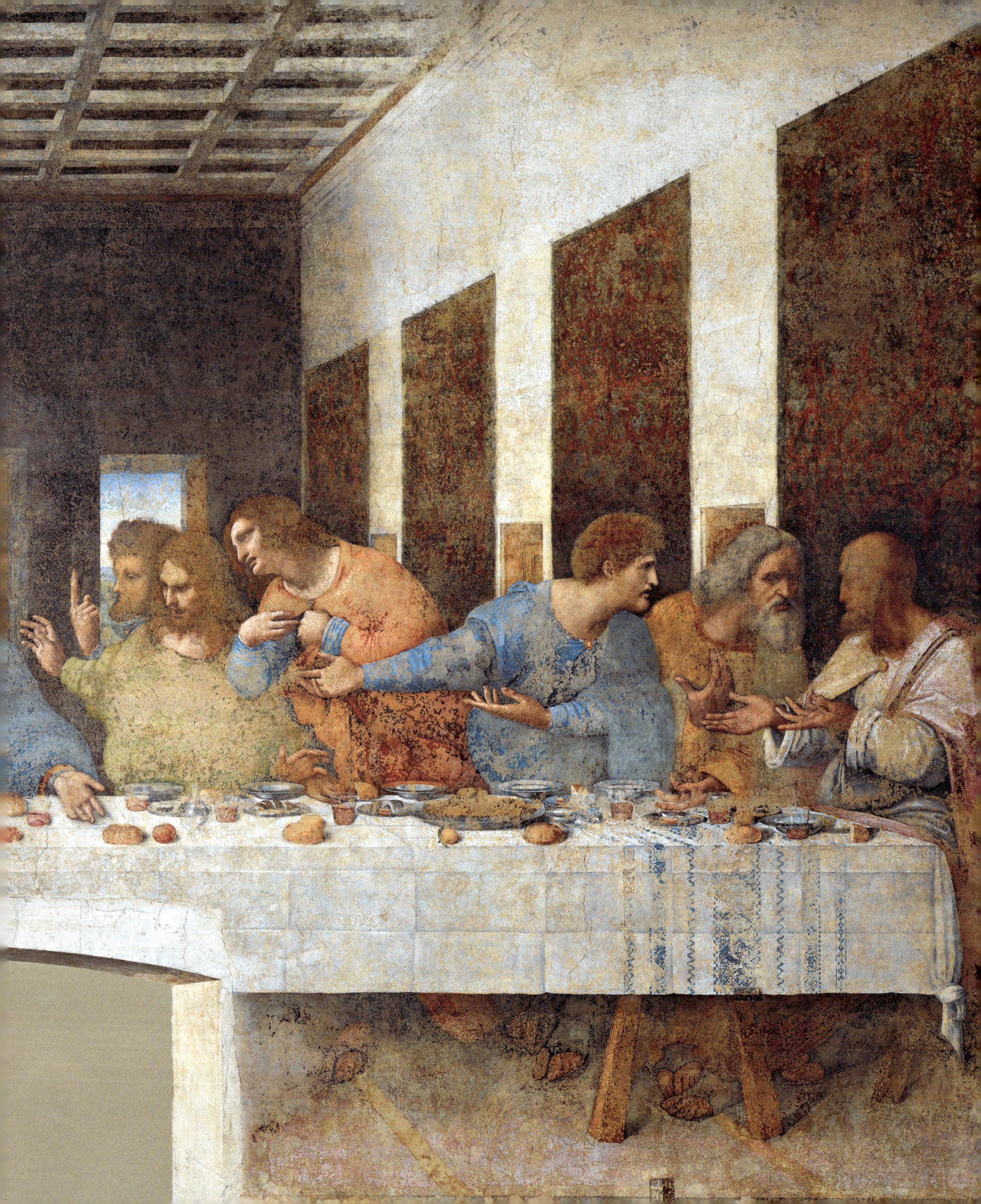

From Anatomy to Emotion: Leonardo da Vinci's *Last Supper*

Christian Lefèvre
Professor of Anatomy at the Faculty of Medicine in Brest

François Gaucher
Surgeon at Quimper General Hospital

Joël Savéan
Technician at the Laboratory of Medical Information Processing in Brest

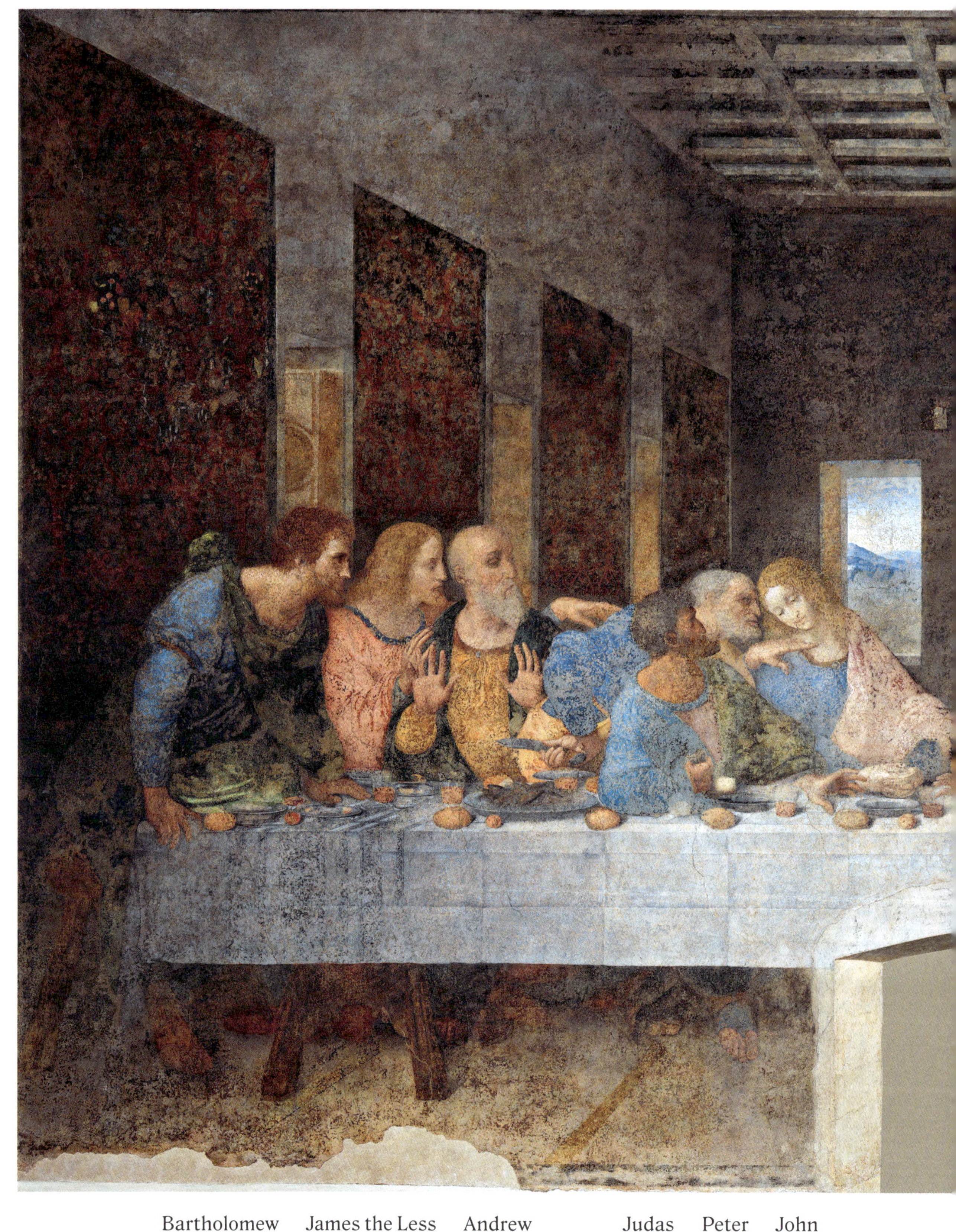

Bartholomew James the Less Andrew Judas Peter John

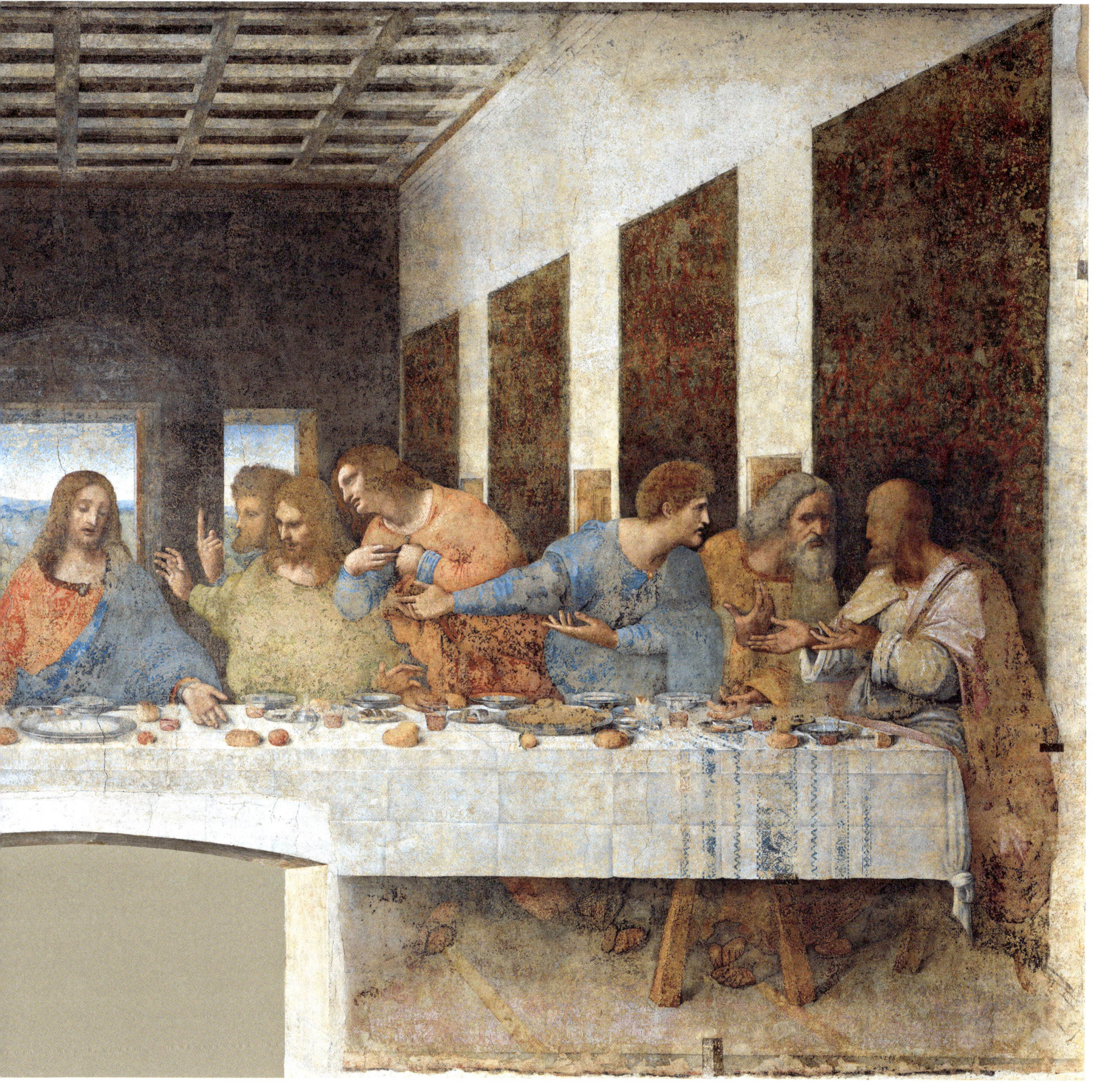

Jesus Thomas James the Greater Philip Matthew Thaddeus Simon

fig. 1—*The Last Supper*, c.1495–98, tempera on gesso, 460 × 880 cm
Museo del Cenacolo, Milan

fig. 2—Kiyoshi Bando, extracts from *The Last Supper* digitised

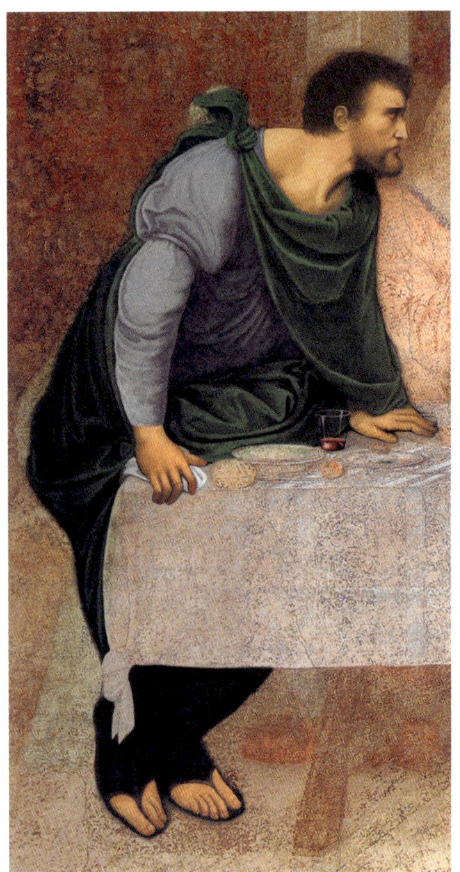

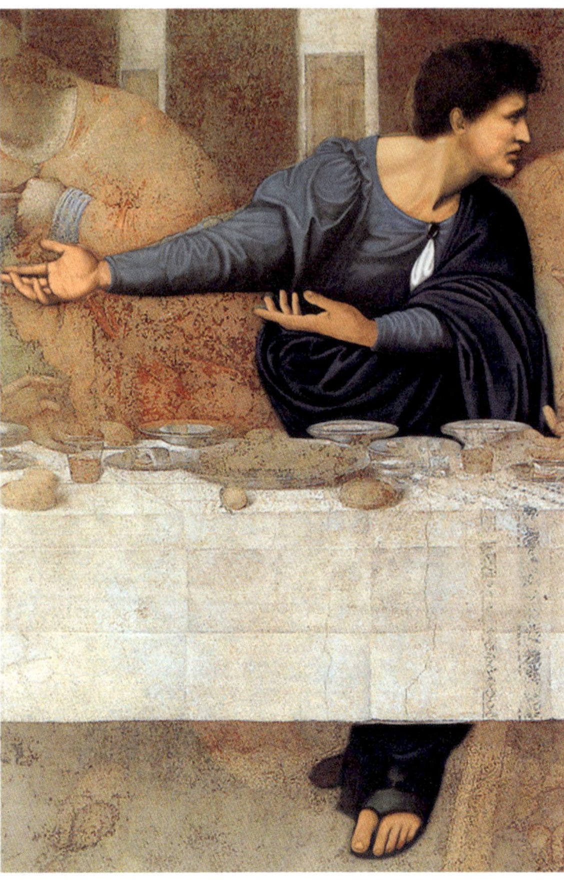

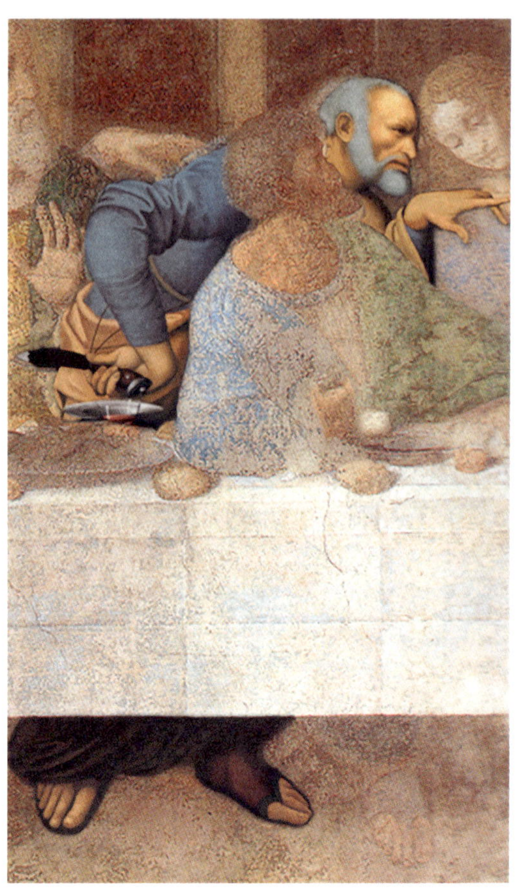

Leonardo da Vinci's paintings are known for being particularly expressive thanks to his knowledge of anatomy gained from his dissections. He understood the musculotendinous mechanisms that create movement, now called biomechanics or the study of movement in living human beings – a discipline that was still unknown in Leonardo's time. Moreover, his remarkable capacity for observation, especially of the simple gestures of everyday life (attitudes, movements, carrying objects, etc.), enabled him to lend a very realistic quality to his paintings. His perfectionist mentality is reflected in his writings:

"A good painter has two chief objects to paint, man and the intention of his soul. The former is easy, the latter hard, for it must be expressed by gestures and the movements of limbs."

Taking his paintings as a starting point, therefore, which are by definition 2D images, Leonardo da Vinci succeeded in producing the perception of spatial movement, to the point of expressing the emotion of his characters.

It is from his famous mural *The Last Supper* ("a moment in motion," according to Isaacson), which depicts Jesus sharing his last meal surrounded by the twelve Apostles (thirteen at table ... a symbol among many others), that we have attempted to elaborate on Leonardo's threefold approach: anatomical, biomechanical and emotional. Originally a commission for the refectory of the monks of the Santa Maria delle Grazie convent in Milan, this painting took four years to complete [fig.1]. It is set high on the north wall of the refectory, and measures 8.80 metres in length and 4.60 metres in height. Jesus' right temple represents the centre of the painting, from which the lines of perspective emanate. Around Jesus, the

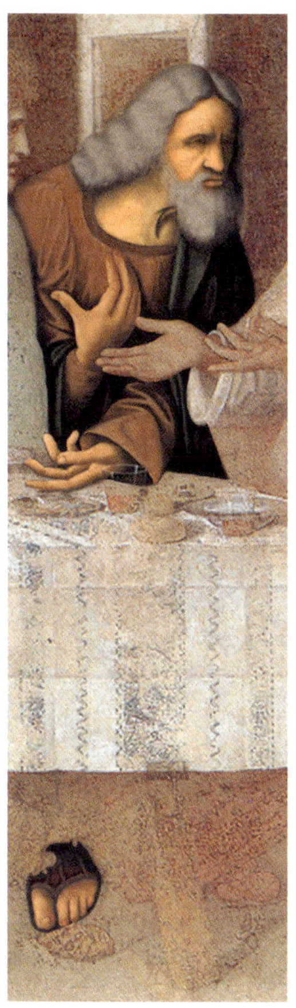
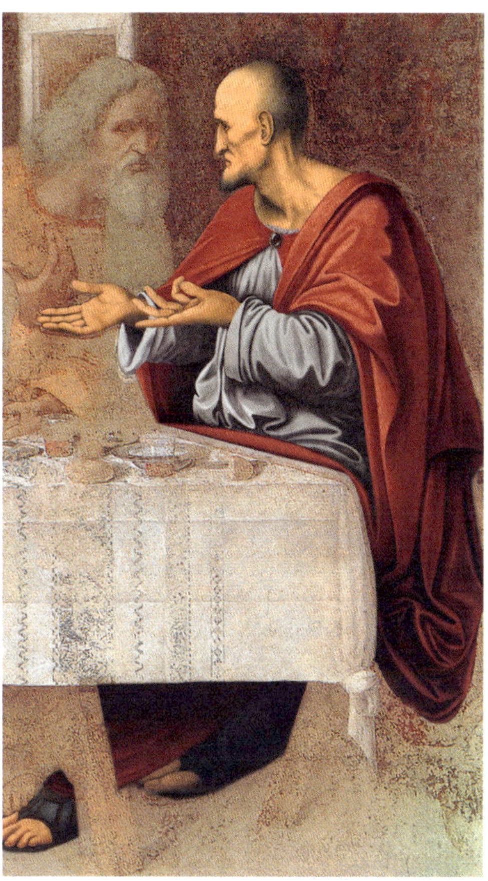

twelve Apostles are arranged symmetrically, in four groups (in reference to the four Gospels) of three figures (in reference to the Trinity). Leonardo showed great skill in using a 'big screen' effect: a scale of 1:4 for his figures and *trompe l'œil* in such a way that the seated monks could observe the fresco from a distance, as if they were, theoretically, at a vantage point 4.5 metres from the ground and 5.3 metres from the painting.

Leonardo chose a particular temporal context for his composition: the moment when Jesus says: "One of you will betray me" (the viewer can even see the still half-open lips of Jesus as he finishes his sentence). One can observe that the state of astonishment of the twelve Apostles is illustrated by a wide variety of spontaneous attitudes, each one reacting in his own way, with his own emotions and gestures.

Methodology

Digital Reconstruction of *The Last Supper* [fig. 2]

In order to analyse more effectively certain details that are sometimes difficult to perceive owing to the severe deterioration of certain areas of the work, we used the digital images of Kiyoshi Bando, who worked meticulously for ten years to create a digital reconstruction of *The Last Supper*. He is a recognised authority in the art world, and the quality and accuracy of his images greatly facilitated our own modelling.

Deformable 3D Skeleton

From a virtual and deformable 3D skeleton, we recalibrated and modelled each character of *The Last Supper* in the form of a skeleton, respecting its precise positioning in the painting and its attitudes in relation to the other characters (work carried out at the Laboratory of Medical Information Processing in Brest). This 3D computer application allowed us to analyse the painting from angles never previously used [fig.3]. It should be noted that all the 3D images obtained in this way, and proposed subsequently, scrupulously respect the exact attitude of each character, as intended by Leonardo.

Using these modern techniques to analyse the original work created 500 years ago, we can illustrate certain notions of biomechanics, so we can admire all the skill of Leonardo, who sometimes cultivates a certain ambiguity in order to allow the observer the freedom to interpret specific details in the painting.

Concept of Muscular Shrouds

Among the figures in *The Last Supper*, the offended Bartholomew [fig.2] rises abruptly leaning forward in a posture made possible by a powerful contraction of the *trapezius*, a posterior support muscle, as evidenced by his clearly visible musculature. Among the anterior support muscles of the neck are the *sternocleidomastoid* muscles.

The combined contraction of the anterior and posterior support muscles of the neck causes a look of transfixed nervous tension that is clearly visible in Judas, a dark, unattractive figure (with a protruding jaw) who, realising that Jesus is talking about him, reacts with a sudden backward movement [fig.4].

Concept of Lever Arms and Muscular Power

Analysing the figure of Matthew [fig.2] shows a right upper limb with elbow extension and shoulder abduction (= away from the body's midline) with a maximum lever arm, hence the clearly visible contraction of his *trapezius-deltoid* muscle. On the other hand, the left side, with the elbow flexed and the shoulder adducted (= brought closer to the body's midline), has a reduced lever arm, putting little strain on the muscles of the left shoulder.

fig. 3—Viewing of *The Last Supper* from specific angles

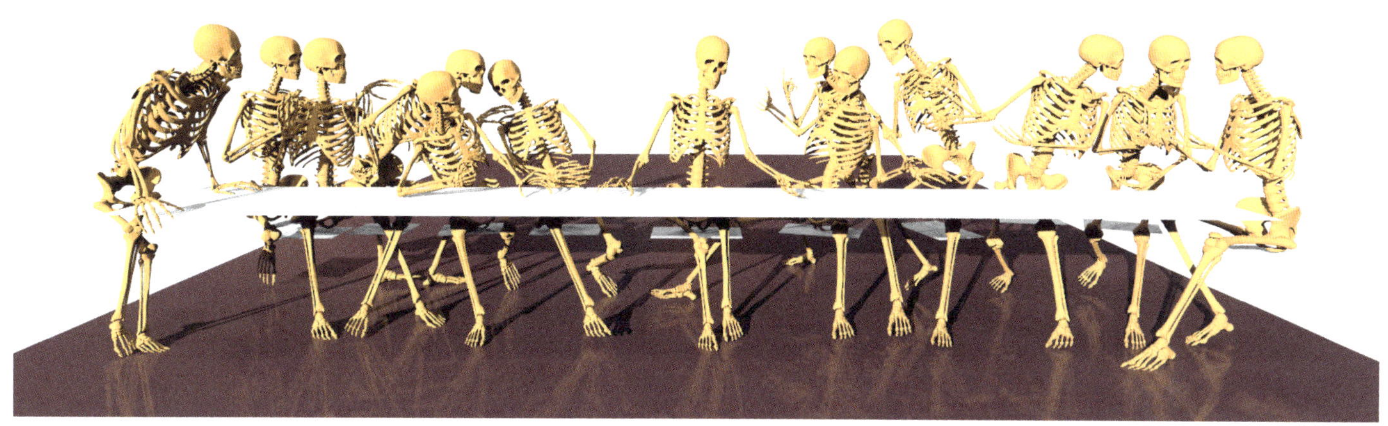

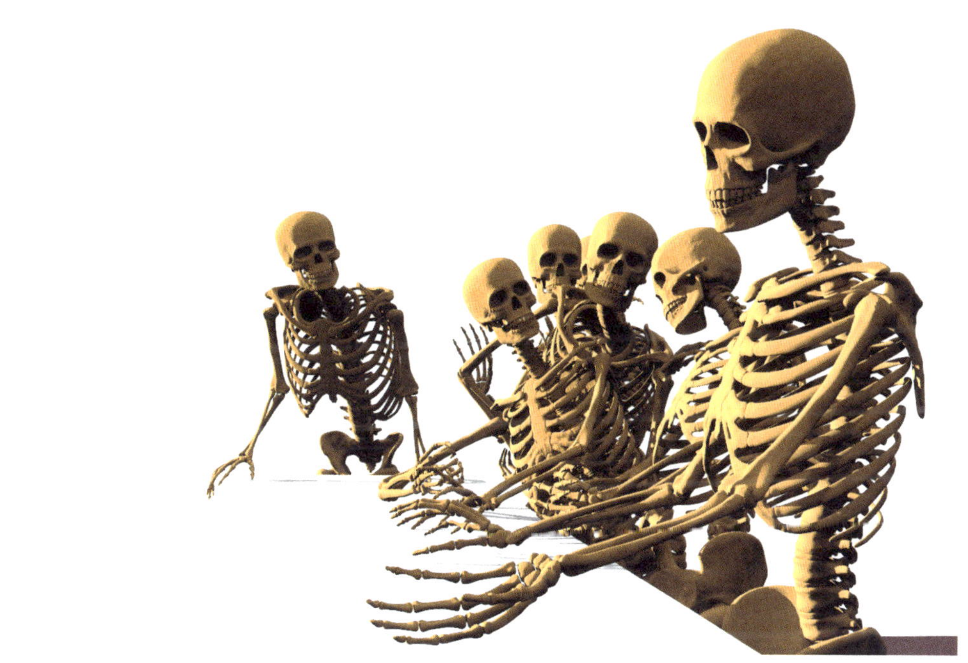

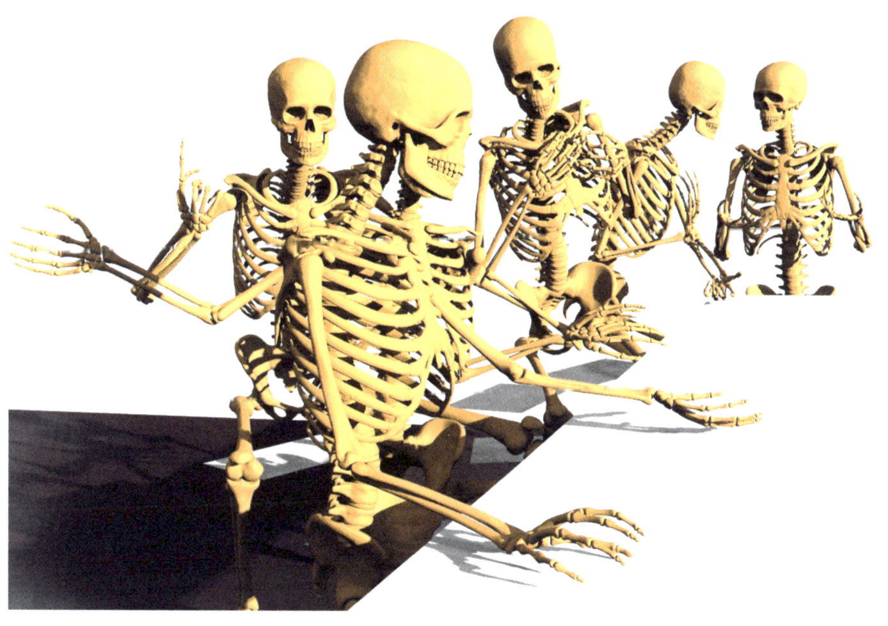

fig. 4 — Judas' attitude of tension

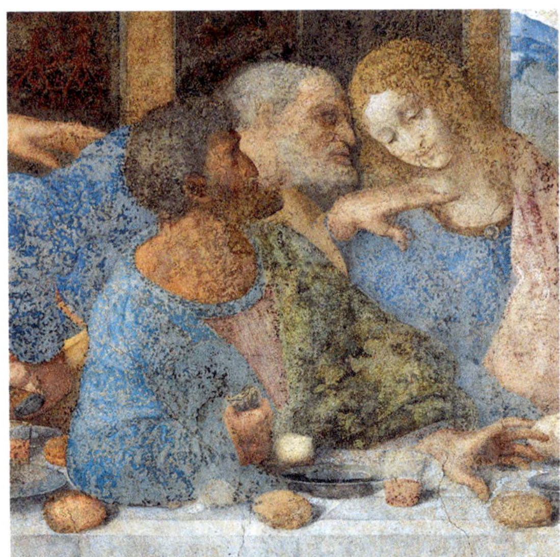

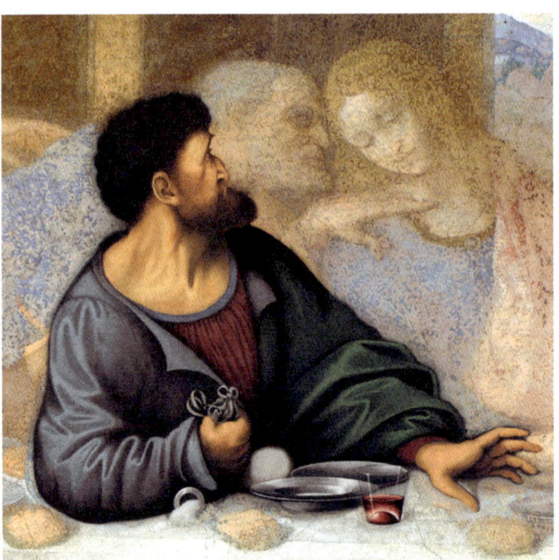

Pronation-supination of the Upper Limb

Remember that supination moves the hand towards the sky, and pronation moves it towards the ground, with the elbow remaining flexed.

Viewers will notice that none of the figures has his hands in the same position. Let us now turn our attention to Jesus: his right upper limb is in pronation, palm towards the ground, the earth, which may allude to his imminent death; in reality, he is reaching for a dish in order to take a piece of bread. On his left side, the hand is in supination, palm towards the sky, which, according to the art historian Michael Ladwein, evokes the act of giving and his future spiritual life. In this way, Leonardo deftly seeks to remind us of the dual human and divine nature of Christ.

One can observe a false supination in Matthew [fig.2], whose left upper limb is with palm upwards, but whose elbow is in extension. The rotation of the left hand here depends only on the shoulder.

The upper right limb of Judas is in the neutral position [fig.4]. His elbow is flexed, the edge of his hand downwards, tightly holding a purse. Leonardo leaves an element of doubt here: is this the reward for his crime, for his betrayal? Judas was also the group's treasurer ... Moreover, when he retreats abruptly, Judas knocks over a salt cellar, traditionally a sign of bad luck. Leonardo's intended symbolism is powerful since it evokes the breaking of a contract of trust, Jesus having said to his disciples: "you are the salt of the earth".

Active pronation-supination (through muscle action) is of lesser amplitude than passive pronation-supination (through forced weight-bearing), which allows extreme amplitudes, as in the case of Peter, whose right hand is in pronation and forced flexion while leaning on the pelvis [fig.2].

The purpose of pronation-supination is the precise spatial orientation of the hand, the last link in the joint chain of the upper limb.

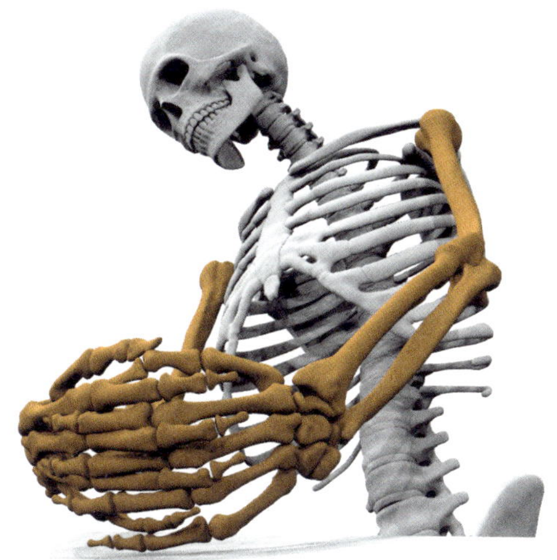

Quietude (John)

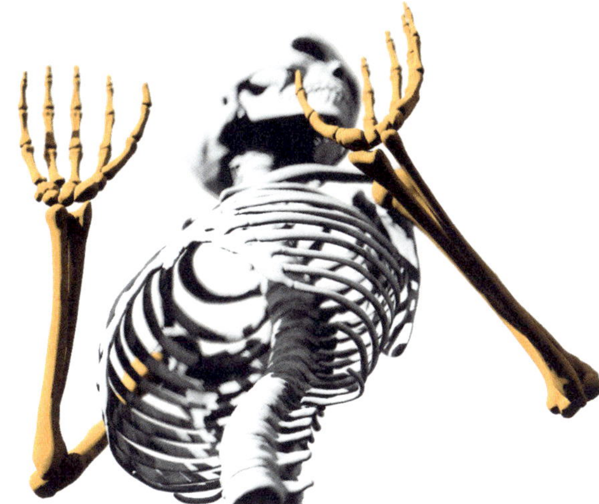

Exoneration (Andrew)

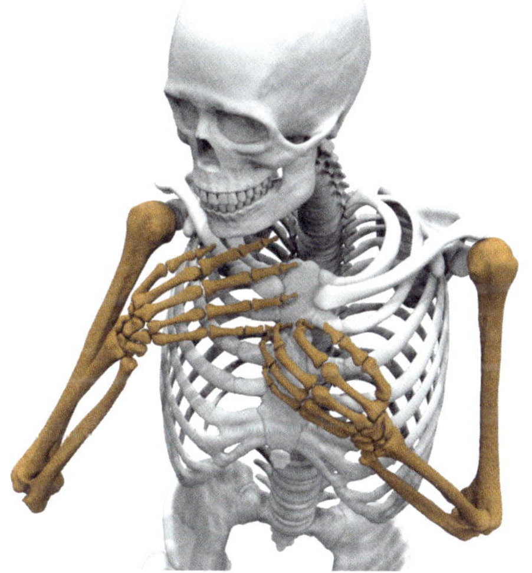

Introspection (Philip)

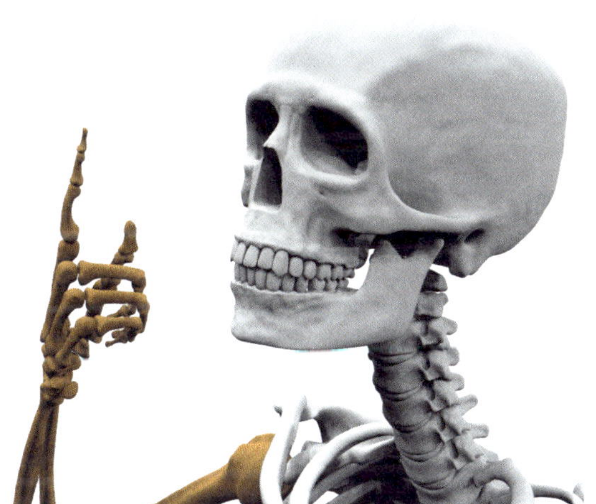

Scepticism (Thomas)

The Symbolism of Hands

Looking at *The Last Supper*, one can but admire Leonardo's great skill in revealing the feelings of each character and enabling their hands 'to speak' [fig.5].

By observing other characters, clearly identified in Kiyoshi Bando's reconstruction [fig.2], one can perceive that Matthew's right hand suggests a direction (towards the presumed traitor?), Thaddeus' left hand suggests vexation, and Simon's hands suggest something evident.

fig. 6—James the Greater leaning back against Thomas

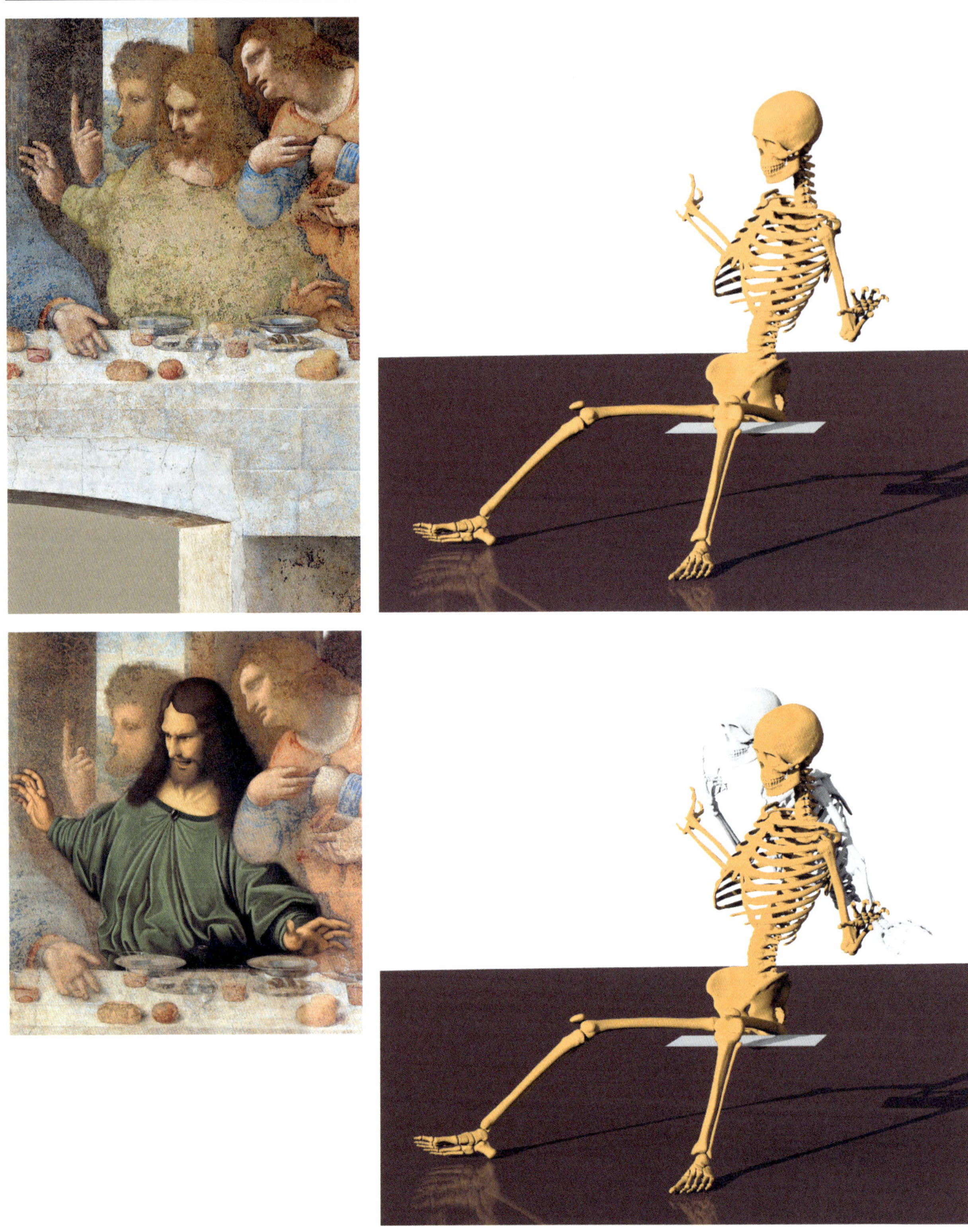

Ideas on Balance

As a keen observer, Leonardo considered the balance of his models' postures. An example of stable balance is seen in Jesus, whose neutral, almost symmetrical seated position conveys wisdom and control despite the gravity of the moment [fig.1].

Sitting to the left of Jesus, James the Greater has heard his words. Shocked, in an outburst of emotion, his attitude expresses surprise and astonishment, with a sudden recoil of the upper body, so much so that he has let his outer garment fall [fig.6]. He therefore needs support from behind, in this instance from Thomas whose extended index finger may represent a threatening finger or the finger of a sceptic ... In a subtle way, Leonardo always leaves the viewer with a choice of interpretations ...

Finally, we should mention Peter, the old Apostle, who probably misheard Jesus' message, and who is leaning forward seeking the stable support of John's right shoulder [fig.2].

Conclusion

3D modelling of *The Last Supper* provides a tool for understanding the work in its third dimension. One can only admire Leonardo's rigorous attention to the anatomy of his models and the balance of their gestures.

"The figure is not praiseworthy if it does not, insofar as is possible, express in gestures the passion of its spirit."

Clearly, Leonardo was a perfectionist. By observing *The Last Supper*, the viewer perceives a scene in motion, almost 'a commotion'. Moreover, Leonardo da Vinci pushed his art to the limits, one might say, of 'perfection', to the point of leaving the emotions of his figures to be revealed simply from their physical attitudes. One word sums up his extraordinary talents: Genius.

✸

Martin Clayton, Ron Philo, *Léonard de Vinci anatomiste*, Arles, Actes Sud, 2018.
Walter Isaacson, *Léonard de Vinci – La biographie*, Lausanne, Presses polytechniques et universitaires romandes, 2019.
Michael Ladwein, *La Cène de Léonard de Vinci – Drame universel et acte de rédemption*, Paris, Triades, 2005.
Frank Zöllner, Johannes Nathan, *Léonard de Vinci – Tout l'œuvre peint et graphique*, Paris, Taschen, 2003.

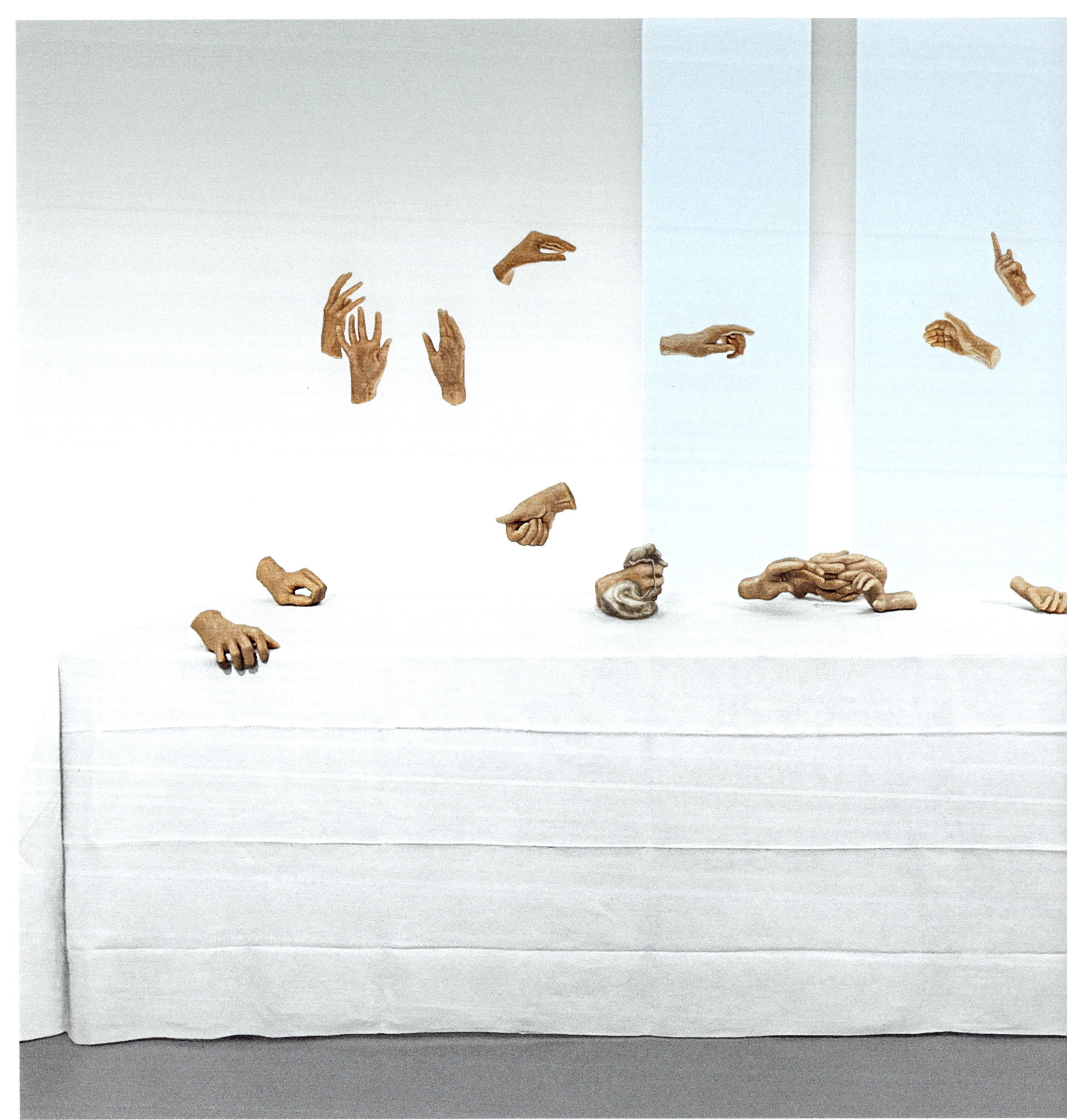

Ivana Gayitch, *The Last Supper*, installation

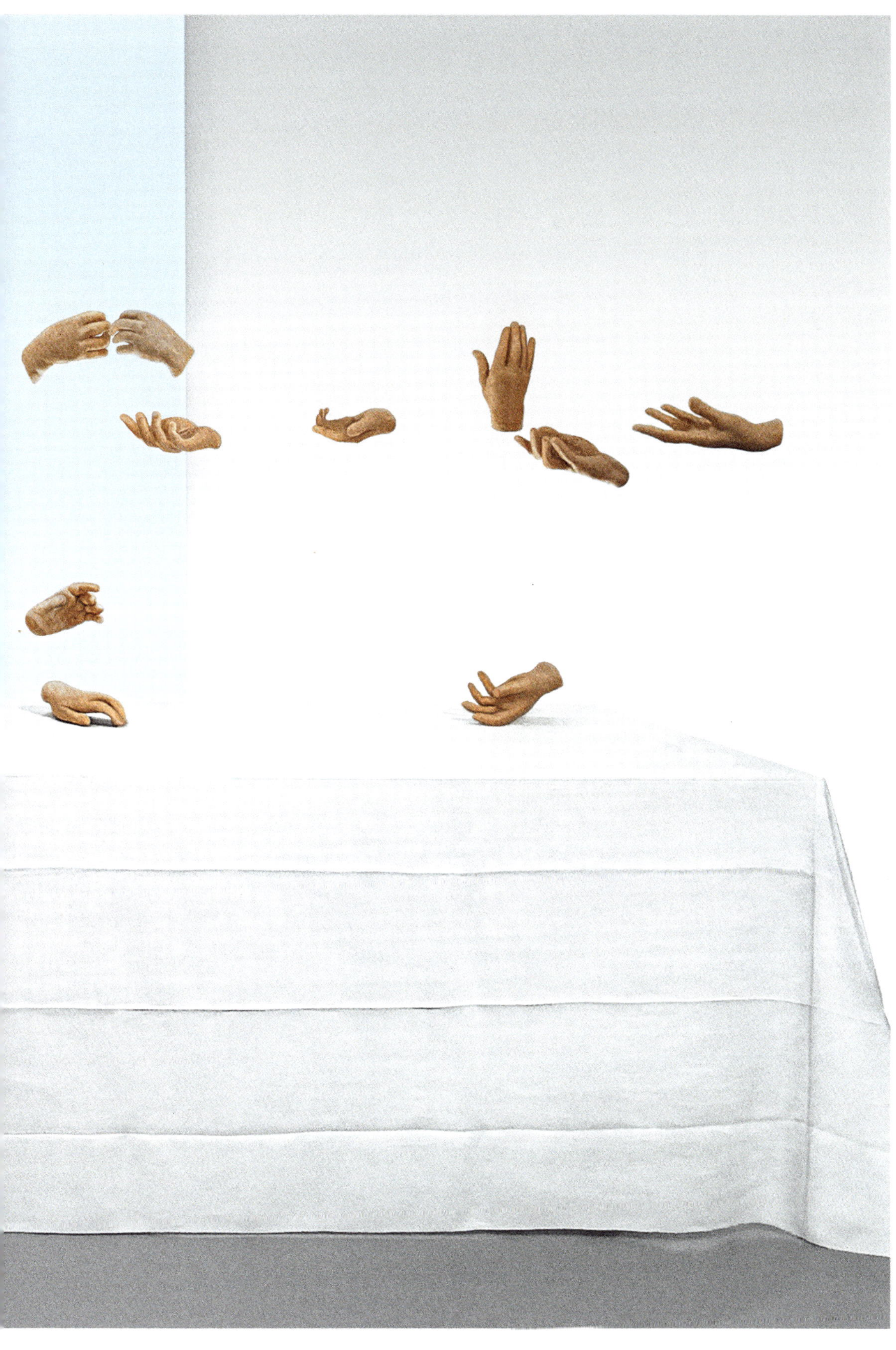

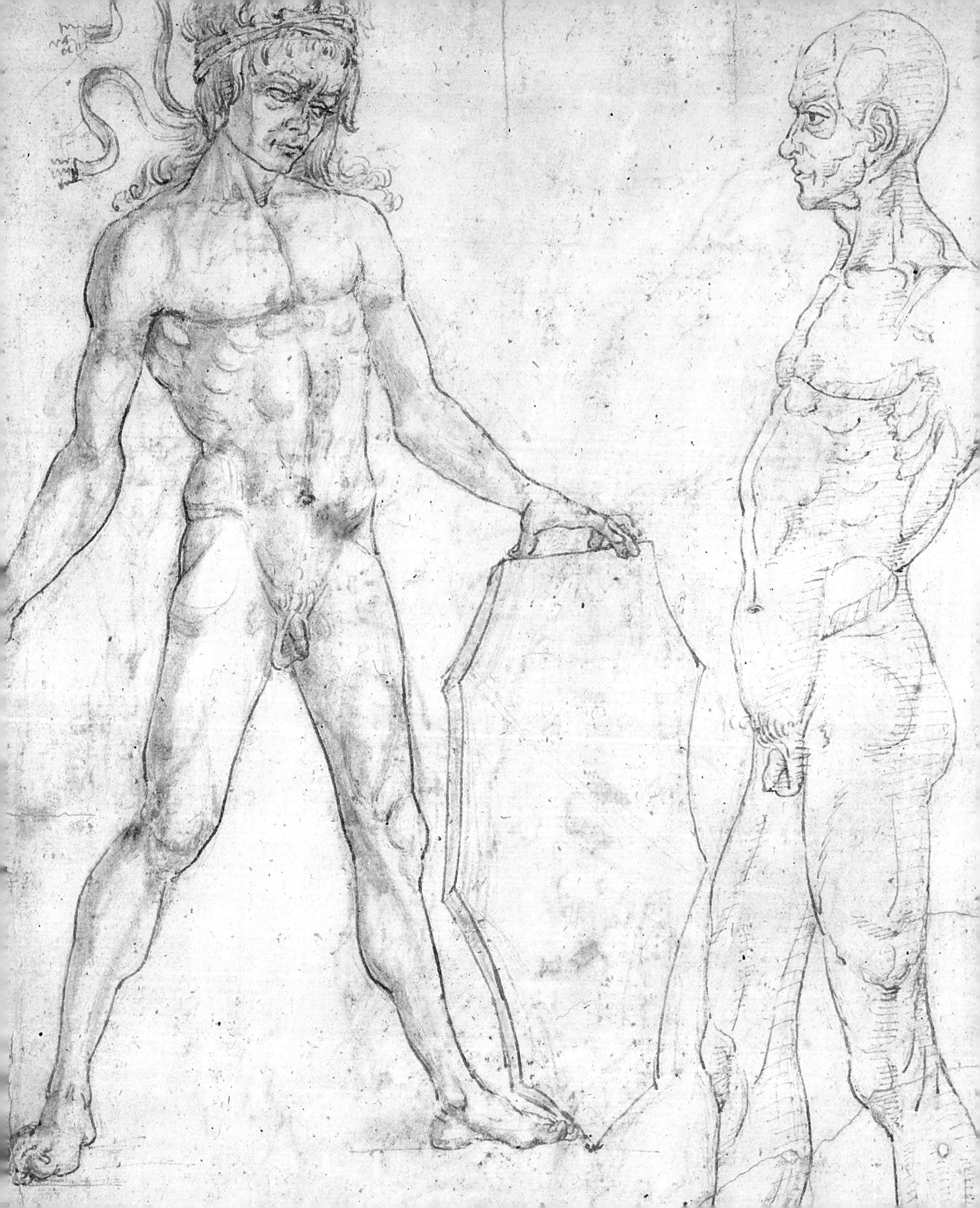

The Anatomical Work of Leonardo: Originality in Repetition

Maëlyss Haddjeri
PhD Student in Art History at the École Pratique des Hautes Etudes, Université Paris Sciences et Lettres

Previous page:

School of Antonio Pollaiuolo, *Studies of two male nudes in front and profile view*, pen and brown ink, black chalk, brown wash (detail)
Florence, GDSU, inv. 269 Ev

The originality of the anatomical work of Leonardo da Vinci (1452–1519) can be perceived from various angles, from a technical, analytical and scientific perspective, considering the artist's personal approach in relation to his predecessors or contemporaries. In this short essay, we shall highlight some of the artistic styles of the Quattrocento on which Leonardo based his anatomical drawings. We shall focus on various traditional forms: drawing techniques, copies after the masters, life drawing and sculpture. This analysis aims to highlight the originality of Leonardo's anatomical work in relation to its reception, affiliations and reinterpretation of works by artists who preceded him.

The drawing in the Royal Collection at Windsor depicting the main organs and vessels of the human body is taken as a starting point to reflect on the singularity of Leonardo's anatomical work [see fig. 1 on p. 57].

This drawing, which reflects his early examinations of the body around 1480–1490, is one of the artist's least original anatomical studies. The figure, represented from the front, references both the model from the artistic culture of the Quattrocento and the anatomical theories developed by Aristotle (384–322BCE) and Galen (c.130CE – c.200/221CE). Leonardo inscribed "the tree of veins" between the legs of the figure, and "spiritual parts" at the top left. In this drawing, he followed Galen's idea that in the cardiovascular system, 'natural spirit' arising from the liver passes through the veins, while 'vital spirit' passes from the heart through the arteries.

The drawing follows a conventional style found in anatomical treatises from the beginning of the 14th century. The use of colour, the brown and green wash, recalls in particular the illustrations of Henri de Mondeville's treatise [fig.2] and the *Bodleian MS. Ashmole (399)* manuscript from Oxford University.

The technique echoes other works on paper by Leonardo, in particular his cartographic representations of Italy, such as those of Imola and Valdichiana, which combine attention to detail with a variety of techniques: pen, ink, black chalk and wash. The drapery studies, preparatory to some of his works, are part of this typology of pictorial drawings and demonstrate his desire to experiment with complex combinations of drawing instruments and coloured paper. Unlike these representations, Leonardo rarely used coloured washes for his anatomical drawings. Along with his drawing of "the tree of veins", another exception to this rule is his anatomical study of the cardiovascular system and major organs of a woman (Windsor, RL 12281). On this large drawing, the pen hatching and yellow wash clarify the depth of the interior of the body and the relationships between organs and vessels. In the drawing of the "tree of veins", Leonardo also reflected on the rendering of depth in the representation of the interior of the body, by juxtaposing vessels at the level of the neck [fig.1]. The figure is drawn on thick lines of black chalk. This technique contrasts with other anatomical studies made by the artist during the same years. A series of drawings on blue prepared paper in the Royal Collection at Windsor was executed with

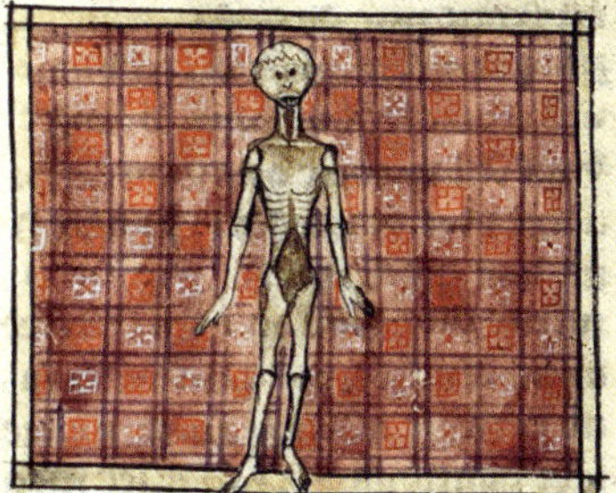

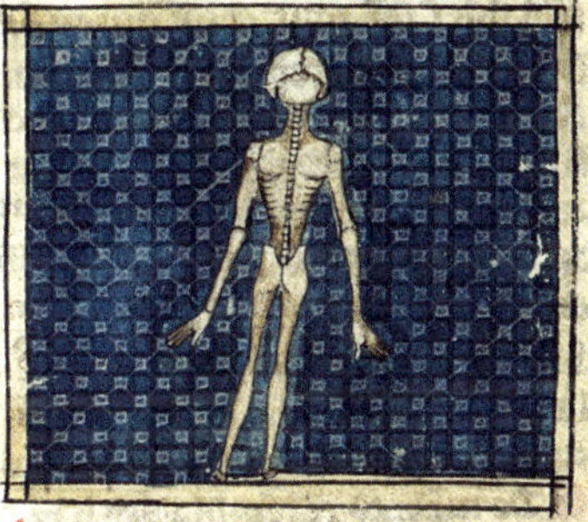

fig. 2 — Henri de Mondeville, *Chirurgie*
Paris, Bibliothèque nationale de France,
French manuscript, inv. 2030, folio 9 v
[fig. 1 – see p. 57]

more care and delicacy in the treatment of the outlines of the motifs, in metalpoint and pen (Windsor, RL 12609; RL 12613; RL 12626).

The model of the body of the figure in "the tree of veins" has often been linked in academic studies to the 'heroic' or 'soldier' figure in the work of Antonio Pollaiuolo (1431–1498). A drawing, held at the Louvre, displays the typology of the male nude that he developed [fig.3].

From the study of a sculpted wax model, Pollaiuolo offered a variety of perspectives on the spatial representation of the human form. The sturdy male figure, with his ample musculature, and the summary, brisk pen strokes are characteristic of this type of drawing, which was very common in Italy during the second half of the 15th and the beginning of the 16th centuries. Many studies similar to the Louvre drawing are now attributed to the Pollaiuolo School (London, British Museum, inv. 1885.0509.1614; Florence, GDSU, inv. 269 E; Venice, Galerie Dell'Accademia, inv. 31; Cambridge, Fogg Museum of Art, inv. 1932.260). Leonardo was likely inspired by the studies of Pollaiuolo and his school for the execution of his drawing of "the tree of veins" [fig. 4].

In his workshop, Leonardo, like his predecessors, produced studies of the body from nudes. Maso Finiguerra (1426–1464), a master of niellowork and goldwork, prolific draughtsman and collaborator of Pollaiuolo, is of interest for his drawings from life. Sometimes attributed to Maso Finiguerra, sometimes to Antonio Pollaiuolo, a drawing showing the study of the arm holding a stick fits into this typology of drawings. As in the drawing of Leonardo's "tree of veins", this study accentuates the representation of the veins of the human body. The anatomy echoes heroic musculature. The pen is schematic, elaborate and controlled [fig.5].

Based on the example of Antonio Pollaiuolo and Maso Finiguerra, Leonardo referred to life models in other studies of the interior of the body. On one of the folios belonging to the series of drawings made on blue prepared paper, held in the Royal Collection at Windsor, he seems to start from the study of the nude to understand the system and mechanism of the inside of the leg. Like an architectural drawing seen in section, the leg is sectioned to show the muscles, tendons and veins (Windsor, RL 12617).

Moreover, Leonardo certainly relied on a wax or terracotta figure to create the "tree of veins" design. This prototype can be found in other studies by the artist. The facial features, as well as the position of the lower limbs, front on; one leg slightly rotated and open to the outside, can be seen in studies that deal with the proportions of the face and the muscles of the lower body (Turin, Royal Library, inv. 15574; Windsor, RL 19003; RL 19018; RL 19029; RL 19014; RL 12631; RL 19006). Sculpted models were reused for his preparatory studies for the *Battle of Anghiari.* In a drawing held in the Royal Collection at Windsor, the model's pose was also likely derived from the memory of Leonardo's lessons under Verrocchio [fig. 6].

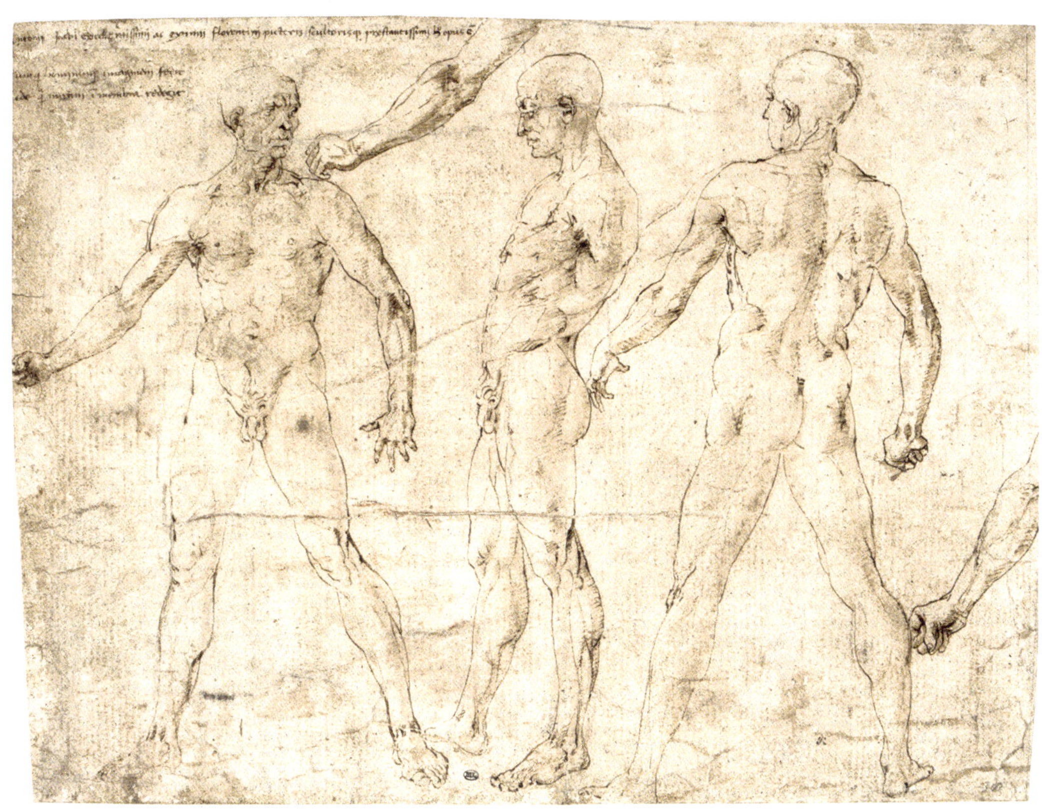

fig. 3 — Antonio Pollaiuolo, *Three male nudes, face, back and profile view; two arm studies*, pen and brown ink, brown wash and stylus, 26.5 × 35.7 cm
Paris, musée du Louvre, inv. 1486

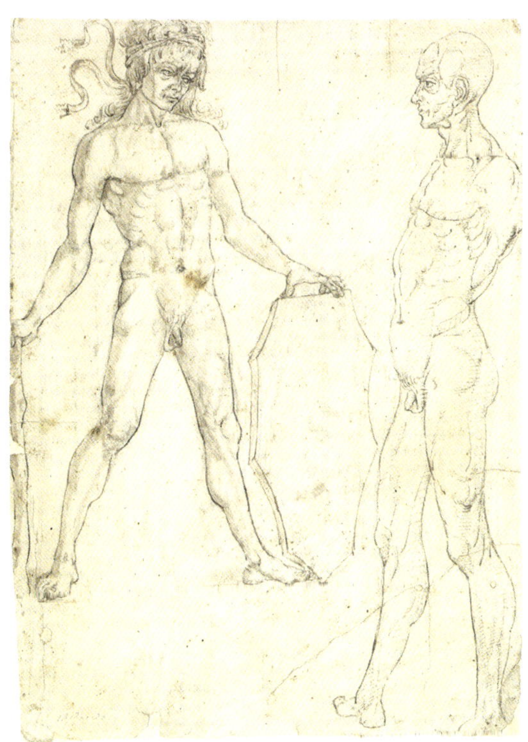

fig. 4 — School of Antonio Pollaiuolo, *Studies of two male nudes in front and profile view*, pen and brown ink, black chalk, brown wash
Florence, GDSU, inv. 269 Ev

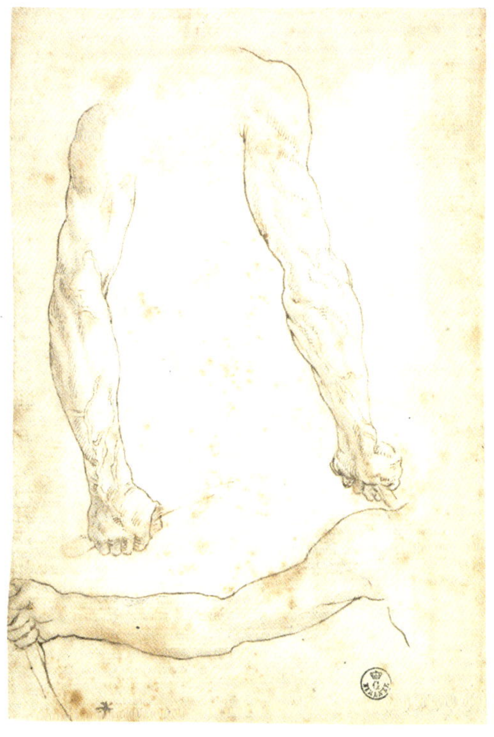

fig. 5 — Antonio Pollaiuolo, *Studies of male arms holding a stick*, pen and brown ink, brown wash, traces of stylus and black chalk, 13.4 × 19.2 cm
Florence, GDSU, inv. 14494 F

Leonardo's creations from his period in the master's workshop, such as his *Saint Jerome in the Wilderness*, attest to the fact that he found key elements while there, enabling him to depict the anatomy of the body in an expressive manner (Vatican, Vatican Museums, inv. 40337).

The pattern of the legs can be compared with the preparatory terracotta model made by Verrocchio for the silver relief figure of the executioner in the *Beheading of Saint John the Baptist* [fig.7]. This figure stands with his back to us, head in profile, right leg forward, in muscular tension.

Following the artistic practices of Pollaiuolo and Verrocchio, Leonardo developed his knowledge of human anatomy during the Renaissance. Although he planned to write a treatise on the subject that was never published in his lifetime, he became the inventor of the vocabulary of modern anatomical drawing. Through affiliation and repetition, Leonardo's work stood out and was enriched by the deepening of his research on the body, his dissections, and the study of living mechanisms. Other artists, such as Michelangelo, who, along with Leonardo da Vinci, enjoyed the greatest fortune, were also instrumental in expressing the same need to render the expressiveness of the body during the Renaissance.

✷

Carmen C. Bambach, *Leonardo da Vinci Rediscovered*, vol. 2, (4 vols.), New Haven, Yale University Press, 2019.
Martin Clayton and Ron Philo, *Leonardo da Vinci: Anatomy*, London, Royal Collection Trust, 2011.
Laurie Smith Fusco, *The nude as protagonist: Pollaiuolo's figural style explicated by Leonardo's study of static anatomy, movement, and functional anatomy*, PhD thesis, Institute of Fine Arts, New York University, 1978.
Domenico Laurenza, *Leonardo – L'anatomia*, Florence, Giunti, 2009.
Lorenza Melli, *Maso Finiguerra*, Florence, Edifir, 1995.

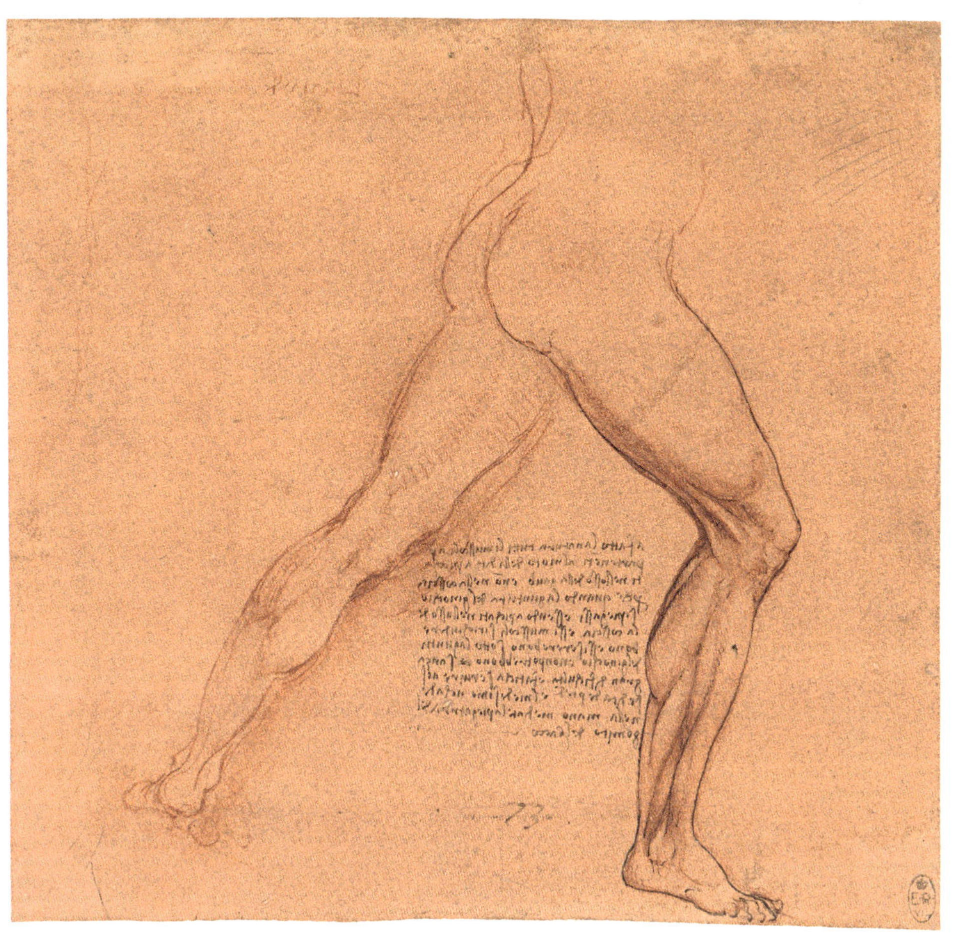

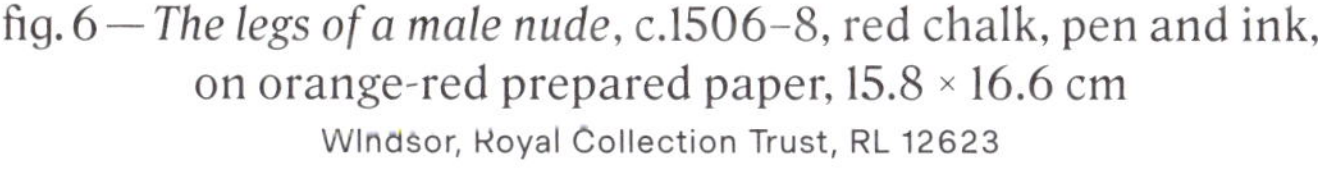

fig. 6 — *The legs of a male nude*, c.1506–8, red chalk, pen and ink, on orange-red prepared paper, 15.8 × 16.6 cm
Windsor, Royal Collection Trust, RL 12623

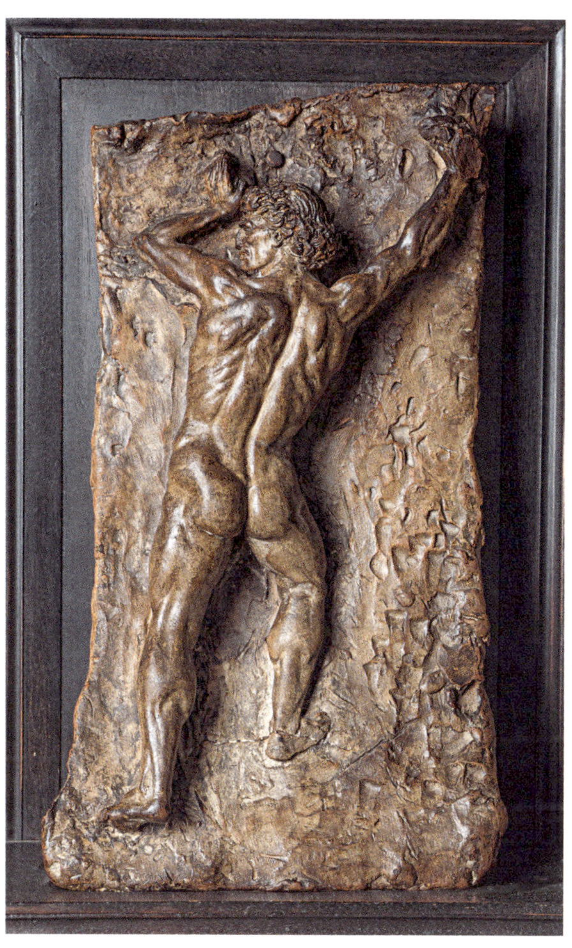

fig. 7 — Andrea del Verrocchio, *Figure of Executioner*, c.1477–1480, terracotta, 27.2 × 16 × 8 cm
Private collection

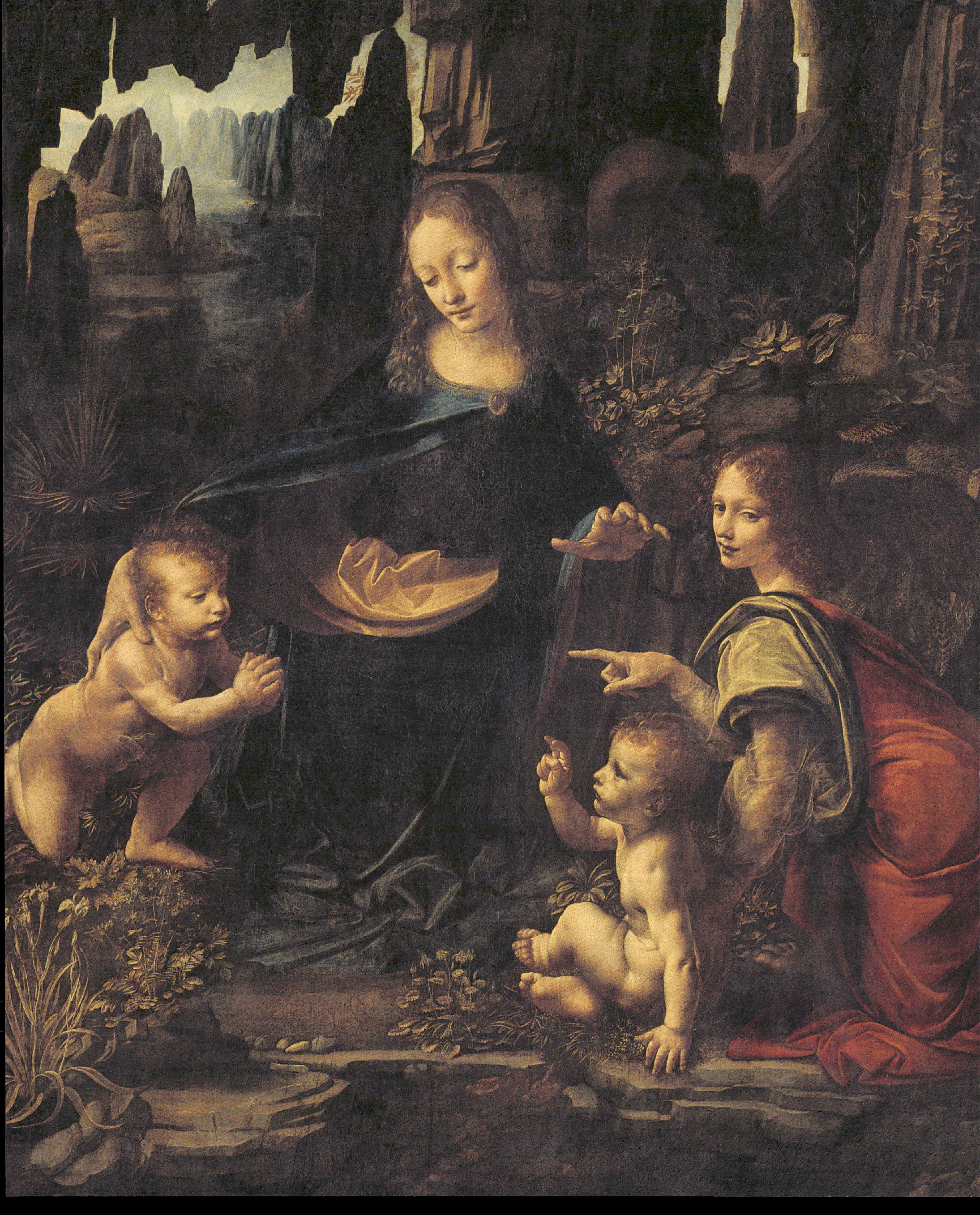

The Power of Analogy: Leonardo's Anatomy of the Earth and his Paintings of Landscape

Frank Zöllner
Professor of Art History at Leipzig University

Previous page:

fig. 1
The Virgin of the Rocks (detail), 1483–1494, oil on canvas, 199.5 × 122 cm
Paris, musée du Louvre, inv. 777

Thinking in analogies runs like a recurring theme through Leonardo da Vinci's studies and written legacy (Marusic/ Broomhall, 2021). Most prominently, it is the human body that he uses for comparison, for example, when he invokes the idea of microcosm and macrocosm already known from antiquity, according to which the human body bears within itself the idea of the entire universe (Richter 1970, § 929; Laurenza 2019). Another example would be Leonardo's studies of human proportions, in which he discusses analogies between the body and its parts (Richter 1970, § 308–349). At the same time, this form of creating analogies is part of anthropomorphic thinking, probably the most widespread form of communicating ideas and interrelationships.

In general, anthropomorphism is not only central to Leonardo's thought, but also important to theory production in the early modern period. But Leonardo also makes use of the figure of thought of analogy in very different individual fields, for example when he compares the role of the architect with that of the physician (Richter 1970, § 1347A). Furthermore, thinking in analogies is not limited to his scientific and theoretical studies; it also creates a direct link to his work as a painter. One of the first examples of this phenomenon is the 1483 *Virgin of the Rocks* [fig. 1], whose strikingly designed background has already been commented on frequently. Of course, iconographically this rocky background has to do with religious ideas of Franciscan piety. But apart from this interpretation, the *Virgin of the Rocks* can also be understood in more artistic terms as an expression of Leonardo's 'scientific' studies. Indeed, the grotto in Leonardo's altarpiece, split into two passageways, with its view of an alpine water reservoir, seems to illustrate those ideas of the earth as a living being that ancient and medieval authors had repeatedly formulated and that Leonardo also repeatedly addressed in his writings some years after he had completed the painting (Zöllner 2019, p. 75; Laurenza 2019). If we follow this reading, the *Virgin of the Rocks* would anticipate precisely those geological and hydrological ideas that the artist would later express in the context of his 'scientific' reflections on the 'body of the earth.' Especially in the *Codex Leicester*, i.e. between 1506 and 1508, but partly also in earlier writings such as Manuscript A, he describes the course of water, which under the surface of the earth in various veins seeks its way up to alpine heights just as the veins in the body of man transport the blood (Richter 1970, §§ 919–1000; Laurenza/ Kemp 2019–20).

One of these fascinating descriptions of Leonardo, with which the presence of a large quantity of water in alpine heights could also be explained, reads as follows:

"Man was called by the ancients a lesser world. Certainly, this designation is quite correct, because since man is composed of earth, water, air and fire, this earth body resembles him. As man has in himself the bones as the support and framework of the flesh, so the world has the rock as the support of the earth. As man has in himself the lake of blood, where the lungs increase and decrease with the breathing, so the body of the earth has its sea of the world, which also decreases and increases every six hours with the breath of the world. As from the aforementioned blood lake the veins go out and branch through the human body, so the world sea feeds the body of the earth through innumerable water veins." (Richter 1970, § 929)

A few years later, in the *Codex Leicester*, Leonardo again describes the earth as a living being:

"The waters circulate with continuous motion from the lowest depths of the seas to the highest summits of the mountains, not obeying the nature of heavy things, and in this case, they act like the blood in the animate things, which always moves from the sea of the heart and flows to the summit of their heads; and if a vein breaks here, as one sees a vein ruptured in the nose, all of the blood rises from below to the height of the broken

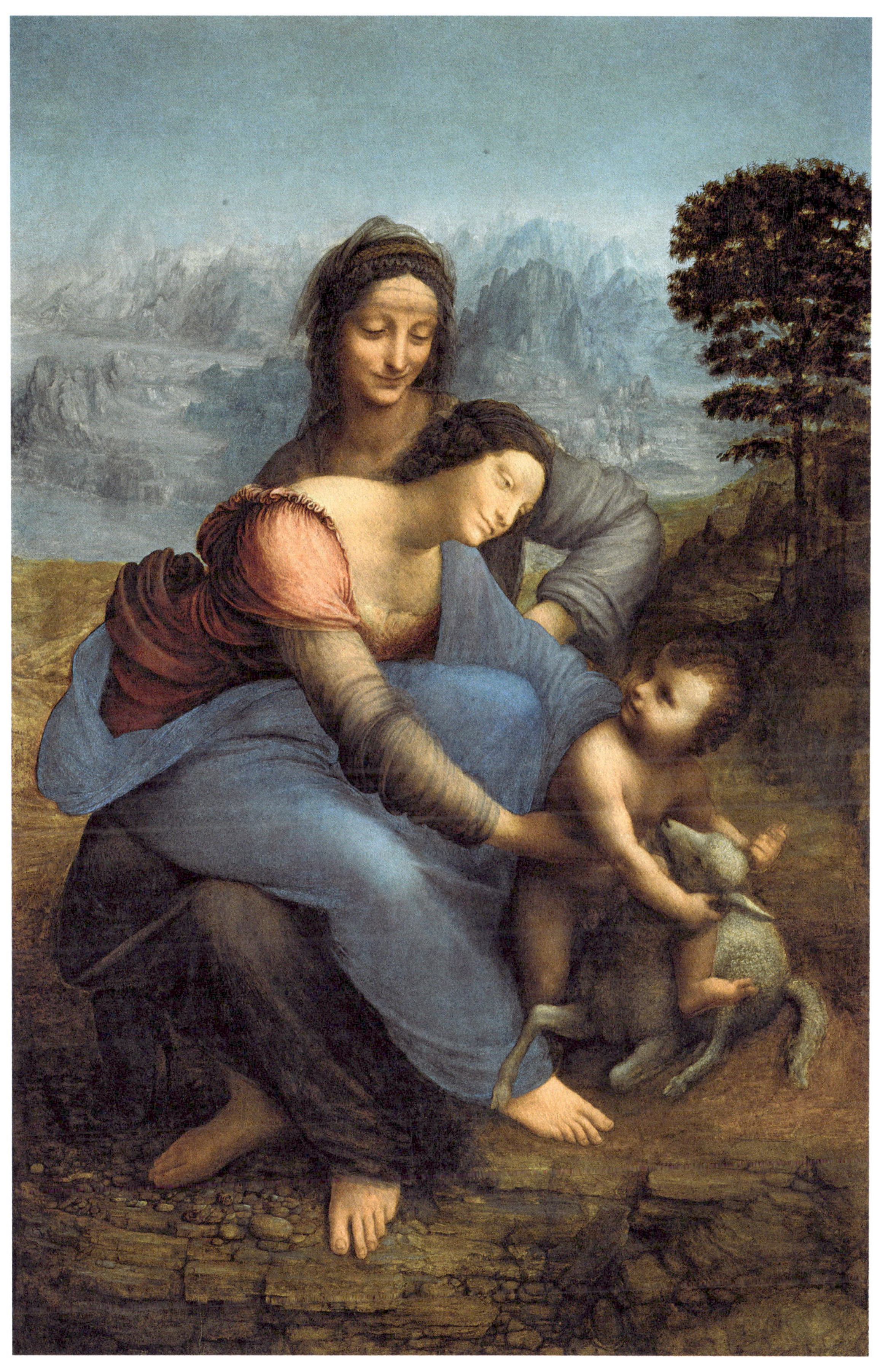

fig. 2 — *The Virgin and Child with Saint Anne*, c.1503–1519, oil on poplar, 168 × 130 cm
Paris, musée du Louvre, inv. 776

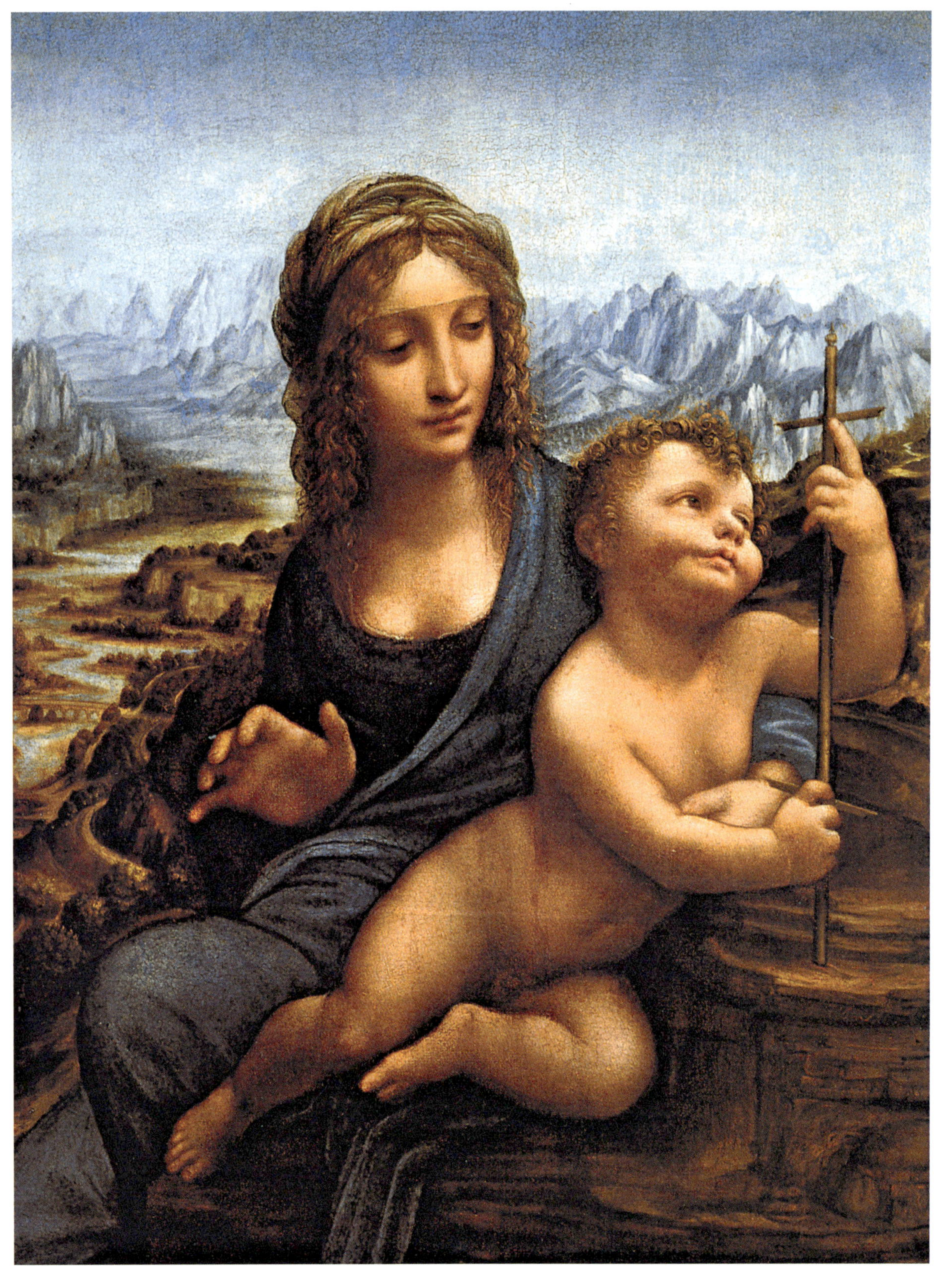

fig. 3 — *Madonna of the Yarnwinder*, c.1501–1507 (?),
oil on panel, after a design by Leonardo, 50.2 × 36.4 cm
New York, private collection

vein ... The veins flow with infinite ramifications through the body of the earth." (*Codex Leicester*, folio 21v; Richter 1970, § 963)

Elsewhere he continues, "The body of the earth like the bodies of animals is interwoven with ramifications of veins, which are all joined together and are formed for the nutrition and vivification of this earth and of its creatures; and they depart from the depths of the sea and to them, after many revolutions, have to return through the rivers created by the high rupture of these veins." (*Codex Leicester*, folio 33v)

Leonardo's views, quoted here at length, may thus help to better understand the striking rock formations and the alpine water reservoir of the *Virgin of the Rocks* from the point of view of his purely artistic and 'scientific' ideas: the clefts of the *Virgin of the Rocks*' background provide, so to speak, a deep insight into the anatomy of the earth. In the second version of this painting, at the beginning of the 16th century, Leonardo once again repeated the motif created in the first version, but at the same time a new phase of landscape depiction now began. In their layout, Leonardo's landscapes appear more monumental, atmospheric and suggestive. This is especially true of *Saint Anne* [fig. 2], begun in around 1503, but finished much later.

In addition to the richness of movement in the composition of *Saint Anne*, the mountain landscape that fills the background, appearing as if it has been raised, is particularly striking. The peaks, blurred in the hazy distance, form a high horizon; on the right side of the picture, they even rise above the head of Saint Anne and appear more monumental than in Leonardo's early paintings. This monumentalisation can be related to the artist's geological and hydrological studies or to his views on the eternal cycle of nature and the origin of the earth. Here the mountain ranges of the background would be seen as continents that had emerged in prehistoric times from the primaeval ocean and had eroded in the course of the time (Zöllner 2019, pp. 191–193, 219; Vai 2021, pp. 309–313). Already towards the end of the 1490s, Leonardo asserts in this matter that "the tops of the mountains are always rising over the course of time." (Richter 1970, § 981)

A few years later, in his Manuscript F, he again describes the formation of the mountains and rock layers, which had been created by the erosive action of the draining water. Here he speculates how the mountains had risen over the sea and how streams of water gradually flowing down from the heights had destroyed the banks of the rivers, until the sheaths of these rivers became steep mountains. And after all the water had drained away, these elevations began to dry and form the rock in layers: "And so, once these hills have drained, they begin to dry and to create layers of stone that are greater or lesser, according to the thicknesses of the muds borne into the sea by the rivers, by means of their floods." (Manuscript F, folio 11v; Laurenza 2019)

The rock slabs, which appear to be piled up, and which are visible at the feet of Anne and Mary as well as at the lower edge of the *Virgin of the Rocks*, correspond to this theory from Leonardo's explanation of the formation of the mountains. The background, in turn, looks like the mountain range rising from the primordial ocean, which Leonardo describes in the above-mentioned reflections on the power of erosion. The landscape behind Saint Anne is thus to be understood as the mountain range emerging from the primordial ocean.

Scientific considerations may also have been at the root of the backgrounds of the *Madonna of the Yarnwinder* [fig. 3] and the *Mona Lisa* [fig. 4]. In the *Madonna of the Yarnwinder*, the deep blue colour of the sky is particularly striking, immediately reminiscent of Leonardo's reflections on the blue colour of the air. He writes about this phenomenon: "Between the sun and us there is darkness, and therefore the air appears blue." (Richter 1970, § 868) Elsewhere he goes on to explain that the moisture particles of the air 'catch' the blue of the luminous rays of the sun: "I say that the azure in which the air shows itself is not its own colour, but it is caused by warm humidity, evaporated in very minute and insensible atoms, which catches behind itself the percussion of the solar rays and makes itself luminous under the vast shades of the region of fire, which acts above like a covering." (*Codex Leicester*, folio 4r)

Leonardo explains that the air appears blue because of the darkness above it from the following observations: "Moreover, as an example of the colour of the air, we will adduce the smoke born from dry and old wood, which, coming out of the chimneys, appears to be strongly azure-tinted when it is located between the eye and a dark place." (*Codex Leicester*, folio 4r) Leonardo believes he makes a similar observation in the view of the mountains: "We can also see in the dark shadows of the mountains far from the eye, that the air, which is between the eye and these shadows, appears very azure ...". In addition, the artist explains in the same place why the air directly above the horizon appears white and further up blue, because directly above the horizon there is more air between the eye and the dark fire region of space than in the zone above.

Based on what has been said so far, it seems reasonable to assume that the design of the background of the *Mona Lisa* [fig. 4] is also related to Leonardo's scientific ideas. In the portrait of Lisa Gherardini, begun in 1503, the landscape background suggests greater spatial depth and atmospheric density than is the case in other portraits of the period. The horizon is elevated, thus monumentalising the landscape. Rugged mountain ranges are lost there in the distance against a green-blue sky. The individual elements of the barren landscape are reminiscent of similar rock formations in his religious paintings. He then seems to have devoted himself very intensively to these landscape depictions in the following years: He kept both the portrait of the *Mona Lisa* and the *Saint Anne* with him until the end of his life, revising the landscape. One reason for this constant reflection of the painter on the subject of landscape is probably to be found in his geological and hydrological studies and thus in his ideas on the anatomy of the earth. As Martin Kemp suggested a few years ago, Leonardo was perhaps focusing here on the prehistoric antecedents of the Arno Valley (Kemp 1981, pp. 263–265).

Leonardo's idea of the anatomy of the earth and his thinking in analogies can thus be understood as one of the starting points for his 'science' of painting. In contrast to the mathematical and thus exact concept of analogy of antiquity, however, Leonardo's thought in analogy was primarily a metaphor. Scientific certainty in a modern sense could not be achieved with it. But the formation of these analogies has in any case led to Leonardo being counted among the most innovative artists and fascinating personalities of the early modern period to this day.

✷

Martin Kemp, *Leonardo da Vinci: The Marvellous Works of Nature and Man*, Oxford, Oxford University Press, 1981.
Domenico Laurenza, Martin Kemp (Eds.), *Leonardo da Vinci's Codex Leicester: A New Edition*, 4 vols., Oxford, Oxford University Press, 2019–2020.
Domenico Laurenza, 'Geology and Anatomy in the Sixteenth–Nineteenth Centuries: Some Suggestions towards a Comparative Analysis', in: *Leonardo da Vinci – Nature and Architecture*, ed. by Constance Moffatt and Sara Taglialagamba, Leiden/ Boston, Brill, 2019, pp. 107–122.
Leonardo da Vinci, *The Manuscripts of Leonardo da Vinci in the Institut de France*. Translated and annotated by John Venerella. Manuscript F, Milan, 2002.
Ivan Marusic, Susan Broomhall, 'Leonardo da Vinci and Fluid Mechanics', in: *Annual Review of Fluid Mechanics*, 51, 2021, pp. 1–25 (https://doi.org/10.1146/annurev-fluid-022620-122816 accessed 16 January 2023 – with bibliography).
Jean Paul Richter (Ed.), *The Literary Works of Leonardo da Vinci*, 2 vols, 3rd ed, Oxford, 1970.
Gian Battista Vai, 'Leonardo da Vinci's and Nicolaus Steno's Geology', in: *Earth Sciences History*, 40 (2), 2021, pp. 293–331.
Frank Zöllner, *Leonardo da Vinci, 1492–1519. The Complete Paintings and Drawings*, Cologne, Taschen, 2019.

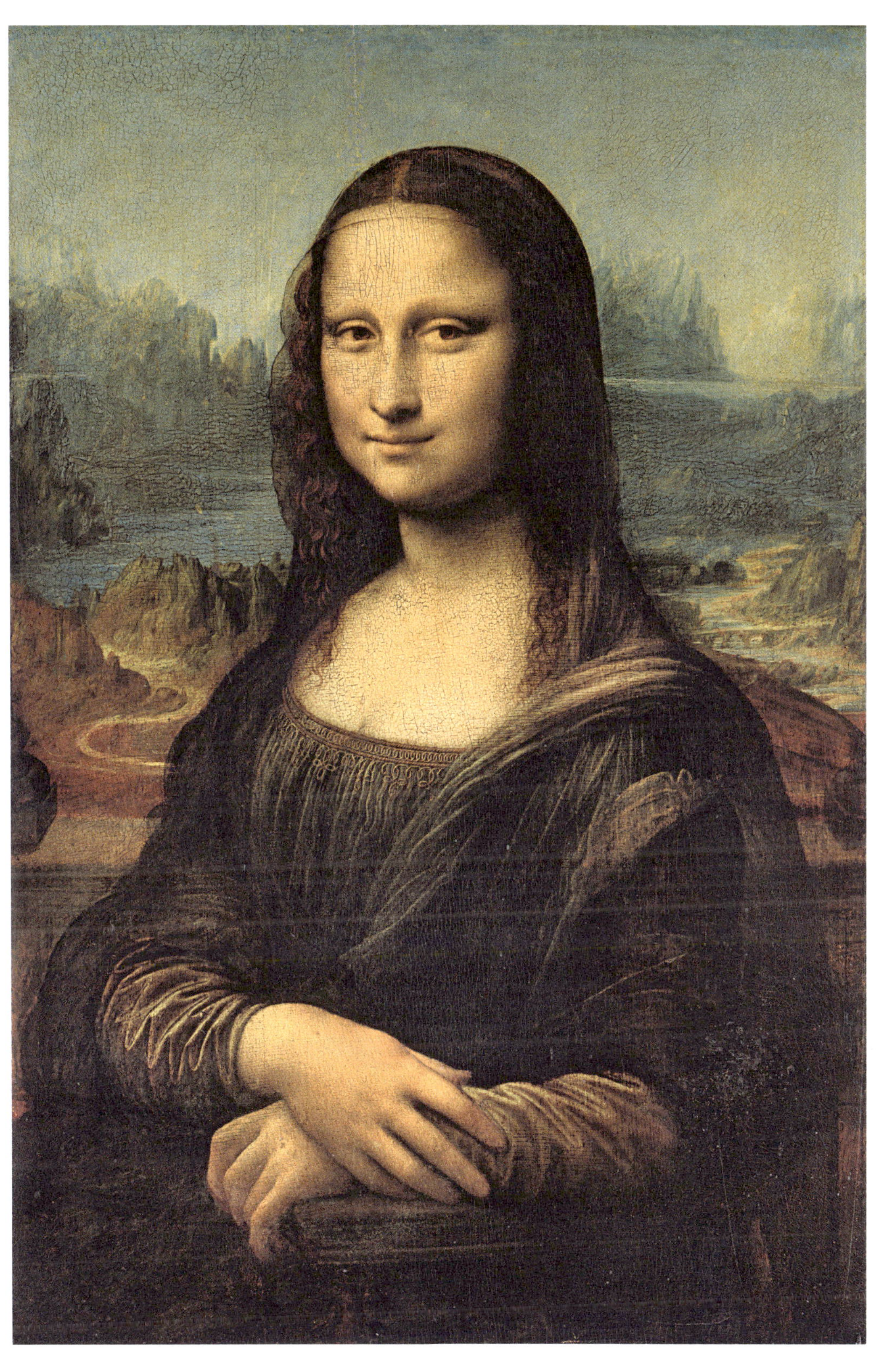

fig. 4 — *Portrait of Lisa del Giocondo* (*Mona Lisa*),
1503–1519, oil on poplar, 79.4 × 53.4 cm
Paris, musée du Louvre, INV 779

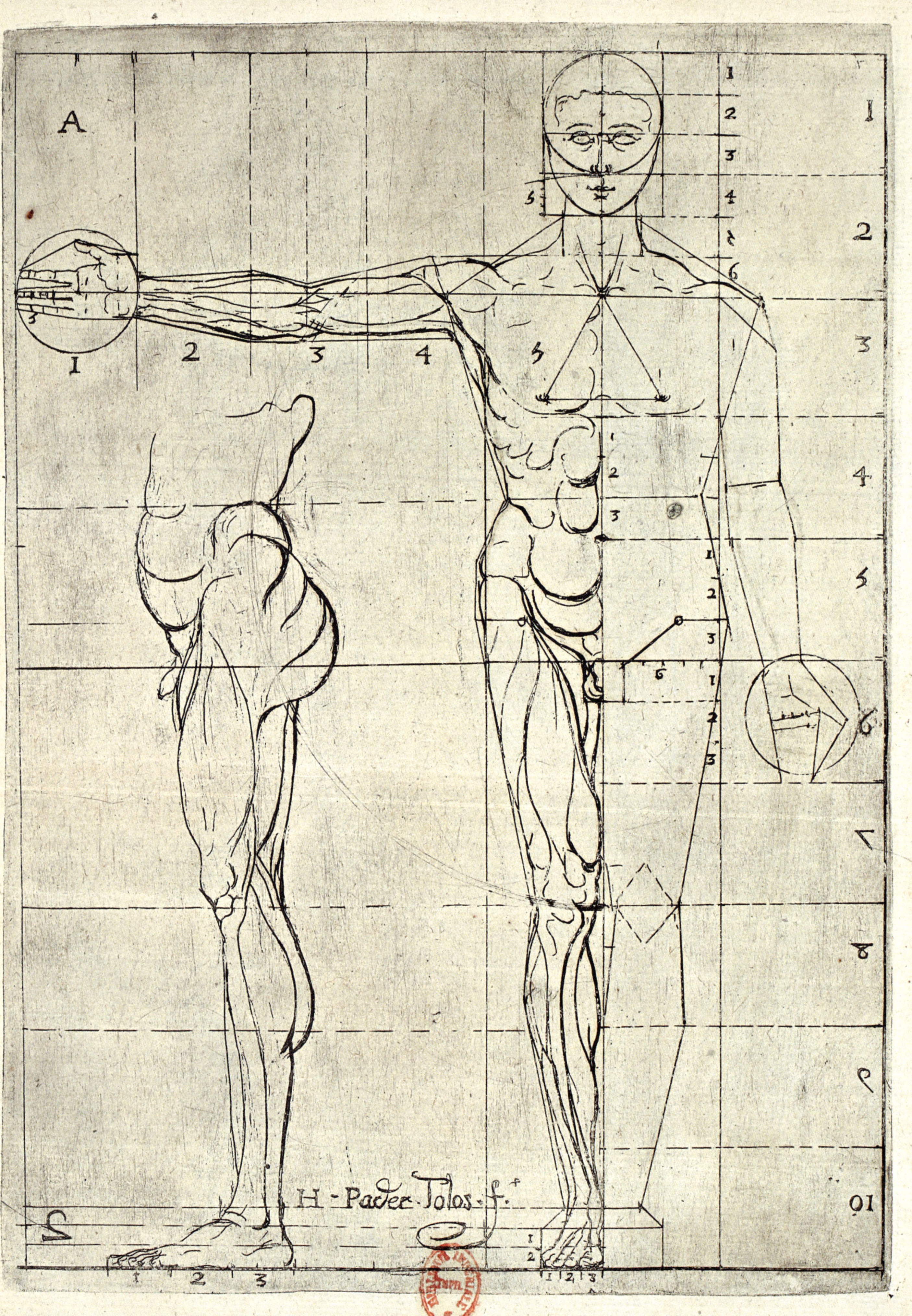
A
H. Pader. Tolos. f.

Representing Anatomy in the *Book on Painting*

Anna Sconza
Lecturer in Italian Studies at Sorbonne-Nouvelle Paris-III University

Previous page:

Treatise on natural and artificial proportion of things, by Jean Pol Lomazzo, translated from Italian to French by Hilaire Pader, 1949, Toulouse, by A. Colomier, pl. [1]

The misfortunes of Leonardo da Vinci as an 'anatomist' are something of a paradox, as critics have shown: although he was an exceptional anatomist, capable of furthering knowledge in this field, he had very little impact on his contemporaries, owing to the limited dissemination of his scientific studies, which remained unpublished, and to the fact that he neither practised officially nor taught in this discipline (Clayton-Philo, 1992). Giorgio Vasari had the rare privilege of seeing Leonardo's anatomical drawings in Vaprio d'Adda, among other folios and manuscripts that his student Francesco Melzi kept as 'treasures'. The biographer describes them with admiration and mentions, in that regard, the friendship between the artist and Marcantonio della Torre, a young professor of anatomy at the University of Pavia in 1509–1510, who died prematurely during the plague of 1511. This meeting with "one of the first to illustrate medical problems through the teachings of Galen" (Vasari, *Lives*, 1568) began Leonardo's reflections on human physiology and allowed him to understand the purposes of organs, including the embryo, which would later have a significant influence on his writings (Laurenza, 2011, pp. 71–72).

During his apprenticeship in Andrea del Verrocchio's studio in Florence, the artist was not familiar with Galen's work, but had probably read Leon Battista Alberti's treatise on painting, which urged painters first to study the skeletal system and then to cover it with muscles and flesh until he reached the superficial anatomy (Alberti, *De pictura*, II, 36; Laurenza, 2003, pp. 34–35). Consistent with these recommendations, Leonardo studied the anatomy on which figurative representation depended, and he placed great emphasis on the importance of learning in detail the muscles and flesh, the nerves and cartilage (*Book on Painting* [106]): "The painter who has obtained a perfect knowledge of the nature of the nerves, muscles and tendons, will know to a certainty, in giving a particular motion to any part of the body, which, and how many of the nerves give rise and contribute to it; and what muscle deflating is the cause of a shortening of the nerves. And what cords, changed into very thin cartilages, surround and contain said muscle."

The *Saint Jerome*, which Leonardo left unfinished when he left Florence in 1482, is the perfect illustration of his early research on the male body of mature years, studied in detail through its bones, nerves and muscles, especially at the clavicle joint.

In the painting treatise conceived by the artist, but produced by his student Francesco Melzi, the question of the representation of anatomy is clearly considered. The composite nature of this *Book on Painting*, a collection of writings that remained in manuscript form, makes it impossible to reconstruct the chronological development of the author's thinking. As the extracts that make up the work express reflections that return to the same subject at different times, the content sometimes appears contradictory. Nevertheless, an understanding of the physiology of the bones that support the flesh was considered a prerequisite to covering the body with drapery. Such thoroughness, nevertheless, does have its limits: only the muscles involved in the movement should be highlighted, if the artist does not want to distort the representation (*Book on Painting* [125]): "O Anatomical Painter! beware lest the too strong indication of the bones, sinews and muscles, be the cause of your becoming wooden in your painting by your wish to make your nude figures display all their feeling. Therefore, in endeavouring to remedy this, look in what manner the muscles clothe or cover their bones in old or lean persons; and besides this, observe the rule as to how these same muscles fill up the spaces of the surface that extend between them ... and which too are the muscles of which the attachments are lost to sight in the very least plumpness."

Even though the study of anatomy may have appeared boundless to Leonardo, like his curiosity, when Melzi organised his master's writings, he kept only what was of use in pictorial representation. The first theoretical part of the *Book* thus likens painting to science and natural philosophy, because of the thorough investigation that characterises it. The discourse then turns to a more practical level in the second part: apprentices must train their hands as well as their memory, knowing that the latter cannot retain all the changes of the body observed during a movement, given that space is a continued quantity divisible *ad infinitum*. It is therefore necessary to hone the eye according to the best conditions of light intensity and with the help of tools allowing the study of the proportions of the body in perspective, such as the *telaio*, illustrated by Albrecht Dürer [fig.1].

Among other themes related to optics and perspective, a wider range of anatomical terms is used in the third part of the *Book*, devoted to the various 'accidents' and movements of the human body, and to the proportions of the limbs. The author focuses in particular on the proportions that evolve with age (measurement, arrangement of the limbs, proportion, proportionality), on the articulations (bone joints) and the thickness of human and animal muscles, whose size varies according to the mechanical effort produced. Each anatomical part can be measured proportionally: as in architecture, this calculation is based on a chosen unit of measurement, the head, according to the traditional nomenclature used in the representation of the Vitruvian man (Perissa Torrini, 2009, p. 38). Also in the *Book on Painting*, a well-proportioned body in adulthood corresponds to ten times its head; it is interesting to note that these proportions were still used by Lombard painters long after Leonardo's death, and were taken up by Giovanni P. Lomazzo (*Trattato*, 1585, I, vi), translated and illustrated in the following century by Hilaire Pader (*Traicté*, 1649, chap. VI–VIII), and by Gregorio Comanini (*Il Figino, overo del fine della pittura*, 1591).

Illustrations, although rare, play an essential role in the *Book on Painting*: Melzi copied stylised figures through which an imaginary centre line passes to indicate the *equipoise* (which he also calls *weight*), i.e. the point of equilibrium of one or several bodies [fig.2]. Once the balance is disrupted, owing to a twisting movement, an imbalance or a major physical

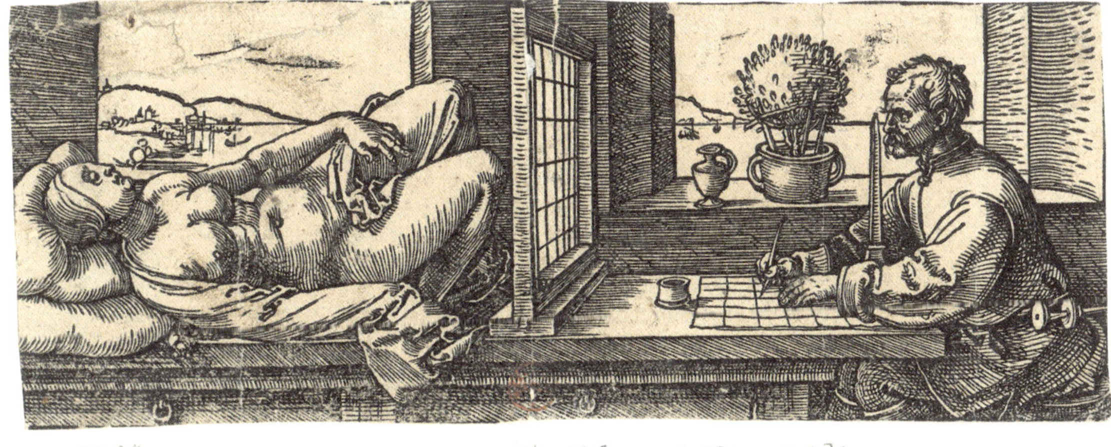

fig. 1 — Albrecht Dürer, *Draughtsman Making a Perspective Drawing of a Reclining Woman*, 1525, wood engraving, 7.5 × 21.5 cm

fig. 2 — *Libro di pittura*, Biblioteca Apostolica Vaticana, *Codex Urbinas Latinus 1270*, folio 128 v, 20.4 × 15 cm

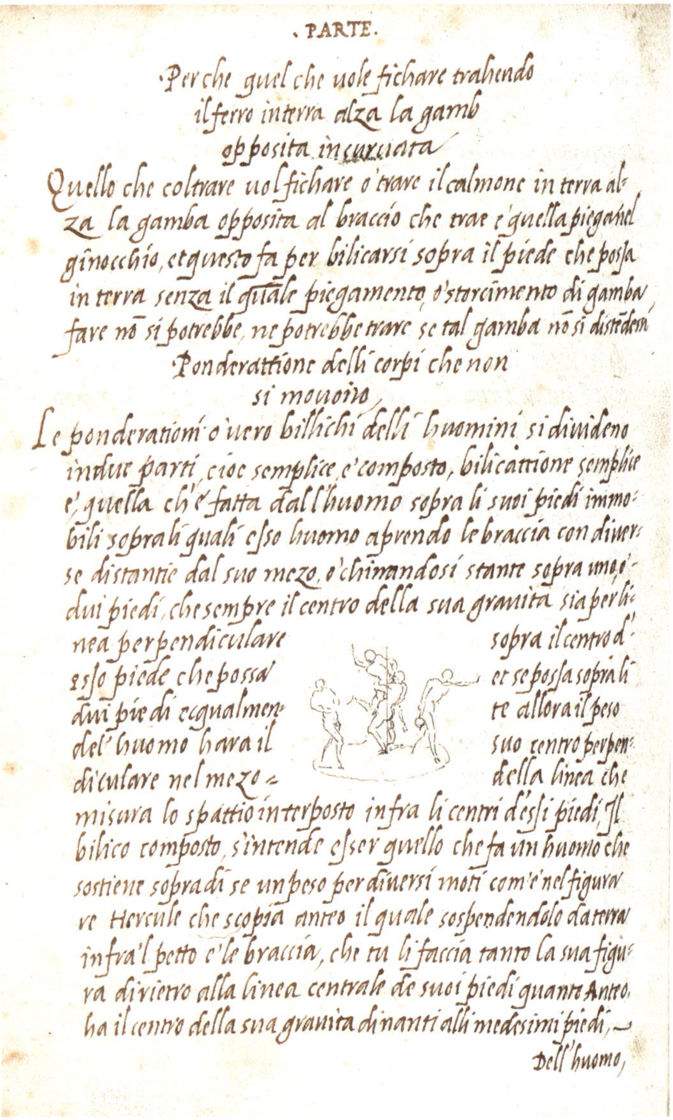

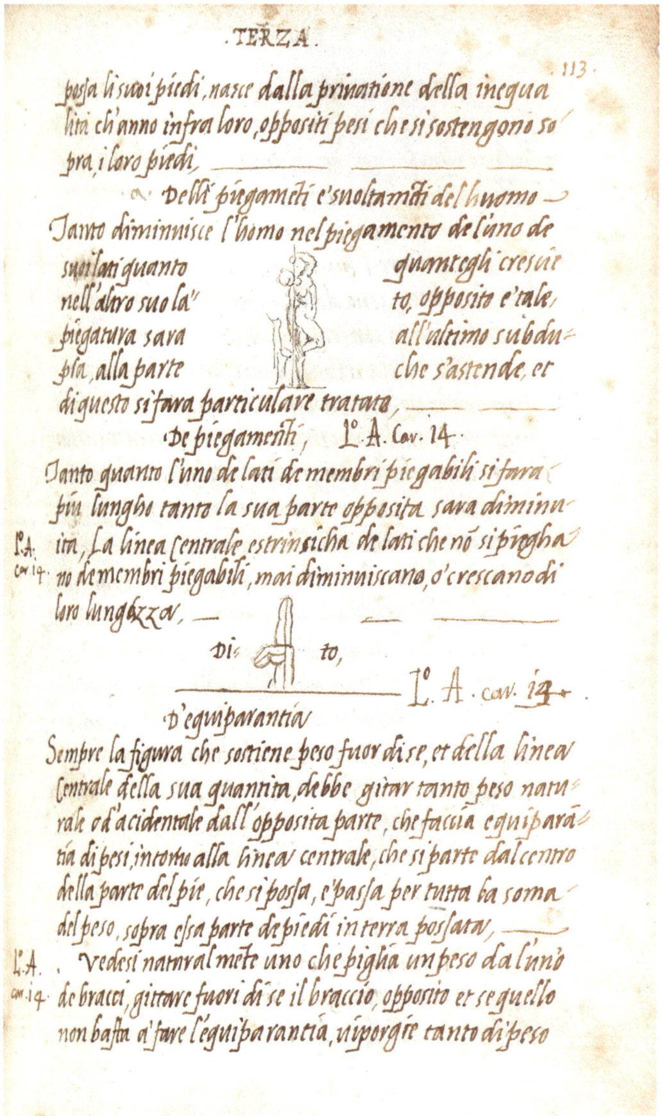

fig. 3 — *Libro di pittura*, Biblioteca Apostolica Vaticana, *Codex Urbinas Latinus 1270*, c.113 r, 20.4 × 15 cm

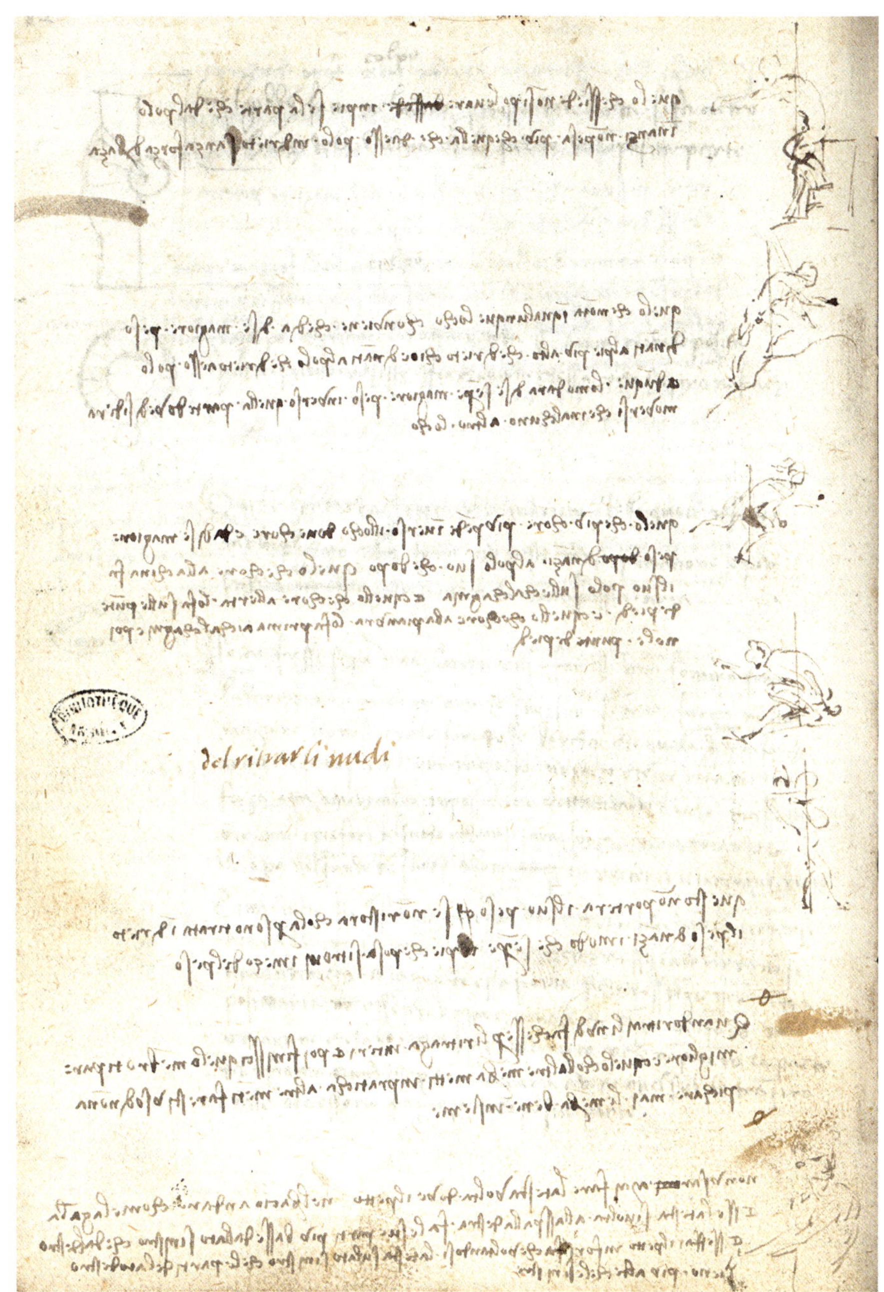

fig. 4 — Manuscript A, Institut de France, folio 28 v

effort, the body's attitude must be broken down using different reference lines, for example the one that goes from the throat to the foot [fig.3], in order to identify all the relevant heights of the limbs in the mechanics of the movement. The theme is so dense that Leonardo intended to make it a treatise in its own right, and reflected in his notebooks both in words and images: the few details identified in short comments, such as on the supporting foot, the inclination of the limbs, the lines of force of a movement, are reproduced through the dynamics of the movement in sketches that give the impression of having been taken from life [fig.4]. Melzi takes up this double language when he transcribes texts that would otherwise have been lost, accompanying them with drawings [fig.5]. The third part of the *Book* is, therefore, illustrated with a succinct collection of small drawings and geometric diagrams explaining the mechanics of the muscles that give rise to movement. This is, of course, a far cry from the highly detailed drawings of the Anatomical Manuscript A, which separate the skeletal and nervous systems from the other anatomical elements and reconstruct the data collected from the dissection of cadavers in extremely accurate illustrations (Laurenza, 2003, pp. 50–52). Such plates could have illustrated an anatomical treatise using copperplate engravings ('*typis æneis*'), as suggested by Paolo Giovio in his *Life* of Leonardo da Vinci (1527); however, the cost and time required for this elaborate technique may explain why such a project to create a map of the human body was abandoned. This left the field clear for the groundbreaking work of Andreas Vesalius, the influential *De humani corporis fabrica*, published in Basel in 1543. Probably in these same years, Francesco Melzi also began preparing the treatise on painting planned by his master, with the intention of including, albeit not in a systematic manner, thoughts on artistic anatomy. When drawing the rough sketches, Leonardo may have kept in mind the technical problem of reproducing the illustrations and, foregoing the calligraphic precision of his anatomical drawings, drew human figures of reduced size with intense movements, as well as diagrams that would be easy to engrave on wood (Pedretti, 1964, p. 140).

The cause of the representation also includes the 'inner motor' that generates the action, namely the emotions or *affections of the soul*: they are to be apprehended in their effects, that range from folds of the body to the expressions of the face, that also reflect the nature of the individual. They are in this case movements triggered by the brain, *acts* or *accidents of the mind*, analogous to the atmospheric *accidents* that disrupt the equilibrium of the Earth (Laurenza, 2001, p. 158–159). In order to capture the scene being observed more quickly, Leonardo advises apprentices to build up a repertoire of physiognomic details useful for reconstructing the figure after observation, and gives the example of various types of nose. With the vivacity of living beings as his goal, Leonardo suggests studying the body language of mutes in the representation of figures. By applying, in this way, the topos of the mute eloquence of painting to the letter, the artist should learn from those who express their thoughts by the gestures of their hands, the movements of their eyes, the frown of their eyebrows, and by their whole body. Indeed, a detailed study of the face, in the imperceptible passage from laughter to tears for example, adds to the appropriateness of the gestures (*harmony of the actions*) in everyday movements, and ensures at the same time the variety necessary for the composition.

✸

Martin Clayton, Ron Philo, *Leonardo da Vinci. The Anatomy of Man*, trans. by Caroline Rivolier, Paris, Seuil, 1992.
Domenico Laurenza, *De figura umana. Fisiognomica, anatomia e arte in Leonardo*, Florence, Olschki, 2001.
Domenico Laurenza, *La ricerca dell'armonia. Rappresentazioni anatomiche nel Rinascimento*, Florence, Olschki, 2003.
Domenico Laurenza, 'In Search of a Phantom. Marcantonio della Torre and Leonardo's Late Anatomical Studies', in *Leonardo da Vinci's anatomical world*, ed. A. Nova and D. Laurenza, Proceedings of the Florence colloquium (Kunsthistorisches Institut in Florenz, Max-Planck-Institut), Venice, Marsilio, pp. 61–77.
Carlo Pedretti, *Leonardo da Vinci on Painting. A lost book (libro A)*, intro. K. Clark, Berkeley and Los Angeles, University of California Press, 1964.
Leonardo l'uomo Vitruviano fra arte e scienza, ed. A. Perissa Torrini, exhibition catalogue, Venice, Gallerie Dell'Accademia, Venice, Marsilio, 2009.

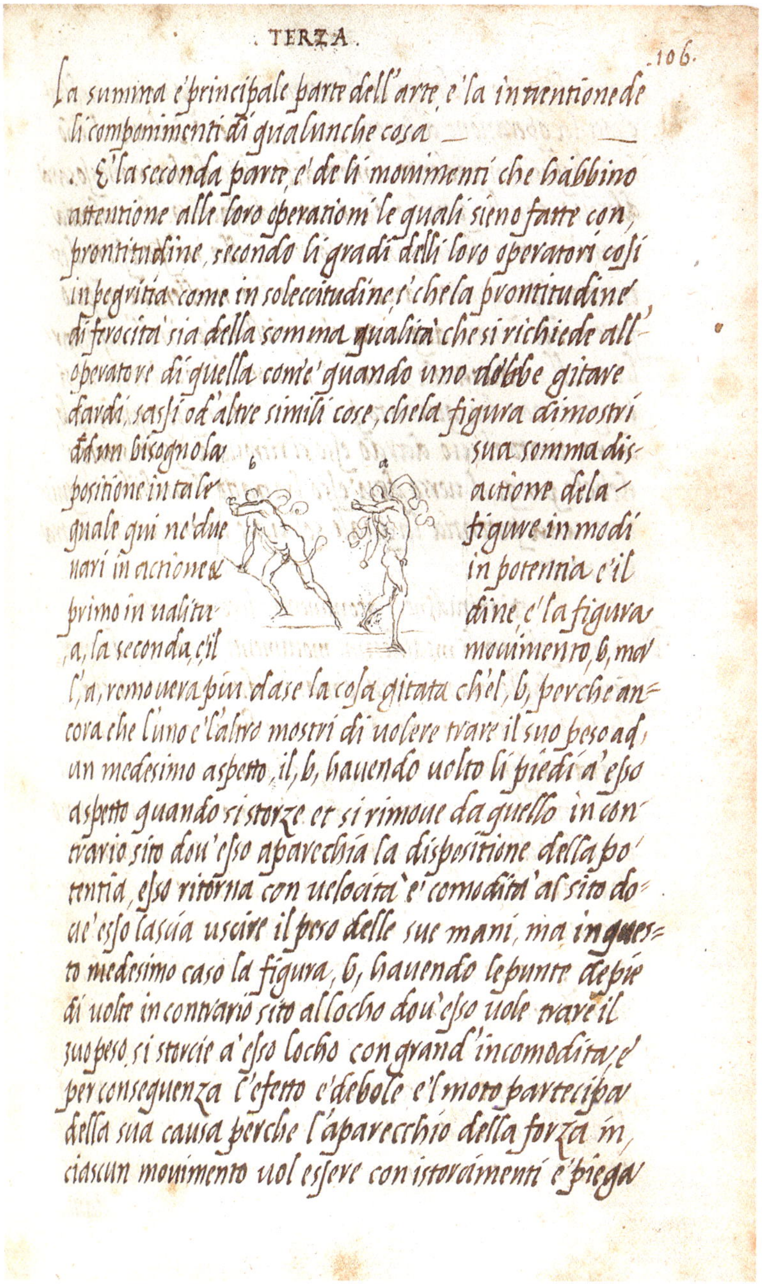

. TERZA . .106.

La summa e principale parte dell'arte, e la intentione de li componimenti di qualunche cosa

E la seconda parte, e de li mouimenti che habbino attentione alle loro operationi le quali sieno fatte con prontitudine, secondo li gradi delli loro operatori così in pegritia come in solecitudine, e che la prontitudine di ferocità sia della somma qualità che si richiede all'operatore di quella, come quando uno debbe gitare dardi, sassi od altre simili cose, che la figura dimostri d'un bisogno la sua somma dispositione in tale actione de la quale qui ne due figure in modi vari in actione e in potentia, e'l primo in ualitudine, e la figura a, la seconda, e'l mouimento, b, ma l'a, remouera più da se la cosa gitata ch'el, b, perche ancora che l'uno e l'altro mostri di uolere trare il suo peso ad un medesimo aspetto, il, b, hauendo uolto li piedi a esso aspetto quando si storze et si rimoue da quello in contrario sito dov'esso aparecchia la dispositione della potentia, esso ritorna con uelocità e comodità al sito doue esso lascia uscire il peso delle sue mani, ma in questo medesimo caso la figura, b, hauendo le punte de piedi uolte in contrario sito al locho dou'esso uole trare il suo peso, si storcie a esso locho con grand'incomodità, e per consequenza l'effetto e debole e'l moto partecipa della sua causa perche l'aparecchio della forza in ciascun mouimento uol essere con istorcimenti e piega

fig. 5 — *Libro di pittura*, Biblioteca Apostolica Vaticana, *Codex Urbinas Latinus 1270*, c.106 r, 20.4 × 15 cm

Building on the Past to Create the Future

Laetitia Guezennec
Marketing and Communication Manager, Dassault Systèmes

Dassault Systèmes, a leading company providing solutions for innovation, offers exclusive experiences – such as the creation of virtual worlds – for its customers and partners. Its aim is to achieve a new development model to address the major challenges facing the world today, drawing on practical solutions and various branches of science – mathematics, biology, chemistry, physics, geology. For 30 years, the company has led the global field in multidisciplinary, multiscale solutions.

In early 2023, Professor Pascal Brioist asked Dassault Systèmes to create video materials for the exhibition *Leonardo da Vinci and Anatomy, the Mechanics of Life* that he was co-curating, to take place in June 2023 at Château du Clos Lucé. The objective was to animate Leonardo da Vinci's anatomical drawings, focusing in particular on the shoulder and on the heart.

Recreating Leonardo da Vinci's sketches in 3D was a way of showcasing to the world the power of virtual twin technology, while also demonstrating how vastly ahead of his time Leonardo da Vinci was in his knowledge of blood circulation. Moreover, this software can also be used to create educational materials and resources to help medical professionals and patients, as well as innovators, designers and engineers, to gain a deeper understanding of the human body.

The Process of Recreating Leonardo da Vinci's Sketches in 3D

The recreation of the drawings into 3D models was performed by the 3DEXPERIENCE Lab team in India, who leveraged useful 3D apps as well as powerful hardware, with which it was possible to create such video clips.

The process and workflow were very straightforward. The very first step was to examine as many details as possible from the drawings and then compare them with actual scientific or biological images available today. There are some areas of the body that Leonardo did not draw or did not provide information on, so in this case reference images come in handy.

The engineers went on aligning the available images in the 3DEXPERIENCE platform with the help of Sketch Tracer, which has various options to import, align and transform images. With those images on the platform, they began shaping the base structure for both the models in CATIA's Imagine & Shape tool.

X-Shape was also handy in this process, as the engineers could model on the browser itself. Once the base model was complete, more details could be added onto it such as striations in muscles, veins, etc. The most useful feature in CATIA Imagine & Shape is the capability of importing/exporting decimated subdivision surfaces in .obj file format along with material.

In the subsequent steps, the engineers sculpted on top of the base mesh adding more details. Now the fine sculpt can be given a re-topology work, unwrapped, textured and animated. The 3DEXPERIENCE platform allows such models to be imported as common sharable formats together with the UV mapping data.

Next, the image sequence of the animation was rendered and merged together to form the video.

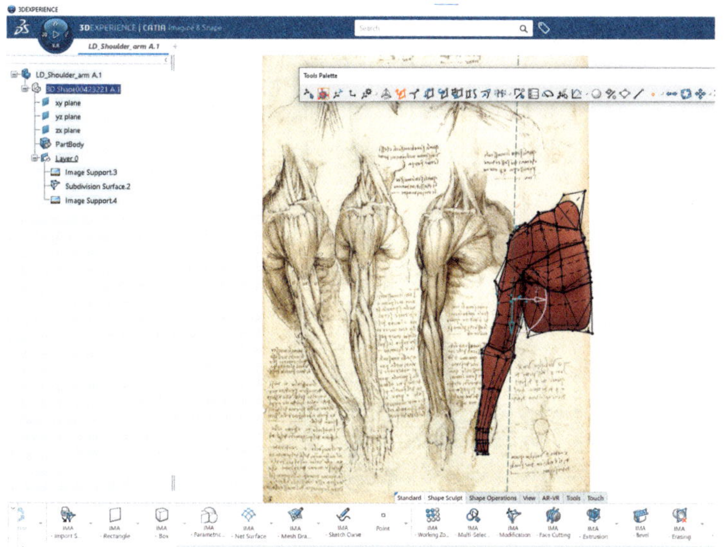

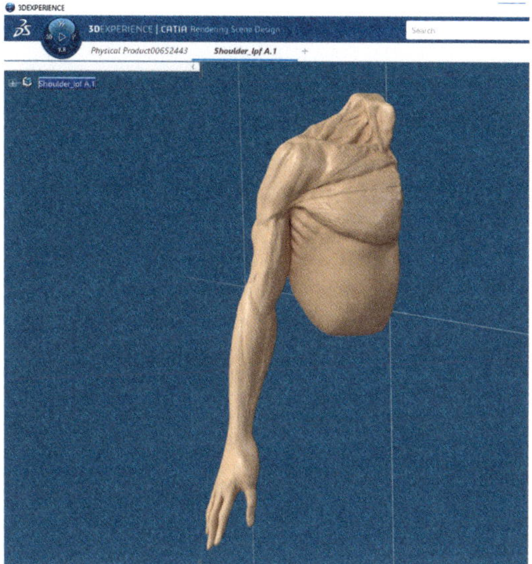

Living Heart Project: The Process of Creating a Realistic 3D Model of a Human Heart

The Living Heart Project aims to advance the development of safe and effective cardiovascular products and treatments by combining engineering, scientific and biomedical expertise to translate cutting-edge science into improved patient care. Through simulation and the creation of validated models, the project aims to provide personalised, interventional patient care.

The Living Heart Project is bringing together leading cardiovascular researchers, educators, medical device developers, regulatory agencies and practising cardiologists on a shared mission to develop and validate highly accurate personalised digital human heart models. These models will establish a unified foundation for cardiovascular *in silico* medicine and serve as a common technology base for education and training, medical device design, testing, clinical diagnosis and regulatory science. This will forge an effective path for rapidly translating current and future cutting-edge innovations directly into improved patient care.

The Living Heart Project allows practitioners to visualise what they cannot see through precise 3D modelling and simulation of an actual heart. The Living Heart Human Model is a high-fidelity multi-physics model of a healthy, 4-chamber adult human heart and proximal vasculature. The response of the Living Heart is governed by realistic electrical, structural and fluid flow physics.

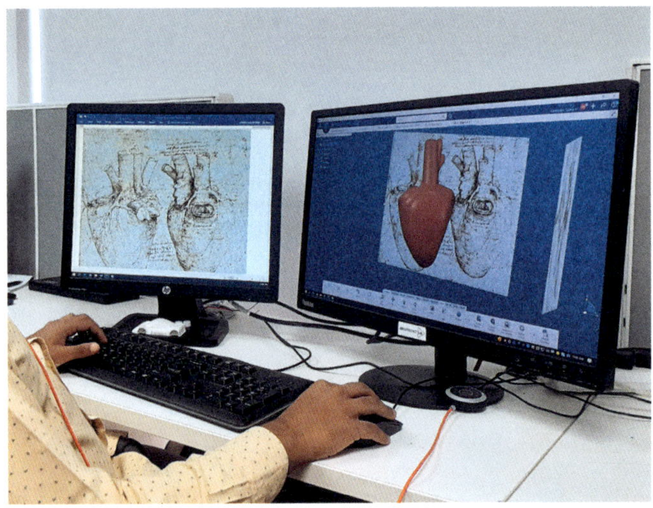

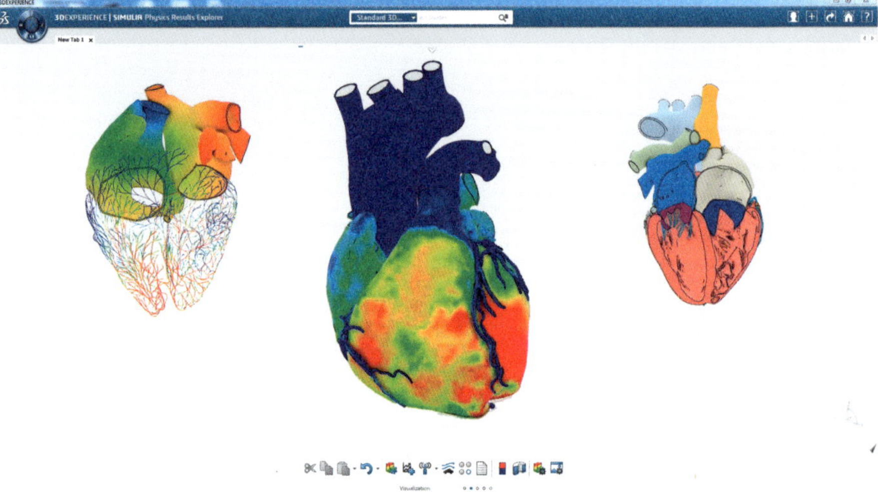

The model comprises a ready-to-execute dynamic, electro-mechanical simulation; refined geometry; a blood flow model; and a complete characterisation of cardiac tissues including passive and active behaviours, its fibrous nature, and electrical pathways.

Backed by the power of the SIMULIA Realistic Simulation software suite, the Living Heart can readily be used to study cardiac defects and diseased states and explore treatment options. Model attributes can be modified or redefined entirely, including the geometry, loads and boundary conditions, and material properties.

The Living Heart Project was launched in 2014 by Steven Levine, Senior Director of Virtual Human Modeling for Dassault Systèmes, following a very personal experience. Levine's daughter was diagnosed with heart disease at a young age, and at that time doctors anticipated that her life would be cut short from the condition. As an engineer working with virtual simulation technology, Levine believed that the heart could be better understood through a different set of tools than the traditional diagnostic methods available at the time.

Leonardo da Vinci, in his time, had sketched the anatomy of the heart and inspired many engineers and scientists. Five hundred years later, the power of virtual twin technology enables scientific simulation including very precise blood flow simulations so that we can better understand how the heart functions, and that can be used for education and training, medical device design, medication testing and clinical diagnosis.

The future will benefit from these new technologies: clinicians and surgeons will have access to a realistic model of a patient's heart, which could greatly improve the level of personalised care they can offer patients.

3DEXPERIENCE Lab by Dassault Systèmes

The 3DEXPERIENCE Lab is the open innovation lab of Dassault Systèmes. It operates worldwide thanks to international networks and locations. It accelerates disruptive startups and innovations that positively impact people and society. It reveals talents, promotes technologies that generate changes, and nurtures collaborative and community projects to experience the unexpected.

The 3DEXPERIENCE Lab supports projects that transform society in a positive way and thus help to achieve the United Nations' Sustainable Development Goals. It aims to be a strategic partner for breakthrough innovations that help to change the world while reducing the ecological footprint. The 3DEXPERIENCE Lab thus supports projects based on themes from everyday life, i.e. cities, lifestyles or life sciences, calling on various innovation levers such as additive manufacturing, big data or virtual reality.

The Partnership between Dassault Systèmes and Château du Clos Lucé

The partnership between Dassault Systèmes and Château du Clos Lucé began more than ten years ago with a digital challenge called the Open Codex project. This project aimed to digitally reconstruct Leonardo da Vinci's inventions from his codex in 3D and put them into 3D experiences. This open innovation approach brings people from different backgrounds together to share their knowledge and recreate da Vinci's machines in 3D to better understand the heritage he left us. The project started in 2012. Thanks to the collective intelligence of the community, it has achieved excellent results. The Open Codex project has brought together enthusiasts and designers from around the world to digitally recreate da Vinci's machines in 3D, including Chuck Ridley, Brian Law, Antonio Camberos, Alain Dugousset, Thibault Waltzer, Vinay Reddy, Aleks Marjanovic, Namkarn Munprasit, Josue Blanco, and Juan Mauricio Zaleta.

Conclusion

The 3DEXPERIENCE Lab would like to thank Professor Pascal Brioist for this opportunity to put its software and technologies at the service of art, history, and Leonardo da Vinci. The 3D videos created have helped promote the partnership between Château du Clos Lucé and Dassault Systèmes.

✷

Selective List of Exhibited Works

Drawing No. 509 A includes two anatomical studies: those of the left half show the neck, shoulders, chest and right arm with the back of the hand of a male body, precisely marked in all the muscular bundles. Those of the right half show the upper part of a male body. The protrusion of the clavicle bone is very evident and in the right upper limb all the muscle bundles are clearly visible. This drawing is related to Leonardo's original, held at Windsor Castle, RL 19008. Moreover, the shoulder, which maintains the arm semi-open to the outside, is also represented in plate RL 19013 in the Royal Library, dated 1508–1511. Both drawings, however, repeat the same sequence on the verso of folio RL 19008: the first on the right is more open, the second, which is also very similar to folio RL 19005 r, is part of the Anatomy Manuscript A, in which the neck, chest and lower limb are studied, from different positions, with the muscles clearly highlighted. The copyist leaves the hands barely sketched, while faithfully respecting the arrangement of the parts of the human body, slightly increasing the space, which Leonardo had filled with his handwritten notes. The copyist repeats the individual parts of the same sheet, drawing them on two distinct supports, but in the spirit of the original as if they were recto and verso.

Drawing 509 B represents anatomical studies of the male lower limbs. It focuses on muscle bundles, the shoulder and neck muscles. The two folios 509 A and 509 B "do not reflect Leonardo's manner" (Pietro Selvatico, 1854). These anatomical drawings, however, do represent a valuable testimony to the 'Vinciano's' interest in anatomical studies. This interest may have been stimulated by the publication of the plates of Vesalius' groundbreaking work, *De humani corporis fabrica*, published in Venice in 1538, a volume that may have encouraged creations of this type in the second half of the century (Luisa Cogliati Arano, 1980). The studies are linked to the verso of Leonardo's drawing RL 19008, which shows, on the right, the same part of the torso and neck, this time without the head, which is turned more to the front. Both reproduce the precise dissections of the neck, typical of the master's anatomical studies, highlighting the *sternocleidomastoid* muscle that divides the neck into two anterior and posterior triangles. The complete study of the bust was engraved by Hollar in 1651. The lower limb replicates with extreme precision the one drawn by Leonardo on the recto of the Windsor, RL 19002 of 1510 also repeated on RL 12627 r. The male half-bust in profile is based on the anatomical study in the lower left quarter of the verso of the same folio in the Royal Library at Windsor.

Domenico Laurenza speculates that both drawings may derive from a variation of Leonardo's now lost Anatomical Manuscript A drawings, perhaps part of that "book drawn in red chalk and stippled with pen" mentioned by Vasari.

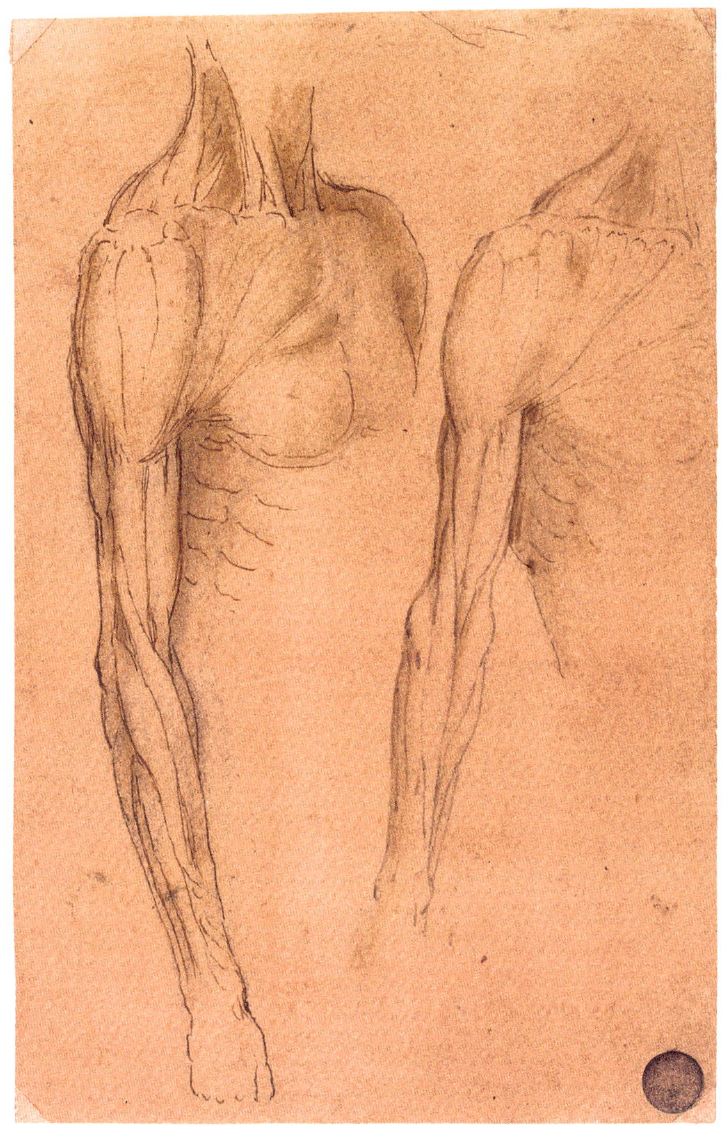

Anonymous 16th century follower of Leonardo
Anatomical studies, first half of 16th century
Inks, black stone on dyed pink paper
20.3 × 13.2 cm
Gallerie dell'Accademia di Venezia,
Cabinet of Drawings and Prints, inv. 509 A

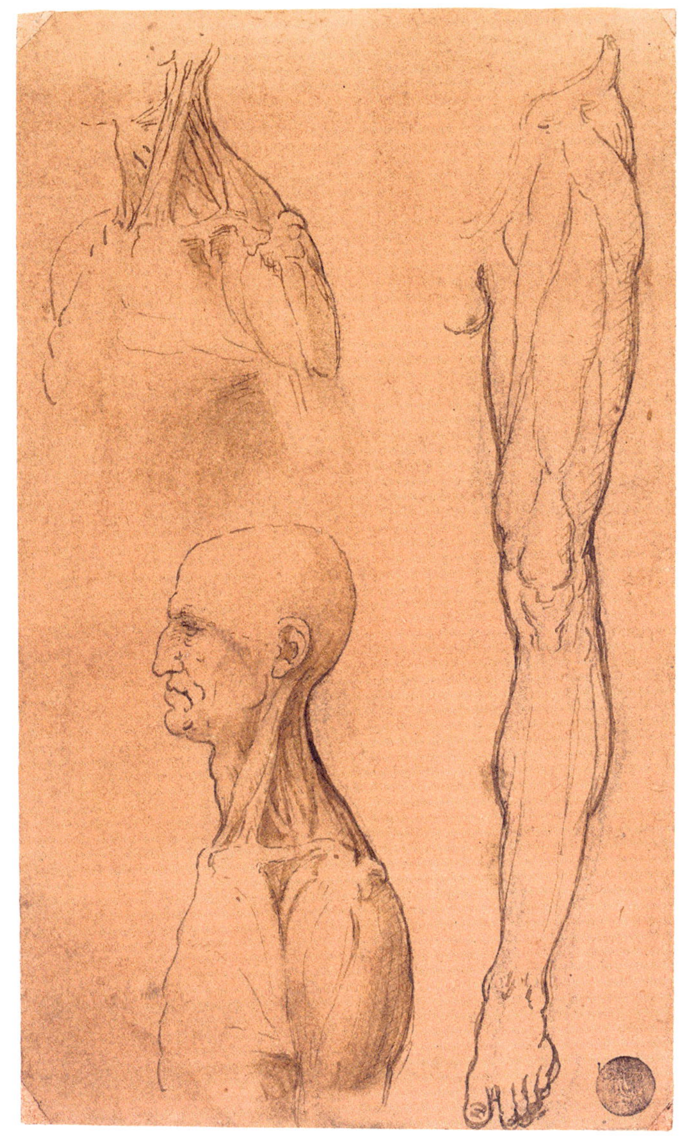

Anonymous 16th century follower of Leonardo
Anatomical studies, first half of 16th century
Inks, watercolour ink, black stone
on dyed pink paper, 21.1 × 12.9 cm
Gallerie dell'Accademia di Venezia,
Cabinet of Drawings and Prints, inv. 509 B

Provenance: Francesco Melzi collection; Cardinal Cesare Monti 1770; Venanzio de' Pagave 1777; Giuseppe Bossi 1818; Luigi Celotti 1822. Collectible stamps: Accademia (Lugt 188). Bibliography: *Drawings by Leonardo* 1966, p. 64; Klee, Pedretti, 1979, III, p. 3; *Drawings by Leonardo* 1980, p. 19, p. 25; Pedretti 2000, p. 145; A. Perissa Torrini, in *Drawings by Leonardo* 2003, No. 57. Exhibitions: Venice 1980, Nos. 28 and 29.

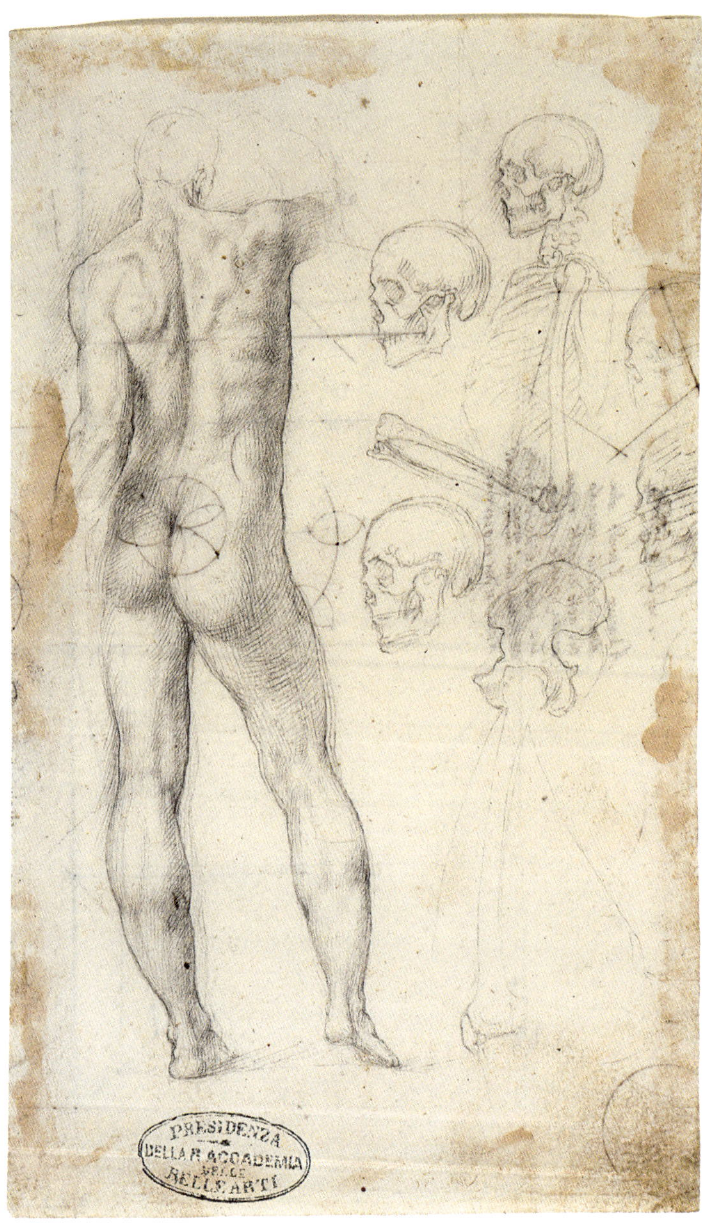

Giovanni Ambrogio Figino
Study of a figure from behind, c.1587
Lunulae, skeletons, black stone on paper, 23.5 × 14.2 cm
Gallerie dell'Accademia di Venezia, Cabinet of Drawings and Prints, inv. 943

Giovanni Ambrogio Figino (1552/1553–1608) is a Milanese student of Giovanni Paolo Lomazzo, who collaborated on fresco and altarpiece projects with some of Leonardo's disciples, including Bernardino Luini. Figino is known for his vast graphic output; 430 drawings can be attributed to him. Conversely, the number of his pictorial works is low. Figino learned from Lomazzo the revered traditions of Leonardo, which his master encouraged, in particular, with his work as a writer of treatises. The anatomical drawings of his youth, although influenced in their thematic choices and their modes of presentation by the famous originals of Leonardo, are recognisable for their graphic control and their *chiaroscuro* counterpoint. Thus they appear perfectly aligned with the drawings of the end of the 16th century in their Tuscan-Roman manner, more akin to Michelangelo. Figino, who draws in the manner of Leonardo, does not hesitate to express his own graphic style, as did Cesare da Sesto, also a disciple of Leonardo.

Drawn on the right side of the folio are a skeleton, in profile, to the knee joint, and four skulls in profile, two of which are partially sketched. A male nude, seen from behind, occupies the left side. He is shown with a double contour line, one lighter, the other stronger, common to many drawings, well highlighted as is the rendering of the profile of the right thigh. The figure, with its distinctive twisted form, is constructed with vigorous and elegant strokes of *chiaroscuro*. Note the considerable muscular tension in maintaining the position assumed by the figure, with the weight of the body borne on the left leg and the back slightly arched, in keeping the right arm raised forward. The body is skilfully modelled through shading, short and compact lines where many short muscles are involved, such as those of the back and shoulders and longer at the level of the legs, whose lines are often hatched. The posture of the figure depicted clearly references that of an *écorché* figure that appears in a panel from Andrea Vesalius' *De humanis corporis fabrica*, book VI, plate I, from the epitome published by Plantin in 1566. The image was later included in the 1568 edition of Valverde's *Anatomia*. This folio would seem to be attributable to Giovanni Ambrogio Figino's early maturity.

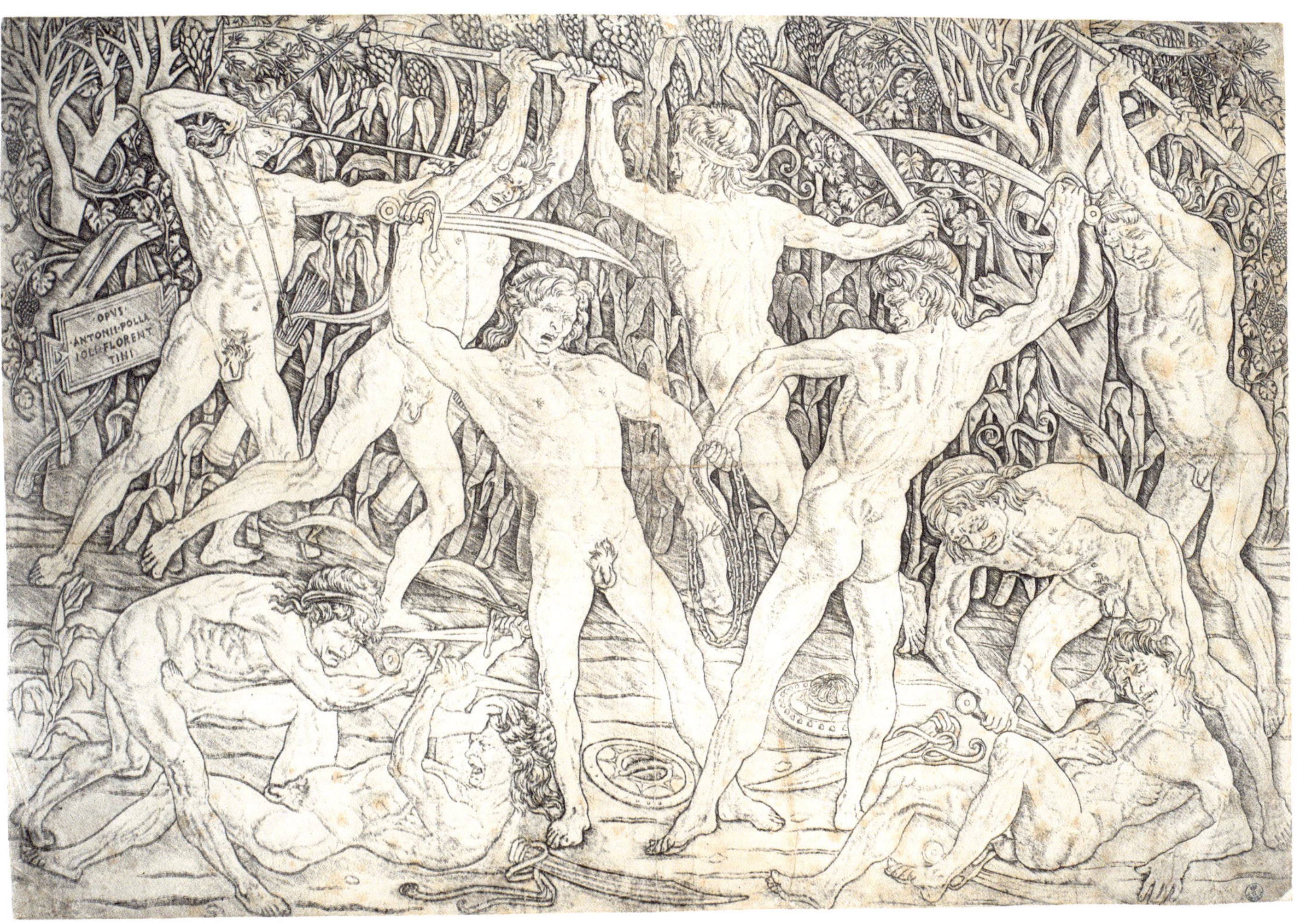

Antonio Benci, also known as Antonio del Pollaiolo or Pollaiuolo
Battle of the Nudes, c.1460-1475, burin engraving , 38.3 × 59.5 cm
Gallerie degli Uffizi, Department of Prints and Drawings, No. 124e. sc.

Battle of the Nudes highlights a type of heroic figure common in Pollaiuolo's (1431/1432–1498) work. It is probably the most famous and highly regarded image of early Italian engravings. What sets Pollaiuolo apart is his rigorous expression of the nude form, whose musculature is well defined, almost sculptural.

Not since antiquity had so much importance been given to the mere appearance of the human body stripped of all artifice, nor had such potential for expression been recognised. Henceforth in the Renaissance, no one could contemplate depicting a clothed or draped figure without having first studied the naked form.

Several features mark this engraving as a major work of art: the burin technique exalts the silhouette of the figures (Pollaiuolo, a great connoisseur of human anatomy, is the first to show how to represent the muscles in a realistic and accurate manner); the use of vegetation in the background, as in tapestries; the monumental figures with faces distorted by violence and hatred expressing a high degree of dramatic intensity...

Although the schematic form of the nude does not reflect the interior of the human body (an aspect that was fundamental in Leonardo's work), according to Giorgio Vasari in his *Lives of Artists*, Pollaiuolo was thought to be the first Renaissance artist to have dissected a human cadaver.

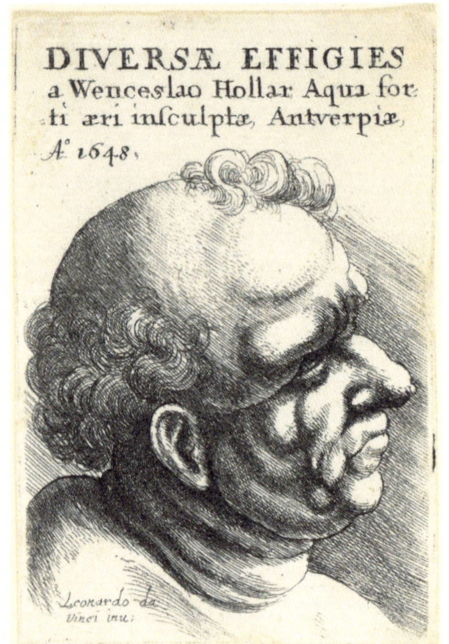

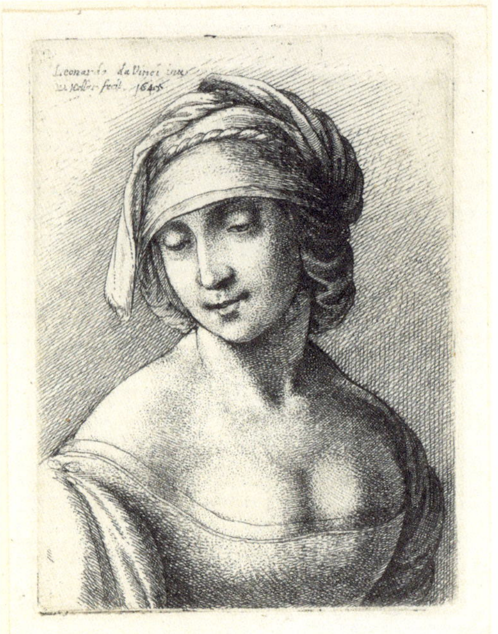
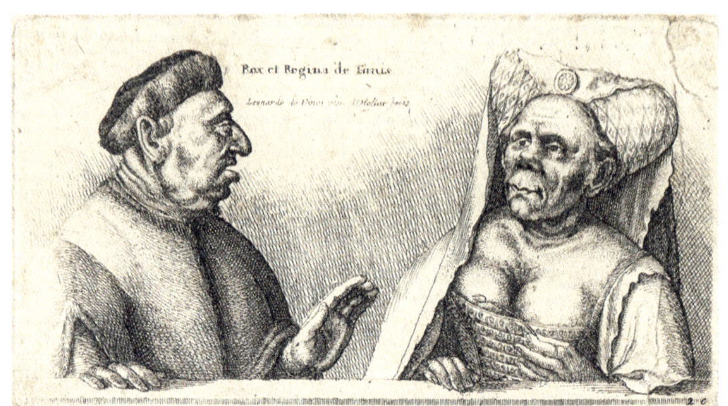
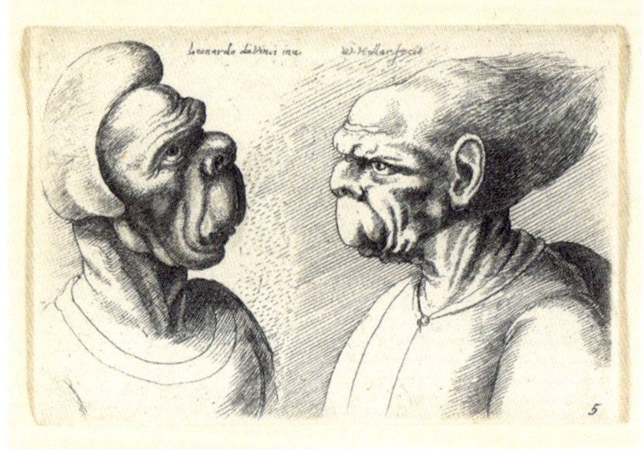
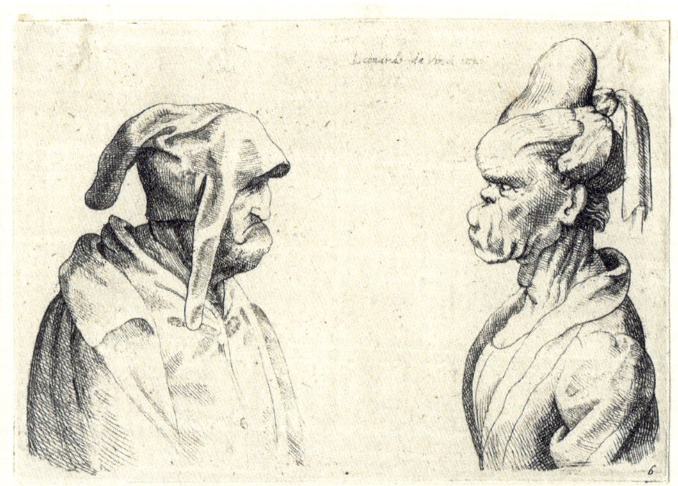

Wenceslaus Hollar
Etchings taken from Lord Arundel's collection, displaying grotesque heads, 1645
Etchings, various dimensions
Private collection, Château du Clos Lucé

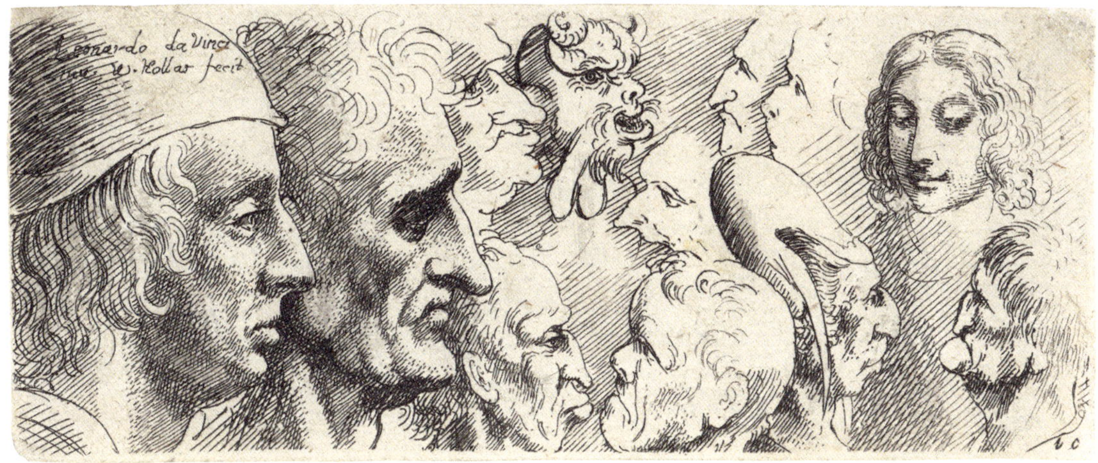

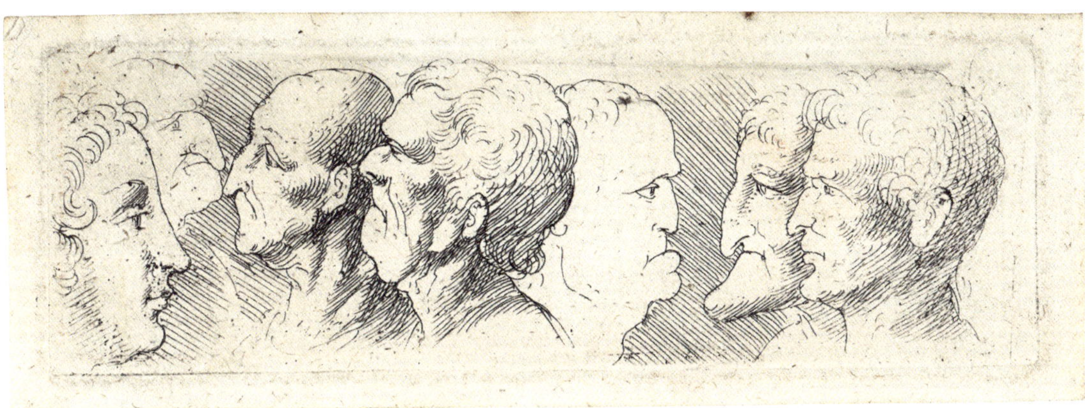

In 1645, the Bohemian artist Wenceslaus Hollar (1607–1667) published some thirty-one etchings in Antwerp based on drawings of grotesque heads by Leonardo present in London in the collection of Thomas Howard, Earl of Arundel, for whom he worked over the period 1636–42. The etchings were produced by Hollar in 1645 in Holland, where the Earl died in 1646, after which his collection of drawings was broken up. There were about sixty-three etchings from Leonardo drawings according to the research carried out by Pennington (1982), listed in his catalogue of Hollar's engravings from number 1558 to 1610B and 1768 to 1774, but further investigations could still bring more to light.

Hollar's *Varie Figurae* are based on what were recognised as autograph drawings by Leonardo da Vinci, as attested by the reference 'ex collezione Arundelliana' for each etching, referring to their former owner.

The best-known model among Hollar's etchings is that of a 'dialogue' between two juxtaposed figures, generally one male and one female, characterized by deformed and sometimes monstrous features. Hollar also made etchings from the master's original drawings of anatomical details, children's heads and religious subjects, such as the well-known *Salvator Mundi* and the head of St Anne. His etchings do not follow the drawings exactly but interpret their most striking characteristics, not least through the choice of by no means fortuitous combinations, such as the juxtaposition of young and old or male and female heads, working nearly always through difference and practically never through similarity.

A significant example is the one entitled *Rex et Regina de Tunisi*, where the two figures are engaged through gestural accentuation in an authentic dialogue. While the 'king' in profile displays no particular physical aberrations, his normality is offset by the grotesque appearance of the 'queen' in a bizarre two-horned headdress delicately holding a slender flower. While the original by Leonardo has been lost, there is a copy in the Royal Collection at Windsor (RL 12492) attributed to Francesco Melzi. The subject enjoyed great popularity, reappearing in an engraving by Pastorini for Chamberlaine's series of drawings from the Royal Collection, published in London in 1806, and in an illustration by John Tenniel for Lewis Carroll's *Alice's Adventures in Wonderland* (Vezzosi, 1999, p. 52).

With their deft modulation of line to create *chiaroscuro*, Hollar's etchings offer a model for the reproduction of drawings not confined to those of Leonardo. The publication of 1645 was followed by further etchings of grotesque drawings, such as the one dated 1646 of five male heads based on an original in the Royal Library at Windsor (RL 12495 r). This clearly satirical composition, bearing the indication 'ex raccolta Arundelliana', could represent the chaos and madness of humankind surrounding a dignified central figure iconographically similar to a classical profile of the Caesar kind.

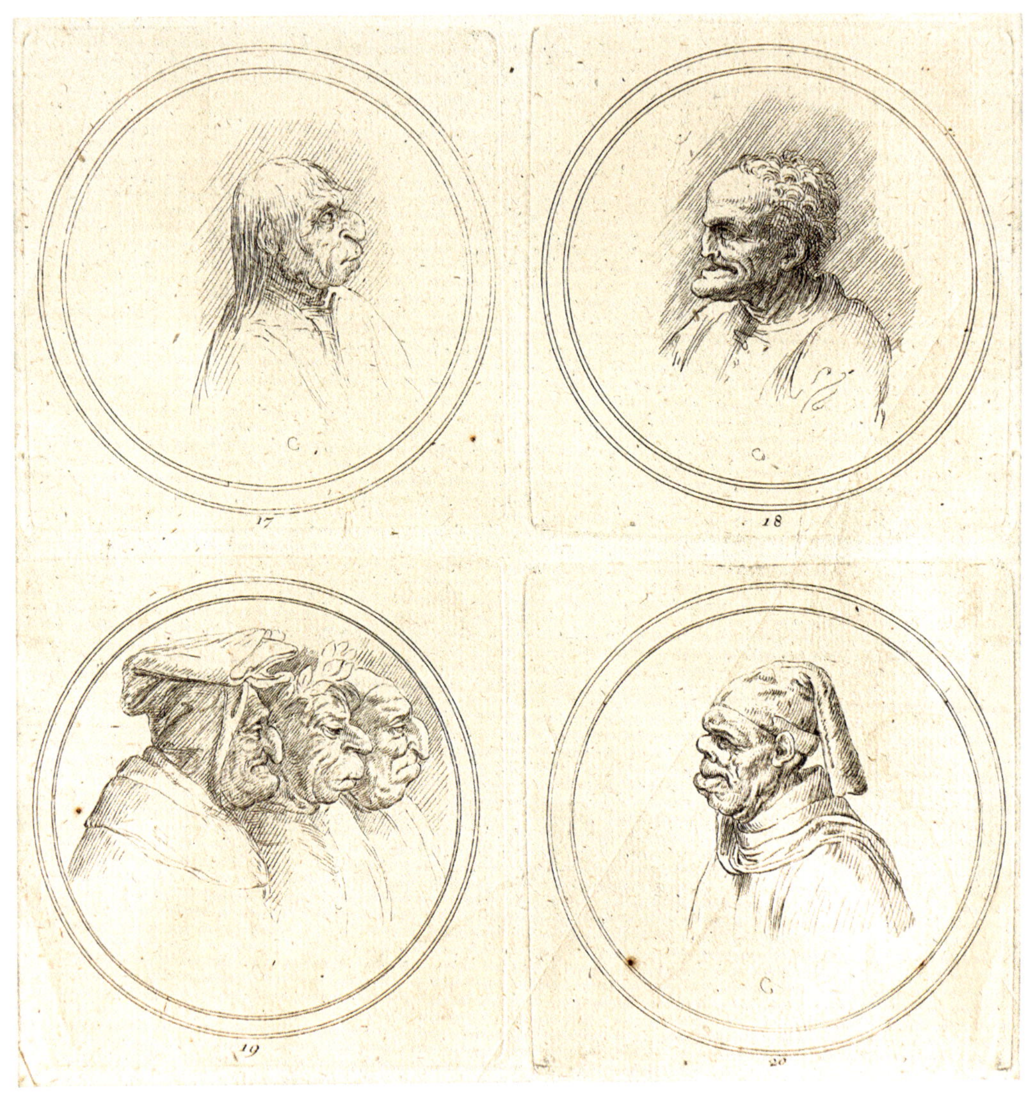

Collection of Grotesque Heads and Caricatures
drawn by the Florentine Leonardo da Vinci
and engraved by M. le C. de C., known as the "Caylus Album", 1730
Etchings
Private collection, Château du Clos Lucé, folio 22 R (n° 17, 18), folio 23 R (n° 19, 20)

The album consists of fifty-one folios. The sixty-seven etchings that it contains are engraved by Anne-Claude-Philippe de Tubières de Grimoard de Pestels de Lévis, count de Caylus, based on the collection of drawings owned by Pierre-Jean Mariette, and adhering to the same dimensions. They are numbered and follow the order of the album of drawings up to number 38.

The plates are numbered from 1 to 59, but only numbers 1 to 54 and folio 45, the *Cigoli*, are based on drawings of the Mariette Album. Numbers 39 to 52 are square for the drawings and circular for the prints (most have the initial C for Caylus engraved at the bottom, sometimes inside, sometimes outside the circles surrounding the composition).

In the catalogue, Mariette speaks of the album of fifty-nine plates that he had made by Caylus. The collection in the Louvre contains sixty-seven plates; the other copies of the 1730 edition all have some variations. This practice was common before the mechanisation of printing.

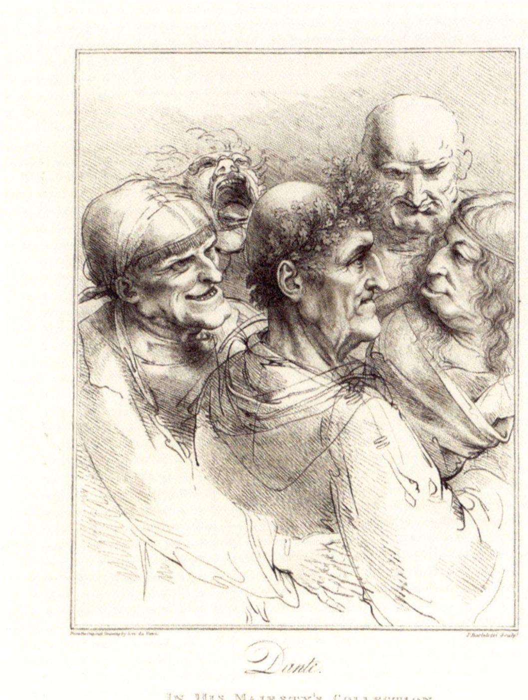

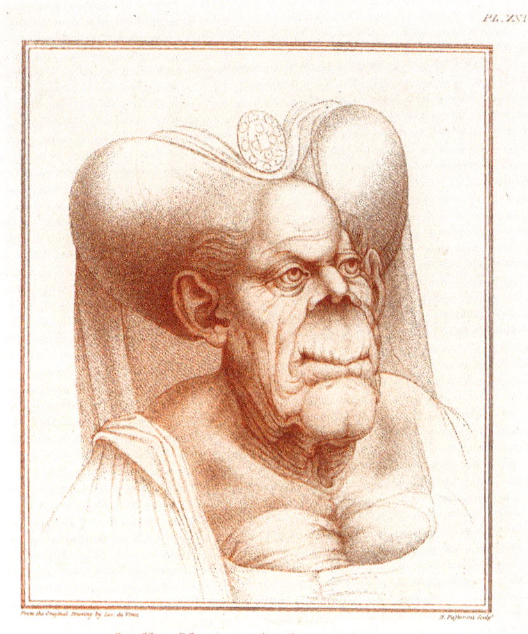

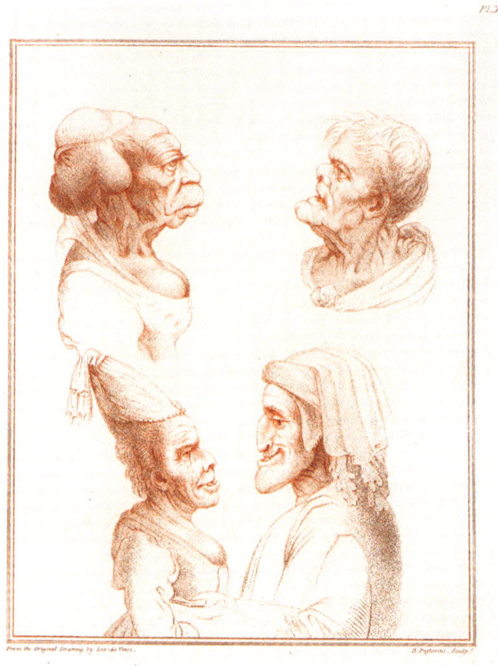

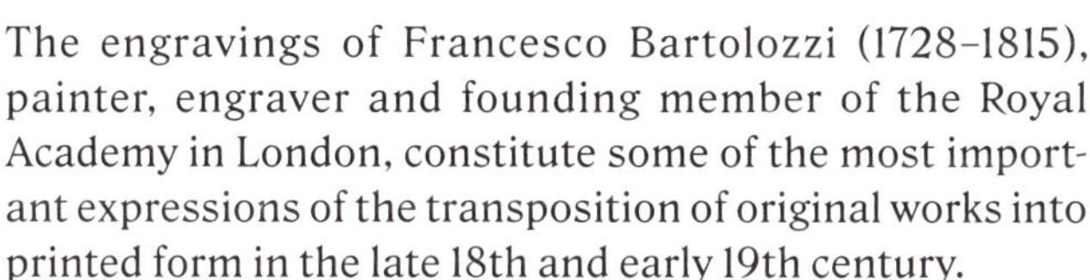

The engravings of Francesco Bartolozzi (1728–1815), painter, engraver and founding member of the Royal Academy in London, constitute some of the most important expressions of the transposition of original works into printed form in the late 18th and early 19th century.

In 1764, Bartolozzi moved to London, where he was elected to the Royal Academy as a painter rather than an engraver despite the fact that he showed only his engravings and drawings on a regular basis. It was in London that Bartolozzi developed the stipple technique. In 1796, the English antiquary John Chamberlaine published a series of drawings on various subjects (*Single Figures, Heads, Compositions, Horses, And Other Animals; Optics, Perspective, Gunnery, Hydraulics, Mechanics*) attributed to Leonardo da Vinci, engraved by Bartolozzi, "Historical Engraver to his Majesty", by means of different techniques depending on the graphic media of the originals. The exceptional quality of Bartolozzi's engravings is the result of his particular graphic sensitivity in following every detail of the original. The outlines are developed so as to construct the figures in a way that corresponds perfectly to the original strokes in the rendering of the whole. After Gerli (1784) and Mantelli (1785) in Milan, Bartolozzi's works are among the most interesting examples of printmaking, not least for the techniques employed with black and red ink. The stipple technique enabled Bartolozzi to reproduce the soft lines of the *sfumato* effect present in some of the originals and achieve a superior rendering of volumes, particularly in profiles like that of Leonardo himself and the head of St Anne. Bartolozzi's collection of engravings also includes some works addressed by others, like the caricature heads engraved by Hollar 1645, accompanied by the title *Dante* in the case of the group of five male caricatures (Windsor, RL 12495).

Francesco Bartolozzi
Imitations of Original Designs by Leonardo da Vinci. Consisting of various Drawings of Single Figures, Heads, Compositions, Horses, and other Animals; Optics, Perspective, Gunnery, Hydraulics, Mechanics; and in particular of very accurate Delineations, with a most spirited Pen, of a Variety of Anatomical Subjects. In His Majesty's Collection. Published by John Chamberlaine, Keeper of The King's Drawings and Medals, And F.S.A. London, Printed by W. Bulmer and Co. and sold by George Nicol, Bookseller to His Majesty; Edwards, Pall-Mall; Robson Bond-Street; and Messrs. White, Fleet-Street, 1796.
Private collection, Château du Clos Lucé

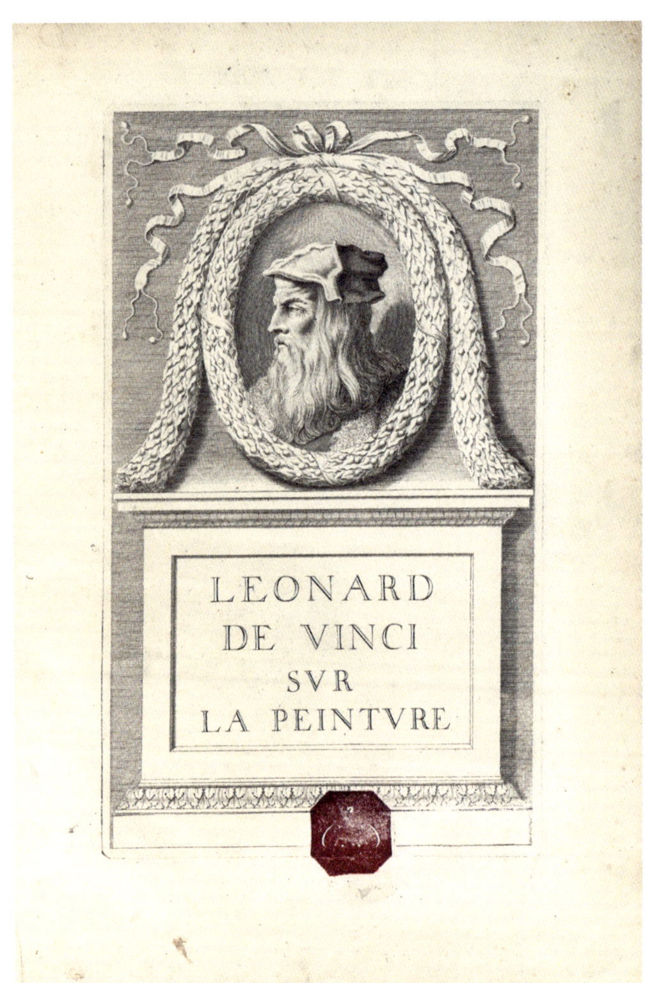

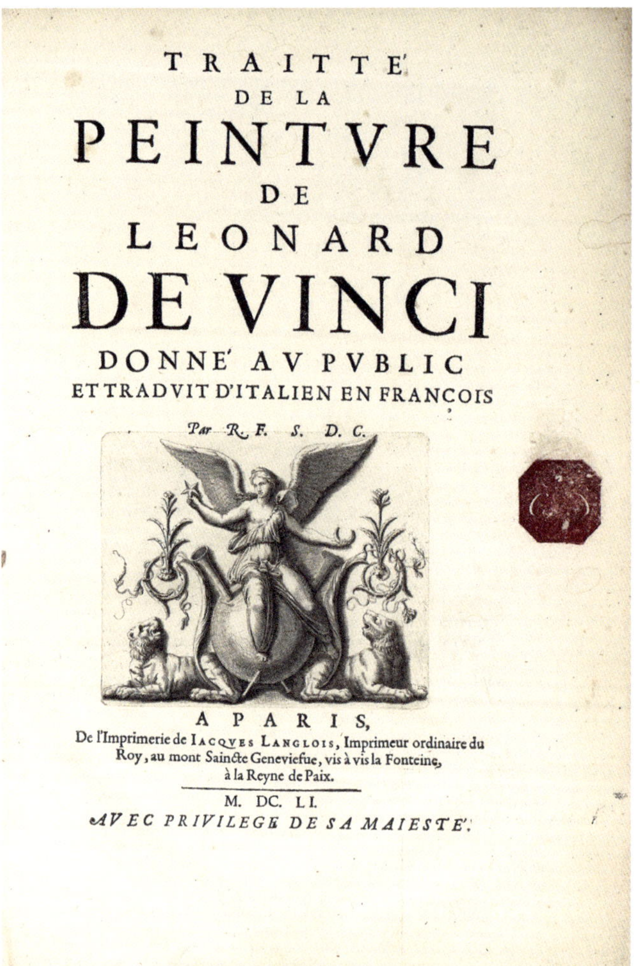

Traitté de la peinture de Léonard de Vinci, donné au public et traduit d'italien en françois par R.F.S.D.C. [Roland Fréart, sieur de Chambray] à Paris, De l'Imprimerie de Jacques Langlois, Imprimeur ordinaire du Roy, au mont Saincte Geneviefue, vis à vis la Fonteine, à la Reyne de Paix. M.DC.LI. Avec privilège de sa Maiesté. 1651
Ten unnumbered leaves of plates; 128 p., 37.5 × 25 cm
Private collection, Château du Clos Lucé

The first printed edition of the *Trattato della pittura* was born out of Cassiano dal Pozzo's studies on the theoretical reflections and scientific investigations of Leonardo da Vinci and appeared in Paris in 1651. The examination of original materials by Leonardo and apographs from the *Libro di pittura*, composed by Francesco Melzi after the master's death, enabled Cassiano dal Pozzo to compile a selection of texts on painting that were to constitute the theoretical basis of the *Trattato della pittura.* The simple line drawings in the series of apographs circulating in the 16th and 17th century in the *Libro di pittura* found classicistic adaptation in the illustrations of Nicolas Poussin. An example of the versions of the *Trattato della pittura* produced by Cassiano dal Pozzo is provided by his own personal copy (Milan, Biblioteca Ambrosiana, H 228 inf.), where the *Opinioni di Lionardo da Vinci circa il modo di dipingere prospettive, ombre, lontananze, altezze, bassezze, d'appresso et da discosto, et altro* contain twenty-seven original pen drawings in bistre on pasteboard by Poussin.

Around 1640, when his plans to print the work in Italy had fallen through, Cassiano dal Pozzo offered a copy of his work with the illustrations by Poussin to his French correspondents Paul Fréart de Chantelou and Raphael Trichet Du Fresne, who published the first edition of the *Trattato della pittura* in Paris in Italian and French in 1651.

Both editions were printed in an elegant folio format and opened with the portrait of Leonardo by René Lochon, engraver of all the plates for the illustrations. They included a wealth of illustrations derived from the drawings by Poussin. Chapter 287, *Ce qu'il faut faire pour que les visages ayent du relief avec de la grâce* (p. 94), includes the first engraving of the *Mona Lisa*, half-length and with the addition of elements not present in the original, such as drapery on the right shoulder, which does not appear in the Italian edition.

SELECTIVE LIST OF EXHIBITED WORKS

Anonymous 16th century follower of Leonardo
Anatomical studies
First half of the 16th century
Gallerie dell'Accademia di Venezia
Cat. 509 A

Anonymous 16th century follower of Leonardo
Anatomical studies
First half of the 16th century
Gallerie dell'Accademia di Venezia
Cat. 509 B

Giovanni Ambrogio Figino
Study of a figure from behind
c.1587
Gallerie dell'Accademia di Venezia
Cat. 943

Antonio Pollaiuolo
Battle of the Nudes
c.1460-1475
Gallerie degli Uffizi, Department of Prints and Drawings, Florence
No. 124e. sc.

Antonio de Béatis
Itinerario di Monsignor Reverendissimo et Illustrissimo il cardinale de Aragona
1522
Biblioteca Nazionale "Vittorio Emanuele III", Naples

Leonardo da Vinci
Traitté de la peinture [Treatise on Painting](given to the public and translated from Italian into French by R.F.S.D.C. [Roland Fréart, Sieur de Chambray] in Paris, by l'Imprimerie de Jacques Langlois, printer in ordinary to the king, at mont Saincte Geneviefue, vis à vis la Fonteine,à la Reyne de Paix. M.DC.LI. With the privilege of His Majesty)
Private Collection, Château du Clos Lucé

Aristotle
De Animalibus
Parisiis: Printed by Simon de Collines, 1533
Bibliothèque municipale, Grenoble
B.2380

Aristotle
De Anima
1548
Bibliothèque municipale, Le Havre
R1362

Francesco Bartolozzi
Imitation of Original Designs by Leonardo da Vinci
published by John Chamberlaine, 1796
Private Collection, Château du Clos Lucé

Comte de Caylus, *Collection of Grotesque Heads and Caricatures drawn by the Florentine Leonardo da Vinci and engraved by M. le C. de C., known as the "Caylus Album"*
1730
Private Collection, Château du Clos Lucé
folio 22 R (n°17, 18), folio 23 R (n°19, 20)

Guy de Chauliac
Treatise on Surgery. The Book of Guidon
Early 15th century
Bibliothèque municipale, Dijon

Nicholas of Cusa (also known as Nicholas of Kues)
Haec accurata recognitio trium voluminum operum clariss
P. Nicolai Cusae cardinalis
1514
Bibliothèque humaniste, Sélestat
No. B.H.S, K-937

Claudius Galen
Frontispiece of *De usu partium corporis humani libri XVII, universo hominum generi apprime necessarii, Nicolao Regio Calabro interprete. Tertio exactiore cura ad Graeci exemplaris veritatem castigati, per Jacobum Sylvium medicum & Martinum Gregorium. Huc accessit ejusdem Jacobi Sylvii brevis Isagoge, partis ususque rationem edisserens*, 1543
Bibliothèque interuniversitaire Santé Médecine, université Paris-Cité

Wenceslaus Hollar
Etchings taken from Lord Arundel's collection, displaying grotesque heads
1645
Private Collection, Château du Clos Lucé

Johannes de Ketham
Fasciculus medicinae
Venice: Jean and Grégoire de Gregoriis, 1500
Bibliothèque Carré d'Art, Nîmes
Inc. 25

Girolamo Manfredi
Liber de homine: cuius sunt libri duo
1474
Art and History Collections, Fondazione Cassa di Risparmio, Bologna
Inv. 47896

Jean Pecham
Perspectiva Communis
1482-1483?
Bibliothèque de l'Institut national d'histoire de l'art, Paris

Prancing Horse
Based on a wax model by Leonardo da Vinci
Bronze with black patina
Italy, 17th century
Private collection, Château du Clos Lucé

Emilio Quadrelli
Bust of Leonardo da Vinci
Patinated bronze sculpture
Celebration of the 400th anniversary of Leonardo da Vinci's death
1919
Private collection, Château du Clos Lucé

David after Verrocchio
Replica in bronze, 19th century
Private collection, Château du Clos Lucé

David after Donatello
Replica in bronze, 19th century
Private collection, Château du Clos Lucé

Photographic credits :
© Louis de Leusse, p. 159 (right) / © Léonard de Serres, p. 13, p. 27 (upper right), p. 37 (bottom), p. 38 (top), p. 41 / © René-Gabriel Ojeda, p. 163 / © Éric Sander, p. 34, p. 37 (top), p. 43 / © Michel Urtado, p. 31, p. 160, p. 157, p. 167 (top)

Copyrights institutions and individuals:
© Biblioteca Apostolica Vaticana, p. 172, p. 175 / © Biblioteca nazionale "Vittorio Emanuele III", Naples, p. 38 (bottom) / Bibliothèque Carré d'Art, Nîmes, p. 50 / Bibliothèque municipale, Grenoble, p. 49 (right) / Bibliothèques virtuelles humanistes, CESR, Tours – private collection, p. 80 / Bibliothèque interuniversitaire Santé Médecine, université Paris-Cité, p. 49 (left) / © British Museum, p. 27 (lower left) / © Château du Clos Lucé – Parc Leonardo da Vinci, Amboise, p. 13, p. 16, p. 34, p. 37, p. 38 (top), p. 41, p. 43, p.186-190 / © CHRU BREST, p. 72 / © Gabinetto fotografico delle Gallerie degli Uffizi – *Su concessione del Ministero della Cultura*, p.185 / © Gallerie dell'Accademia, Venise, Italie/Bridgeman Images, p. 8 / © gallica.bnf.fr/Bibliothèque nationale de France, p. 155, p. 168, p. 171 / © G.A.VE – Archivio fotografico – "*su concessione del Ministero della Cultura*", p. 182-184 / Image détenue par la Biblioteca Nacional de España, p. 47 / Klassik Stiftung Weimar, p. 107, p. 112, p. 123 / © Museo del Cenacolo, p. 14, p. 15, p. 138, p. 140, p. 141, p. 146, p. 148 / © RMN-Grand Palais/Institut de France, p. 26, p. 173 / Royal Collection Trust/© His Majesty King Charles III, 2023, p. 20, p. 23, p. 25, p. 30, p. 33, p. 54, p. 57, p. 60, p. 61, p. 63, p. 64, p. 66 (top), p. 68, p. 70, p. 71, p. 73, p. 75, p. 77, p. 81, p. 85, p. 86, p. 88, p. 91, p. 92, p. 93, p. 94, p. 96 (middle top), p. 98 (top), p. 100, p. 104, p. 105, p. 108, p. 111, p. 115, p. 116, p. 118, p. 119, p. 120, p. 124, p. 127, p. 128, p. 132, p. 133, p. 134, p. 135, p. 136, p. 137, p. 159 (left) / © The Morgan Library & Museum. 2006. Purchased in 1938, p. 78, p. 82 / © Veneranda Biblioteca Ambrosiana/Metis e Mida Informatica/Mondadori Portfolio, p. 96 (middle top), p. 99 / © Wellcome Collection 23690i, p. 58 / © Kiyoshi Bando, p. 142, p. 143, p. 146, p. 148 / © Ronan Bouttier CHRU BREST, p. 66 (lower left), p. 69 (top) / Courtesy of Professor Robin P. Choudhury, p. 131 / © Bertrand Debono, p. 117 / © Marc Garetier HIA BREST, p. 24, p. 66 (lower right) / © Ivana Gayitch, p. 150, p. 151 / © Jacky Laulan et Dominique Le Nen, p. 95 / © Christian Lefèvre, François Gaucher, Joël Savéan, LATIM BREST, p. 74 / © Dominique Le Nen, p. 69 (bottom), p. 96 (upper right and bottom), p. 98 (bottom) / © Jean-Louis Pironio, p. 27 / © François Rozet, p. 103

ÉDITIONS SKIRA PARIS
14, rue Serpente
75006 Paris
www.skira.net

Senior editor
Nathalie Prat-Couadau

Project manager and editorial coordinator
Juliette Chambon

Commercial and editorial projects manager
Meryl Mason

Editorial assistants
Samaa Mohamed Ali Abdelaal
Roxanne Rebours

Translation
Martin Lewis
Clément Martin

Copyediting and proofreading
Etty Payne

Colour separation
Litho Art New, Turin

ISBN 978-2-37074-214-8

Printed in June 2023 by Graphius,
Gent, Belgium
Legal deposit June 2023